Charles River

Charles River

Essays and Meditations for Daily Reading

ROBERT ALLAN HILL

RESOURCE *Publications* • Eugene, Oregon

CHARLES RIVER
Essays and Meditations for Daily Reading

Resource Publications
An Imprint of Wipf and Stock Publishers
199 W. 8th Ave., Suite 3
Eugene, OR 97401

www.wipfandstock.com

ISBN 13: 978-1-62564-981-2

Manufactured in the U.S.A.
02/10/2015

I dedicate this book, and in truth all the others, currently eleven, to my beloved wife, Jan. Janette Lee Pennock Hill, whom I have known forty-five years, to whom I have been married for thirty-seven, and by whom, day by day, I have been given, shown, taught, and embraced in love.

In addition, I want to thank Mr. Jason Ford for the unstinting, excellent editing he has provided this volume, as he so well did for my earlier book on John, *The Courageous Gospel*. Further, I want to thank my dear friend and colleague over many years, the Rev. Susan S. Shafer, for the original gift that inspired the development of this collection.

Contents

Preface

A few years ago, a dear friend gave me as a Christmas gift a book of writings by Dietrich Bonhoeffer. The collection was assembled for daily reading. Each was about 200 words, most of them short essays in thought, some of them prayers or poems or meditations.

I had never had a morning reading collection of the sort. Sometime in the early winter I put Bonhoeffer's essays on my bureau. I found I could finish dressing, fill my suit pockets with various assorted pens and notebooks and wallet and what not, adjust my tie, and all the while truly enjoy reading his words. They were not a daily devotional, but they were a daily help. I used the collection to my advantage all year long.

Eberhard Bethge joined us for dinner one evening at Union Theological Seminary, ten of us around a table in Hastings Hall, with the Broadway traffic rattling past, in November of 1976. He told us about Bonhoeffer, his teacher and friend. It was the quiet Bonhoeffer, the reflective, ruminating mind, the man who had been young himself in Hastings Hall forty years earlier, who deeply impressed me, as Bethge spoke during that simple dinner. The daily essays returned me to that introduction, nearly forty years later. A decade, four decades, eight decades—hardly any time at all.

I resolved at the end of the year to try to put together such an assortment of essays and other pieces. Perhaps they will be a help to some others, as his were to me. The collection is one part homiletical, one part pedagogical, one part devotional, even as my current role at Boston University is part preacher, part professor, part pastor—Dean of Marsh Chapel, Professor of New Testament, and University Chaplain. In our ninth year of sojourn in Boston, along the River Charles, shimmering at night, rolling in the morning, historic and iconic and bucolic in every season, I name the essays for the river, the river that runs to the sea, and to the sea that is never full.

January

Bill Huber

Once when our son was ten years old, he accompanied me during a visit with two parishioners. Mary and Bill had married just after the Second World War. They raised four daughters, who all had become vibrant, creative, caring adults. In addition they found time to prepare the Altar for Sunday, to sit through various Worship Committee meetings, to take an interest in local politics, to read and learn and grow in change, as faith intersected with life.

During the October that Bill was dying, our son Ben went with me once to see him. On an earlier visit, Bill had told me about his experience in the war. At age 20 Bill had become a pilot, and had flown 30 missions from England into and over Germany. His plane had been shot down once. He had survived, though not all of his crew had survived. He had carried responsibility for an airplane, a crew, many missions, and to some small but human degree, the outcome of the war itself. He was honored and decorated when the war ended. 30 missions later, several deaths later, many hours of anxious service later, many buildings and bridges destroyed later, after three years in command in England in the air in the war, he came home. He was 22. Bill was 22 years old, when the war ended, and he came home.

I cannot remember how this happened, but our son either asked to see or was offered to see Bill's flight jacket. It was a heavy, worn, brown leather flight jacket, waist long with an old center zipper. At age 10, and I do not remember how this happened, whether he asked or was offered, Ben donned the jacket. He was small in it, but Bill himself was somewhat small, and the jacket fit, if poorly. Here was a moment when Mary, soon to be a widow, and Bill, soon to be dead, and Ben, soon to be 11, and I, soon to conduct a funeral, were fully quiet together. With that jacket Bill came home, 30 missions later, a war won, at 22 years of age. 22. A young man. Bill worked the next 40 years as a public relations writer for a small manufacturing company, a quiet life of backroom pencil sharpening, phoning, rewriting, and mailing.

Some moments stand frozen in time. Our son in Bill's jacket is one. Bill's primary work, his main adult life, as he reflected on all of his life, was completed by age 22. Which leads to a question: Where did we ever get the idea that young people are not capable of great things?

January 1

A Teacher's Influence

Somehow, with four growing children and a preacher's meager salary, my parents managed to give us all piano lessons. My teacher was a farm wife, thirty years younger than her husband. The distance from the barn to the house, from the manger to the piano, was very short, in both geographic and olfactory senses. I feel the warmth of that space and that tutelage today, even though those precious parsonage dollars were almost entirely wasted on me, to my regret. I can't play a scale, after at least 5 years of lessons. I can though appreciate the difficulty of what others do. And there was something more, somewhere between Lewis and Freud, in those afternoon lessons, which usually began with an honest question: "Did you practice?" and a less than honest response: "Some."

You know, looking back that was one of the few places and times, week by week, when I was in the sole presence of a non-parental adult: honest, trustworthy, kind, caring. Now where the farm was there is an auto dealer and a pizza parlor. But the hay, the barn, the milking, the home, the warmth, the music, the teaching, the—may I call it friendship—live on. In her forties she died of cancer, three fine children, one great marriage, several years of crops and evenings and mornings of milking, and some less than stellar piano students later. At her funeral the minister preached this sermon: "You Are A Song That God Is Singing." That itself is thirty years ago, but I remember it in full. "You Are A Song That God Is Singing." You are too. And so are you. And so are you.

January 2

Schweitzer

Maybe we need to remember Albert Schweitzer.

A child organ prodigy, a youthful New Testament scholar, a young principal in his Alsatian theological seminary, a man whose books and articles I used with profit in my own dissertation a few years ago, Schweitzer's life changed on the reading of a Paris Mission Society Magazine.

As a scholar, he wrote: "He comes to us as one unknown, without a name, as of old, by the lakeside, He came to those men who knew Him not. He speaks to us the same word, 'Follow me!' and sets us to the tasks which He has to fulfill for our time. He commands. And to those who obey Him, whether they be wise or simple, He will reveal himself in the toils, the conflicts, the sufferings which they shall pass through in His fellowship, and, as an ineffable mystery, they shall learn in their own experience Who He is."[1]

What he wrote of Jesus became his life. He left organ and desk, studied medicine, and practiced in Africa for 35 years, calling his philosophy, 'a reverence for life.'

Vocation leads to God. A decision about vocation leads to nearness to the divine.

January 3

1. Albert Schweitzer, *The Quest for the Historical Jesus,* 389.

Preaching: Irving G Hill

Preaching is not Bible study, but
It does require Biblical understanding
Preaching is not theology, but
There must be theology in it.
Preaching is not biography, but
It does require an understanding of people.
Preaching is not teaching, but
It is instructional.
Preaching is not social ethics, but
It must point to social responsibility.
Preaching is one vehicle God has chosen
That can grow life.
Preaching is humbling,
Frightening,
And Rewarding!

January 4

Bird Song

The gospel is our spoken gift of faith.

Every bird sings faith, over the globe, through all time. Thurman loved penguins, odd and remote. Listen. Along the Charles, in the spring, make way for goslings and ducklings. Mid-island in Bermuda, I hear the song: Early in the summer mornings, out in the land currently under the death cloud of possible fracking, where we live, at dawn a rooster. Two eagles—they too mate for life, as in Christian marriage—soaring, I only imagine their music. The owl at night. A swan song, a silver swan, who living had no note. The gospel is a bird in song, and all nature sings. Even if or when the preaching of the gospel by human imperfection abates, as it does threaten to do, birdsong will carry the tune.

Just as there are so many, sorry, reasons to skip church, so too there are many, sorry, reasons, in the space of 4000 earthly Sundays, to skip faith. Faith is only real gold, real faith, when it is all you have to go on.

January 5

6

Capital Campaign Invocation 2012: Boston University

Gracious God, Holy and Just
Thou whose greatness is formed in goodness, and whose goodness is the pathway
To greatness
We pause at the outset of our shared journey, along the banks of the River Charles
To lift of a word of thanks and to ask for a measure of blessing.
Tonight, we pause to give thanks
For this good place, Boston University
For its long, good history in learning and virtue and piety
For the goodness of its people and leaders and laborers in the current season
For all the good heart and minds of the devoted people in this room
Who together are trying to shape a better future through this good University
On the cusp of this campaign for all that we have inherited from those who came
Before us, we offer our heartfelt thanks.
Tonight, we pause to seek a blessing
We need a blessing if we are to choose to be great
We need a blessing if we are to dare to do something new and big and noble
We need a blessing if we are to struggle toward an impressive great goal
We need a blessing if we are to work together for a school we love, and for a
Future that surpasses our past
Lord, we shall need a blessing for this adventure, this journey, this
On the cusp of this campaign we open ourselves to the possibilities of blessings
Both divine and human
Now as we break bread together around a common table, over a fine meal, and in a
spirit of familiarity and humility, we offer our thanks and seek thy blessing, Thou whose
greatness is formed in goodness, and who goodness is the pathway to greatness. A prayer
of thanks and blessing.
Amen.

January 6

Choral Synoptics

Each Synoptic passage is like a choral piece, including four voices. There is the Soprano voice of Jesus of Nazareth, embedded somewhere in the full harmonic mix. In Matthew 9, Jesus conflicts with the Pharisaic aversion to pagan inscriptions and iconography. There is the alto voice of the primitive church, arguably always the most important of the four voices, that which carries the forming of the passage in the needs of the community. From Mark to Matthew an insertion has arisen, the citation of Hosea 6:6. Evidently, the earliest church needed the fuller support of the prophetic tradition—mercy not sacrifice, compassion not holiness—as it moved farther out and away from the memory of Jesus. The tenor line is that of the evangelist. Matthew is here, marking his own appearance in the record. His work seems to reflect a connection to school, to scribes, perhaps as Stendahl said from across the river, years ago, to Qumran. The baritone is borne by later interpretation, beginning soon with Irenaeus, Against Heresies: "What doctor, when wishing to cure a sick man, would act in accordance with the desires of the patient, and not in accordance with the requirements of medicine?"[1] If our church music carries only one line, we may be tempted to interpret our Scripture with only one voice, and miss the SATB harmonies therein, to our detriment.

January 7

---

1. Irenaeus, Adv. Haer., in *Early Christian Fathers,* edited by Cyril C. Richardson (New York: Touchstone, 1996), 377.

Dean James Stamas Dinner

Invocation
Romans 12: 9
Gracious God
Pausing at table, enthralled with this evening's welcome, we again recall the grace of hospitality.

We remember those in our families who taught us by example.

We recall mothers' hands that held us and fed us and welcomed us into the world, before we could speak.

We see again fathers' tables around which we were fed, in spirit and in body.

We remember the moments of intimate candle light, of quiet promise, of spirited mirth, given us by friends and loved ones.

We are personally grateful for the example of Dean James Stamas, in work and life, in profession and in person, a Dean of Hospitality and a hospitable Dean.

At twilight tonight we see those who this week have broken a month long fast about a common table, and those who honor days high and holy around a common table, and those who revere the memory of a borrowed upper room and a common table.

Tonight we feel again the beauty of creation, the starry heavens above and the moral law within. We warm ourselves before the embers of memory and under the stars of hope, before the embers and under the stars.

Make of us we pray a joyously hospitable people, who remember those in need, who remember the call to live in the service of the city, in the heart of the city.

Amen.

January 8

E-Trouble

One day you encounter e-trouble. My son knows I think the world gets better one conversation at a time, and worse one email at a time. He clerks for a federal judge. One morning my son called me with this story. "I knew you would enjoy it Dad," he said. "It involves trouble and email." Well, apparently in the judicial employment system, when one falls ill and runs out of sick days, others can take from their account and give to the need. A worker received days from about twenty others, healed, and went back to work. The colleague who organized the sick day bank support assayed to write a thank you note, which she did. It was a very simple note, graciously thanking the donors, reporting on the healing, and wishing all well. This would have been no problem. Except that in mailing the thank you note, she hit the wrong key, and sent to the wrong list, not a list of twenty donors, but a general list of 200,000 judicial employees. Here is a trouble, a day's own trouble, organically designed for the tweeter, list serve, email, website 21st century. Oops. Yet even this would also have been no problem. Except that a lawyer in Arizona took umbrage at the e-incursion, and said so in a curtly written note: "not my issue, not my problem, you invaded my space, thanks but no thanks, plus I really do not agree with this whole socialist sick day swapping anyway."

Which would have been alright, too. Except that she hit 'reply all,' and, in the next hour, said my son, he had 100 emails in his box. Yes, Sick Day Bank! No Arizona! Yes Thank You Note! No To Rude Response! Yes to Liberty, No to Obama (I have no idea how he got in there) . . . Until one kindly attorney from the St Lawrence River area shouted out: "STOP. This is what makes people suspicious of lawyers in general and federal workers in particular. We have better things to do with our time." This also would have been no problem. Except. Except that before he signed off he wrote: "PS, while I have your attention, I want you to know that I am an amateur chef, and I would like to take this opportunity to share with you all *my favorite recipe for cooking salmon.*" Yes, he hit reply all. And on the day went: Salmon Yes! Salmon No! Amateur Chef Yes! Email recipe, NO! . . .

January 9

Reflections on E. Kohak:
The Embers and the Stars

We shall dig again the wells of our Fathers.

"Words do not contain the truth, they point to it and evoke it." 19.

The winter is the season when things seem dead, but they are not.

"Humans grow angry so easily, so heedlessly venting their anger at those nearest and most vulnerable, needlessly, wantonly injuring what is most precious and most fragile."86.

"Humans are not only humans, moral subjects and vital organisms. They are also *Persons*, capable of fusing eternity and time in the precious, anguished reality of a love that would be eternal amid the concreteness of time. A person is a being through whom eternity enters time." 121.

We are as insensitive to history as we are to nature, 159.

There is self-discovery in remembrance.

"The echo of a word of the Lord not yet spoken."

"How can humans live with what they can neither accept nor escape?" 162

We have a sense of history. But we have lost a sense of eternity.

"European thought has been profoundly affected by collapsing into each other two dimensions of being human which humans had long treated as distinct: the line of temporal progression, from before to after, and the line of moral judgment, between good and evil. Whatever else may be true of it, ours is a time for which later has acquired a sense of better—while better has been drained of all meaning except that of later." 164

The authentic relation between beings is the personal encounter of mutual respect. 208

Most of the time we possess and covet far more than we can care for and cherish. 212

Generosity personalizes as greed depersonalizes.

Wear it in, wear it out, make it do or do without.

We need to rediscover ourselves as persons, not as need gratifying organisms. 215

Havel: "To Live In Truth."

"Their great achievement is that, before all eternity, they have spoken the word of truth in time."

"The chief task of philosophy is to write footnotes to the text of experience." 219

January 10

Four-part Harmony

So, this morning, as Jesus greets the children, we hear four voices, a choral harmony. Here is the light lead voice, the soprano melody, the remaining fragrant essence of Jesus of Nazareth, who suffered the children to come to him. Here is the strong formative voice, the alto and most important voice, that of the primitive church, which remembered Jesus, remembered his word, but remembered in way that was formed in their own life, out of their own need, the need to address the community needs of children. Here is the tenor voice, that of the writer, Mark, who places this passage among others of similar type, others related to the needs of the community. Here is the baritone voice of the church, remembering and re-rendering this same gospel text, for two thousand years, beginning with Matthew and Luke, twenty years after Mark.

January 11

Genuine Generosity

The eye of the Lord today rests for a moment upon a genuine generosity. If we follow his gaze our eyes too may rest for a moment upon genuine generosity. We too by the lenses of the Scripture may for a moment see what Jesus sees, imagine what he imagines, today. His vision may shape our own. Then in his light we may see light. Follow in the mind's eye for a moment the angle of vision, the dominical angle of vision, now registered for us and all time in St. Luke's generous gospel, Chapter 13. Hum the tune, some months before Christmastide: Do you see what he sees. In water on the Sabbath, simple refreshment of those who emerge from the manger, he sees and honors genuine generosity. Can we do otherwise? The next time you are tempted, as you consider a generous act, to think that no one sees, that no one shares, that no fruit falls, remember today's gospel of water on the Sabbath. Follow the eye of the Lord, resting for a moment today on generosity. He teaches us about visible generosity. He delights us with religious generosity. He persuades us of the power of generosity.

January 12

Hope and Pam Brush

In 1985 Jan and I were assigned to a city church nearby a large nominally Methodist university. On the first Sunday, in a building with 50 rooms, whose sanctuary seated 600, there were 35 people, all but two of whom would be dead before we moved. A grand, once great pulpit. Here is the church. Where are the people? We noticed that fall an article in the student newspaper: 6,000 students were living in our neighborhood, said the article. So we planned and worked, we advertised a Sunday evening student dinner, we passed the word, beat the drum, fanned the flames, and went to the highways and byways. We cleaned one of those 50 rooms, cooked a turkey dinner, and sat down to wait. You know the feeling. 5:45, no one. 6:00, no one came. 6:05, no one. We were about to close up, when, at 6:10, in walked one woman, Pam Brush. She had seen the notice. She had grown up in the Methodist church on Long Island. She was a sophomore. She thought maybe she'd check out the neighborhood church.

She did not say any of the following: "where is everybody, am I the only one, who else is coming, is this the right place?" Here is what she said: "wow, thanks for the meal, this tastes great, I love turkey, tell me about the two of you, what is there to do in Syracuse, I love this old building, is it haunted, next week I'm bringing my two roommates and their boyfriends, we'll cook, I wish I had a boyfriend, maybe I will by next week, what a great place . . . see you next Sunday!" And out of that one lone child, one lone woman, one lone person on the periphery, over a decade, there grew a Sunday dinner fellowship, the Wesley fellowship, a house and half time ministry and minister, seasonal retreats, a newsletter: *The Epworth News*, service work, fun, fellowship. In the snow some years later, Jan and I slid our way down to Long Island to officiate at Pam's wedding. It is emotionally draining and even painful to remember this, to remember who we are, and what can happen, where Christ is.

To remember Pam Brush in 1985 is to remember that I am a child of God. You too.

January 13

Thurman

Maybe we need to remember Howard Thurman. The first page of his autobiography announces today's gospel, that Jesus empowers his disciples, whose vocations lead to God:

At the end of my first year at the Rochester Theological Seminary, I became assistant to the minister of the First Baptist Church of Roanoke, Virginia. I was to assume the duties as pastor during the month that the minister and his family were away on vacation. I would be on my own. On my first night alone in the parsonage I was awakened by the telephone. The head nurse of the local Negro hospital asked, "May I speak with Dr. James?" I told her he was away. "Dr. James is the hospital chaplain," she explained. "There is a patient here who is dying. He is asking for a minister. Are you a minister?"

In one kaleidoscopic moment I was back again at an old crossroad. A decision of vocation was to be made here, and I felt again the ambivalence of my life and my calling. Finally, I answered. "Yes, I am a minister."

"Please hurry," she said, "or you'll be too late."

In a few minutes I was on my way, but in my excitement and confusion I forgot to take my Bible. At the hospital, the nurse took me immediately into a large ward. The dread curtain was around the bed. She pulled it aside and directed me to stand opposite her. The sick man's eyes were half closed, his mouth open, his breathing labored. The nurse leaned over and, calling him by name, said, "The minister is here."

Slowly he sought to focus his eyes first on her, and then on me. In a barely audible voice he said, "Do you have something to say to a man who is dying? If you have, please say it, and say it in a hurry."

I bowed my head, closed my eyes. There were no words. I poured out the anguish of my desperation in one vast effort. I felt physically I was straining to reach God. At last, I whispered my Amen.

We opened our eyes simultaneously as he breathed, "Thank you. I understand." He died with his hand in mine.[1]

Vocation leads to God.

January 14

---

1. Howard Thurman, *With Head and Heart* (Orlando: Mariner, 1979), 3–4.

I bear witness.

In June I preached in Baltimore, in the fine facility of the Baltimore Marriott Waterfront Hotel. A thousand well quaffed, fashion edged, nicely attired Christians, in black and white, United Methodists, filled the lush ballroom. The next morning we drove north to Scranton PA, to the last full session of the so-called Wyoming Conference. 300 overweight, poorly dressed, all white, largely retirees, met in the unkempt gymnasium of the University of Scranton. Like Solomon's baby, the conference is to be cut in two pieces this year. From southern waterfront to northern wasteland we drove in one morning. In religion, the south has surely risen again. In Scranton, most of the delegates were too old and too heavy to walk from the gym to the cafeteria, less than 300 yards. Golf carts carried the disciples. The ice is melting. Fast.

I bear witness.

I attended my home conference, my spiritual home. As an itinerant preacher, a traveling elder, my church is the gathering of similarly cast about travelers, my conference. My brothers in ministry, my sisters in itinerancy. Hymns to sing. My life goes on in endless song . . . I drove to Clarence Center, near Buffalo, thinking about the plane crash last winter which put the little town on the map. My dark reverie was shaken as I passed a church sign which read: "True peace is found only through Jesus Christ." I do not believe that. Neither do you. Re-read Romans 8 again about the whole creation groaning if you must. Read Acts 10 about all in their own way being saved if you must. Re-read Galatians 3:26 about the end of religious distinctions if you must. Channel John Wesley—if thine heart be as mine then give me thine hand—if you must. Re-read any of Huston Smiths books if you must. Remember Abraham Heschel. Remember Anwar Sadat. Remember Abraham Lincoln. Remember Mahatma Ghandi. Recall the Dalai Lama, if you must. *But must you?* We are not Christofascists, are we? We know in our bones that there are many ways of keeping faith. We know in our guts that in the Father's house there are many rooms. We know in our hearts that the true light that enlightens *every one* has come into the world. Don't we?

I drove on, glad to be arriving at a *magnanimous Methodist* conference wherein there is no east or west, wherein no south or north, but one great fellowship of love throughout the whole wide earth, wherein there is broad peace, peace perfect peace, wherein Wesley is remembered, and remembered to have said, "if thine heart be as mine, give me thine hand." *No.* Not for you, not for us the holier than thou neo-gnostic Unitarianism of the second person of the Trinity, patronizingly triumphalistic, christofascist, exclusivist hatred of such a saying: "True peace is found only in Jesus Christ." No.

But. As you probably already surmise, in the rear view mirror, and beneath the afore-quoated warped proverb, I cringed and wept to read the church's name, Harris Hill United Methodist Church. And. As you may now guess, at the conference itself the opening sermon, an atrocity, gave more than ample cover to such christomonist religious one-up-man ship.

I will try to bear witness.

January 15

I Will Be With You: Irving G Hill, 1953

One balmy spring evening, in the early fifties, I was returning to our apartment at 17 Yarmouth Street in Boston. I had just spend the last two hours in the world of a John Wayne Western. This American genre where right always succeeds and you know the outcome before the film begins. You don't have to think you just allow yourself to be immersed in this world of dreams.

Then, as I walked across Huntington Avenue, I looked to my left and saw the lighted dome of the Christian Science Mother Church. I had seen it many times before. I had taken our youth fellowship there to visit and walk through the giant globe that is there. But this evening as I made that familiar crossing I was struck, not by an auto, but by the reality that in just a few days I would receive my theological degree and become the pastor of the Brewerton Methodist Church.

How could this be? What was I to do? I was only 24 years old. I had never dealt with death except I in theory. I had never sat with a couple after the death of a child. I had never counseled a couple preparing for marriage except in a classroom setting. To my recollection I had never spoken with a person who had no belief in God or saw any reason for one. I had never thought how a church budget was raised or more significantly how my salary would be paid. In a few days, I would be facing all of these things and more.

I recalled a conversation that occurred at the just past annual conference with a committee from the Brewerton church. One of the saints said to me, "Young man, if you get a better offer, you had better take it, I don't know how we will be able to pay your salary." How about that?

Now, I had grown up in the church, attended church school, taught church school. I had been active in the youth fellowship at the local level and the conference level. Marcia and I had spent one summer as life guards at Casowasco. But now I was to be the pastor of a church in a community that I had only driven through.

Of course, I had graduated from a Methodist related university and had the privilege of studying at one of the better theological schools for three years, but on that June evening in the middle of that empty thoroughfare, I was totally lost.

Then I heard, "You don't think you are going to do this all by yourself do you? Surely I will be with you."

I heard that voice as clearly as I have ever heard anything and it has remained with me for these past 53 years.

It has taken the form of a loving, supportive wife, a devoted family, dedicated and crate lay people, inspired bishops, superintendents, and brother and sister clergy. Group commanders, wing chaplains and people of God, just like you.

January 16

Addams

Maybe we need to remember the young woman from Rockford Illinois, Jane Addams. She grew up 130 years ago, in a time and place unfriendly, even hostile, to the leadership that women might provide. But somehow she discovered her mission in life. And with determination she traveled to the windy city and set up Hull House, the most far reaching experiment in social reform that American cities had ever seen. Hull House was born out of a social vision, and nurtured through the generosity of one determined woman. Addams believed fervently that we are responsible for what happens in the world. So Hull House, a place of feminine community and exciting spiritual energy, was born. Addams organized female labor unions. She lobbied for a state office to inspect factories for safety. She built public playgrounds and staged concerts and cared for immigrants. She became politically active and gained a national following on the lecture circuit. She is perhaps the most passionate and most effective advocate for the poor that our country has ever seen.

Addams wrote: "The blessings which we associate with a life of refinement and cultivation must be made universal if they are to be permanent . . . The good we secure for ourselves is precarious and uncertain, is floating in midair, until it is secured for all of us and incorporated into our common life."

Yet it was a Rochesterian who, for me, explained once the puzzle of Jane Addams' fruitful generosity. This was the historian Christopher Lasch. Several times in the 1980's I thought of driving over here to visit him. But I never took the time, and as you know, he died seven years ago. Lasch said of Addams, "Like so many reformers before her, she had discovered some part of herself which, released, freed the rest."

Is there a part of your soul ready today to be released, that then will free the rest of you?

Vocation leads to God.

January 17

Marsh Chapel
9/11 Memorial Service 2006
Meditation on Peace

Today we pause in prayer and quiet to honor those who lost their lives 5 years ago, and those who lost loved ones the same day. We meet this moment, in quiet, to honor and remember. In doing so we do not neglect, we do not forget, we do not side-step, those who have lost life and loved ones since. In service of God and neighbor, in service of God and country, in Tsunami and hurricane and disease, we remember those who have been hurt, in a world of hurt.

Rightly to honor those lost and those loved, and fitly to meet this moment, we shall need briefly to look out toward the far side of trouble. There is, we hope, a far side to trouble. We may watch from the near side, but there is a far side to trouble as well. That is our ancient and future hope. Dewey spoke of a common faith. Thurman preached about a common ground. Today we identify a common hope.

This is the hope of peace. We long for the far side of trouble, for a global community of steady interaction, an international fellowship of accommodation, a world together dedicated to softening the inevitable collisions of life. This is the hope of peace.

Without putting too fine a point upon it, this hope, the vision of the far side of trouble, is the hallmark of the space in which we stand, and the place before which we stand. If nowhere else, here on this plaza, and here before this nave, we may lift our prayer of hope. There is a story here, of peace.

Methodists are like everyone else, only more so, the saying goes—a wide and diffuse denomination, committed to a handshake and a song, and that shared 'creed' of "that which has been believed, always, everywhere, and by everyone" (so, John Wesley).

Mahatmas Ghandi, walking and singing 'Lead Kindly Light,' embodied this common hope. Ghandi wrote: "I am part and parcel of the whole, and cannot find God apart from the rest of humanity." A common hope of peace. Ghandi inspired and taught the earlier Dean of Marsh Chapel, Howard Thurman.

Howard Thurman, hands raised in silence, later wrote: "The events of my days strike a full balance of what seems both good and bad. Whatever may be the tensions and the stresses of a particular day, there is always lurking close at hand the trailing beauty of forgotten joy or unremembered peace." A common hope of peace.

Thurman taught King, whose stentorian voice fills our memory and whose sculpture adorns our village green. King wrote: "I believe that unarmed truth and unconditional love will have the final word in reality." A common hope of peace. Martin Luther King inspired a whole generation of ministers, including the current Dean of this Chapel.

He (Robert Allan Hill) wrote: "We are all more human and more alike than we regularly affirm, all of us on this great globe. We all survive the birth canal, and so have a native survivors' guilt. All six billion. We all need daily two things, bread and a name. (One does not live by bread alone). All six billion. We all grow to a point of separation, a leaving home, a second identity. All six billion. We all love our families, love our children, love our homes, love our grandchildren. All six billion. We all age, and after forty, its maintenance, maintenance, maintenance. All six billion. We all shuffle off this mortal coil en route to that undiscovered country from whose bourn no traveler returns. All six billion."

Today, in memory and honor, we lift our hope for a day to live on the far side of trouble. We remember our ancient and future hope, a hope of peace.

January 18

Odd Experience

Recently a reporter traveled to Alaska. The reporter followed a trail of news, stemming from the announcement that in several Alaskan cities, there lived an abundance of young single men, and a paucity of young single women. An eager editor, seizing a summer moment, sent off his dutiful scribe, to interview the Northern Lights. As I recall, the reporter did confirm the statistical imbalance, far more women than men. 3 men for every woman. 3 to 1. What made the article memorable, however, was a more insightful quotation, with which the report concluded. The reporter interviewed a young woman at a bar, and asked her perspective on this statistical imbalance. "Well," the woman replied. "yes, it is true, look around you, yes, the ratio is heavily weighted. The men outnumber the women. There are something like two three men for every woman. You could say that the odds are good, if you are looking for a relationship. The odds, yes, the odds are good . . . but, on the other hand, again, look around you, the odds are good, but . . . though the odds are good . . . the goods are odd!"

Her experience changed her outlook, modified her perspective, qualified her inherited idea.

January 19

Our Help

D: Whence cometh our help?

S: From the Lord who made heaven and earth. The Creator. The Ground of Being. The God beyond God. The invisible, unknowable, unutterable, unattainable. The first, the last beyond all thought. The Transcendent.

D: What is the point of our lives?

S: To worship God and glorify God forever.

D: How is this possible, in the face of silence, darkness, mystery, accident, pride, immaturity, tragedy and the threat of meaninglessness?

S: By walking in the dark with our Transforming Friend, the Transcript in Time of who God is in eternity, the gift of the Father's unfailing grace, our beacon not our boundary, the presence of the absence of God, Jesus Christ our Kyrios.

D: Given our failures, our gone-wrongness, our sin, what daily hope have we, as those who hope for what we do not see?

S: Where the Spirit of the Lord is, there is freedom. Where there is freedom, there is promise. There is a self-correcting Spirit of Truth loose in the universe. There is a self-correcting Spirit of Truth loose in the universe.

D: How do we follow the trail of the Spirit?

S: By tithing, by ordered Sunday worship, by honest faithfulness in our relationships.

January 20

Public Speaking 101: A Sketch of a Speech

Personal Introduction

Confident Speech: Awareness, Setting, Attire, Delivery, Diction, Ease, Smile, Make others comfortable, Eye Contact, Lift Voice at End of Sentences, "Please Speak Slowly and Distinctly," Good humor, Daniel Marsh, "Good Friends All." Psalm 100.

Clear Speech: 1. Delivery: Audible, Precise, Enough Volume (more than you think). 2. Content: Diamond Point, Some Structure (A story? An image? An argument? A stream?). Three parts. Use Repetition. Third President: Merlin: heart, service. Frost: Road Not Taken

Concise Speech: Be clear, be brief, be seated. Consider the hearer. Eulogies for Adam Robert Engel at Hillel Monday night. KISS. Lincoln, Gettysburg. Brown: "One BU." Shakespeare 66 Sonnet. 10,000 hours.

For example: Say your name, with confident, clear, concise speech, telling us one thing about your name that we would not know.

January 21

Resurrection Light

Friends, resurrection comes from the religion Joanna and others carry with them to the tomb. Resurrection comes from Judaism, and from a particular hope in Judaism, an apocalyptic hope. In the range of religious reality available, to Jesus and Paul and Luke and all, the cosmic apocalyptic hope of resurrection, when the dead would be redeemed from graves, was the nearest best idiom available to say this: Why do you seek the Living One among the dead?

Resurrection from the dead comes from Jewish apocalyptic. It explains, interprets an experience, namely the appearance of Jesus to his disciples. He showed himself. "Resurrection is a reflective interpretation of encounters with the Living One which had the power to convince, to generate new community, to establish authorized leadership, and to commit to mission."

As George Buttrick, across the river years ago, said, "resurrection is the lifting of personal life into a new dimension of light and power . . . not . . . retrogression from the vivid personal into the vague and abstract impersonal . . . the inner evidence is the structure of our personal life; the outer evidence, meeting the inner evidence as light meets the eye, is in Jesus Christ . . . faith . . . beckoning, always freedom for our choosing and response . . . he showed himself to those who loved him . . . by hint and gleam, lest we be coerced."[1]

Resurrection Light uncovers humility.

Christ is Risen! Indeed.

January 22

---

1. George Buttrick, Sermons From A University Pulpit (Nashville: Abingdon Press, 1959), 176.

Retreat Devotion Outline

Psalm
Moment of Silence
A Word of Wonder
Moment of Silence
A Word of Vulnerability
Moment of Silence
A Word of Self-Awareness
Moment of Silence
Hymn
Exhortation

January 23

Salt and Light

To this service of ordered worship, in cantata and sermon, we welcome all. . .

For salt and light we bring learning, virtue and piety

With salt and light we become a heart for the heart of the city, a service in the service of the city

As salt and light, we lift our voice around the globe, discern our vocation in the heart and expand the volume of the Marsh Chapel community

With sisters and brothers in other traditions, traditions ancient and global, we share a longing for atonement and a need of compunction.

A humble contrition, here is today's salt.

A contrite humility, here is today's light.

Let us lift our hearts in personal and collective confession.

You are the salt of the earth. You are the light of the world. Peace, perfect peace, the peace of pardon and joy, be upon you.

January 24

Steeple Jack

Before you work high you build a scaffold to get yourself up there.

Steeple Jacks do not use a scaffold. They use rope and pulleys, and they rightly earn many hundreds of dollars an hour. As one said to me, quoting Scripture, and speaking of the dangers of height, "Jesus said, 'Lo(w) I am with you." Meaning, he continued, "up high you are on your own."

Our first and smaller churches, some five of them, hired Steeple Jacks for the minor tiling, shingling, painting and other repairs required of small church steeples on small steeple churches. One was squat enough (the church I mean not the Jack) that he could go up by ladder. Our sixth church (and the seventh, too) was a "tall steeple church." The trustees tried to get by with a Steeple Jack, every time repairs were needed, but most times, no, they needed to spend more. Once a two hundred pound section of copper plate fell off that steeple onto a University neighborhood street. Exposure, liability, act of God, randomness—these words appeared in sermons later that month. No one was hurt. Scaffolding went up the next week, and stayed up for several expensive days.

The interior space of churches also requires endless attention. As with care of the human body after the age of forty, the motto for sanctuary care must be "maintenance, maintenance, maintenance." Interior scaffolding also comes at a price. Sure you prefer to change light bulbs and paint ceilings with a huge step ladder and a fearless Trustee or hired painter. Sure. But the higher the nave, the, well, I refer you to adage above. "Lo I am with you." Not high.

Even before any paint is spilled, and even before any long lasting bulbs are replaced, there is work, there is cost, there is meaningful preparation.

So it is, as you know, in preaching. The interpreter either swings in the breeze like a Steeple Jack, if the matters of historical interpretation are low fences (Paul's letters come to mind), or, if the height is greater, scaffolding is needed (the Hebrew Scripture, all the Gospels, and especially the Gospel of John come to mind). What you see when the work is done, is the steeple repaired, the roof replaced, the paint (both coats) applied, the bulbs changed. But before that there has been scaffolding up, so that the work could be done.

January 25

The Importance of Condolence:
Letters Received at a Time of Loss

Dear Bob,

At this time you are either at your father's funeral or the burial. I am with you in spirit and prayer. This morning when I was meditating upon you and your relationship with your father I got to reflecting upon how your loss includes the loss of the world that only you and he had together, common understandings and experiences that only a son and father can have, common perceptions, beliefs, and knowings that go beyond words that bound the two of you together. Now that world, which I believe is eternal, is held in this life by your mind and soul, a place where your father continues to speak to you in the silence and essence of his being. I believe that world has an existence beyond this life where he holds you in his eternal soul, the soul that is also the Soul of God where God holds the two of you and your special world. I give thanks for that world knowing it is sacred and so very special. That world has nurtured my world and the world of creation. While you grieve the loss of being with your father in your earthly live, you know better than I that you and he will always be together and nothing, not even death, can destroy that. Thanks be to God and to his Son, Jesus, our Christ.

"About a week after Mary Elizabeth circulated an email informing us of your father's passing, I bought this card. For various reasons, certainly some not known by me, I 'forgot' to write. Some of it has to do with my own grieving (my mother died the day after Christmas, my father died a few years ago—and I've actually repressed the year). However old we get, we will always be the child of our parents, and the memories will appear out of nowhere—some welcome, others not. I hope your mourning unfolds well. I hope the images, thoughts, and feelings that arise unbidden connect you with your father, and even if shaken in this momenbt, you can smile knowing he's there with you."

"I can't quite express my feelings about your loss. Irving was such a huge influence on so many of us—we all grieve with you."

"Our heartfelt condolences on the death of your father. Our thoughts and prayers have been with you. Around 1476 the Spanish Poet Jorge Manrique expressed his sentiments upon his father's death in a poem entitled 'Coplas por la muerte de su padre,' the famous elegy written in the Spanish language. Manrique reminds us not only of the brevity of life but the comfort that comes from knowing his father had lived an exemplary life and moved from time to eternity . . .

Nuestros vidos son los rios
Que van a dar en la mar
Que es el morir
Que querer hombre vivir
Cuando Dios quiere que muera

Es locura
Que aunque la vida perdio
No dejo harto Consuelo su memoria.

January 26

The Technological Society

When you walk down Commonwealth Avenue, make a rough count of the number of people who pass you and are talking on cell phones, texting on Blackberries, or are ear-wired for music. One of the real joys of being alive is the chance to walk, and to watch and look and listen to all that may be alive around you. On such a walk, Jesus met a woman at a well, and made her well. On such a walk, down from Jerusalem to Jericho, a Samaritan saw and helped a man who had fallen among thieves. On such a walk, near Emmaus, the disciples encountered the Risen Christ. On such a walk, outside Damascus (today such a tumultuous city), Paul of Tarsus was blinded, thunderously addressed, and made into a new person. On such a walk, Francis of Assisi crisscrossed Europe and left behind his riches. On such a walk, Marco Polo found China. On such a walk, Isaac Newton saw an apple fall from a tree, and imagined gravity. On such a walk, Benjamin Franklin studied lightening, and later captured electricity. On such a walk, Robert Frost found two roads that diverged. On such a walk, the original San Francisco 49'r discovered gold in those western hills. On such a walk, Johnnie Appleseed filled the country with apple blossoms and apple trees. On such a walk, Martin Luther King changed Birmingham, and so the country. On such a walk, Winston Churchill decided that Commonwealth Avenue, Boston, is the most beautiful in America.

Here is a word of caution from Jacques Ellul: "Technology has two consequences which strike me as the most profound in our time. I call them the suppression of the subject and the suppression of meaning. . .The suppression of the subject is transforming traditional human relations, which require the voice, which require seeing, or which require a physical relationship between one human being and the next. The result is the distant relationship . . . the suppression of meaning: the ends of existence gradually seem to be effaced by the predominance of means . . . the meaning of existence of 'why I am alive' is suppressed as technology so vastly develops its power."[1]

January 27

---

1. Jacques Ellul *Perspectives on Our Age: Jacques Ellul Speaks on his Life and Work* (Seabury Press, 1981) 51.

Whimsy

A man driving across Ireland had car trouble. He emerged from behind the wheel and could see no one, only a horse. Suddenly the horse leaned over the fence and said, "Open the hood, and let me have a look." "You are a talking horse?" "Yes. Clean the gaskets and retry the ignition." The car purred, and off the man drove, terrified. He stopped in a bar to calm his nerves with a drink. "You look terrible said the barkeep. What happened to you?" "You won't believe it. My car broke down. Then a horse came to me and spoke, and fixed my car." "Really? What color was the horse?" "Black. Why?" "Well, you were lucky. There is white horse over there, too. But he doesn't know anything about car mechanics."

January 28

A Sketch on Writing for the Ear[1]

- The test of good writing is permanence, the test of good speech is immediacy.
- Sentences: short and clear; words: familiar and plain.
- Churchill, Roosevelt, Shakespeare, King, (Cuomo).
- The preacher must hear how the words sound.
- Use as few words as possible (Laconic).
- Use words that sound well together (paralysis of analysis, perky jerky).
- Short, strong, clear, familiar words (Anglo Saxon, not Latin).
- Sensuous not abstract, specific not general (not flowers, apple blossoms; not great poets, John Milton; not suffering, blood toil tears sweat "the Bible was the weapon of our souls."
- Sentences, sometimes long (Lincoln).
- Paragraph, or though (move?) more important than sentence.
- The ear is far more tolerant of repetition, reiteration.
- Every sentence has two positions of strength, beginning and end.

You will not acquire mastery of words and sentences by reading about them. You will take them captive by practice.

January 29

---

1. H. Grady Davis, *Design for Preaching* (Minneapolis: Fortress Press, 2013), 265.

Young Man Jesus

Jesus meets us today in the Word. He greets us. He greets us a real human being, fully human.

How shall we say this, today?

You know, for a long time, people have been trying to say the right thing, in the right way, at the right time, about Jesus.

To an unruly church, Matthew said: "Hold it. Jesus was a teacher."

To a suffering church, Mark said: "Remember. Jesus was crucified. He suffered too."

To a settled, more comfortable church, Luke said: "Wait a minute. Jesus loved the poor, those outside."

To a philosophical church, John said: "Stop. God's word became flesh and dwelt among us."

You know, for a long time, groups of people have been trying to say the right thing, in the right way, at the right time, about Jesus.

In 1848, over in Seneca Falls, Jesus was well remembered as an advocate for, a friend of women.

In 1862, in the autumn, as Lincoln pondered the Emancipation Proclamation, Jesus would have been remembered as a person of color, semitic, dark, today we would say black.

In 1933, the only thing worth saying in Berlin and Tubingen about Jesus was that he was a Jew. In fact, Dietrich Bonhoeffer said then that the Christian church in Germany either would be found standing next to for and up for the Jewish community or it did not exist at all.

And today?

Humans have always had problems with Jesus' humanity. The rude manger, innocent and innocuous, we can accept. The empty tomb, divine power and victory, we can accept. It is what lies between Christmas and Easter that is harder for us.

On October 24, 2010, at Boston University Marsh Chapel, amid 4400 freshmen and women, and 40,000 people in a community of learning, what shall we say about the humanity of Jesus?

Just this: He lived and died a *young* man. So he is, as a classmate once wrote, "perpetually ripe."

January 30

Can We Afford It?: Irving G. Hill

From my earliest memory
The question has been
'Can we afford it?'
When I wanted a bicycle, I asked
'Can we afford it?'

My mom said 'no.'
But,
We did!

When the American Youth Hostel recruited me for a work project
In Europe in 1946
'Could we afford it?'
No!
But I went.

When it came time for me to go to college,
'Could we afford it?'
No!
But I graduated from Syracuse University.

My future father in law asked, 'could I afford to marry
His daughter?'
'Weeeel. . .' I answered
But we got married!

Confronted with a growing family
And a month's vacation, we needed
A summer retreat!
'Could we afford it?'
No!
But somehow we did!

After thirty nine years of the Traveling Ministry
At age sixty-two
'could we afford to retire?'
No
Was the answer.
But I did retire!

When it became necessary to purchase a residence
The answer this time was
Yes
With a lot of help!

The next great adventure we face is death.
Can we afford it?
Not willingly, not willingly,
But by faith we will!

January 31

February

A Complete Life

Martin Luther King's own favorite sermon, "The Dimensions of a Complete Life," as Gary Dorrien reminds us, was itself based on a sermon from Boston's own Phillips Brooks.[1] King preached the sermon in 1954, to candidate at Dexter Avenue, and again at Perdue in 1958 before a national UCC convention, and again in 1964 in Westminster Abbey to accept the Nobel Peace Prize. As you learn, preaching on a circuit, what is good the first time, can often be better preached three times or more. The opposite also may be true. King, following Brooks, compared life to a cube, possessing the three dimensions of length, breadth and height. The good life flourishes when all three interact in something like a great triangle. "At one angle stands the individual person, at the other angle stand other persons, and at the top stands the Supreme Infinite Person, God." Length means achieving personal goals, breadth comprises the concern for the well being of others, and height signifies the desire for an upward moving longing for God.

February 1

---

1. Gary Dorrien, *The Making of American Liberal Theology: Crisis, Irony, and Postmodernity* (Louisville: Westminster John Knox Press, 2006), 157.

Groundhog Day

There are no ordinary days, no insignificant holidays.

Emily Webb stands as our fiercest sentinel to the landscape of this, truth, the Gospel of Groundhog Day.

You will remember that she and George were graduated from High School in Grover's Corners. On the basis of a frank talking to over a soda, in which Emily criticizes George for being less than fully humble, George decides not to leave home, not to go to college, but to start working an uncle's farm right away, and to marry Emily, the girl next door. You remember their wedding. "A man looks pretty small at a wedding, all those good women standing shoulder to shoulder, making sure the knot is tied in a mighty public way." You remember that Emily, after just a few years of profoundly happy marriage and life, tragically dies in childbirth. You remember that George finds no way to manage the extreme grief of his loss. Simple Yankee English. Simple reckoning about love, life, death and meaning.

Maybe you also remember, in the playwright's imagination, Emily from the communion of saints looking out on her young husband and wanting to go back.

Others warn her away from the plan: "All I can say Emily, is, don't . . . it isn't wise . . . (If you must do it) Choose an unimportant day. Choose the least important day of your life. It will be important enough."

She chooses February 11, 1899, her 12th birthday. She arrives at dawn. She sees Main Street, the drugstore, the livery stable, and breathes the brightness of a crisp winter morning. Simple. She looks into her own house. Her mother is making breakfast, her father returning from a speech given at Hamilton College. Neighbors pass in the snow. Simple. She sees how young and pretty her mother looks-can't quite believe it. It is 10 below zero. There is fussing to find a blue hair ribbon—"its on the dresser—if it were a snake it would bite you." Simple. Papa enters to give a hug and a kiss and a birthday gift. And others from mother and the boy next door. Simple. "Just for a moment now we're all together. Mama, just for a moment now we're all together. Just for a moment we're happy. Let's look at one another."

Simple. This is the gospel of Groundhog Day, the best holiday of the year, the holiday of the extraordinary ordinary, of the uncommonly common, of the sunlit winter, of the eternal now. Simple. Grover's Corners. Papa. Mama. Clocks ticking. Sunflowers. Food. Coffee. New ironed dresses. Hot baths. Sleeping. Waking up. "Earth, you are too wonderful for anybody to realize you."

Reverence for Life is the beginning of wisdom.

February 2

As If Not

The form of this world is passing away.

So let those who have wives live as if they had none. Let them be married, not in the form of this world, but in the form of the world to come, "as if not . . ."

Once there lived a model couple. Pillars of church and community, they arrived at their mid-fifties in joyful wedlock. They were models of self-giving love. He would arise every morning thinking, "What can I do to make her life brighter today?" She would end every evening with some bright thought for the morning. The minister would pass by that house and smile.

Then one night the preacher had a phone call from the couple, and a distressed question: "Can you come right over?" After some awkwardness and foot shuffling they asked, "Would you marry us?" Well it was a long story. They had begun many years earlier working together, running the town store. Times were tough, so, to save money, they moved in, together to share space. Then they fell in love. People in the town assumed they were married, and, well, what could they say? So, year followed year and decade followed decade. They felt, though, that is time to make if official. A simple, elegant ceremony ensued. The minister would pass by that house, again, with a smile.

About a month after the wedding, the minister received another late night call. Down he went again to visit this model couple, who, for the first time were on the verge of separation. They were at wits end. The wife spoke up: "Nothing has been right since the wedding. It used to be, you know, every day was a new happiness. But since the ceremony and the ring and the certificate, I guess we have started to take each other for granted. There was something about being free to leave, that kept both of us on our toes. We used to really watch out for each other, even serve each other. But now that the knot is tied, we are chaffing at one another."

A long night of conversation followed. Tears and apologies, advice and consolation. There was a return of the old feeling for the old couple. In the wee hours the minister put on his coat to leave. But before he left he forced the couple to make a solemn vow. He made them promise to live together, from that day forward, for better or worse, in sickness and in health, as if they were not married. As if not . . .

Let those who have wives live as if they had none. Let us be married, not in the form of this world, but in that of the world to come. Not in complacency and disregard and a taking for granted—this world. But in surprise and kindness and joy and love—the world to come.

February 3

Auntie Rose: A Listener's Memory of a Moving Eulogy

Auntie Rose loved being Auntie Rose. And the billowing costumes of Masterpiece Theatre.

The drama of the theatre, ballet and lights on Broadway.

PBS, BBC and anything having to do with Jane Austen.

Looking at the costumes, patrons and talking furs of the opera.

Listening to the sopranos' aria at the opera.

Anrea Boccelli, Luciano Pavarrotti, Kathleen Battle, Mahalia Jackson and Sweet Honey and the Rock.

Singing along with the soundtrack from *The Bodyguard*.

Listening to Mozart in her Mazda while driving along the Charles.

The lights of New York City, Chinatown, and bargaining at the open market.

Talking about the market and being savvy.

Watching the pundits on CNN.

Commenting like a pundit on CNN.

Tom Brokaw, Dan Rather, 60 Minutes and the Latest Breaking News.

Watching Charlie Rose, listening to Charlie Rose.

And watching his interviews with Johnny Depp, Denzel Washington and Sean Penn.

Talking about the state of the world.

Being hopeful about the future of the world.

Talking about history and the politicians in the world.

Another niece simply said, "Auntie Rose thought it was more important to look good than to be on time."

February 4

Awakening

To some degree, in the light of the Transfiguration, in the light of truth, the true light that enlightens everyone, we all have responsibility to bear witness. In fact, our saving possibility lies in the very challenge and calling we have to try to respond to the light, however dim, the true light, however dusky.

Your awakening to faith, your Christian reawakening as my friend put it, may occur, may arrive on the witness stand.

You are a junior in college. What have you seen? What have you heard? What have you experienced of wisdom and love?

You are a man without a job. 85% of jobs lost have been men's in the great mancession. What have you seen? What have you heard? What have you experienced of wisdom and love?

You are a professional. Necessarily an institution has a claim on you. Adult life is invariably institutional, whether or not you are institutionalized. What have you seen? What have you heard? What have you experienced of wisdom and love?

You are an elder of many moons and many moccasins. If someone spares the time to ask your testimony, what will it be? What have you seen? What have you heard? What have you experienced of wisdom and love?

February 5

G. B. Caird Starts Over

This summer I discovered in an old box, a prize possession, a copy of a sermon from 60 years ago.

It is GB Caird's inaugural sermon as a professor of New Testament at McGill University, Montreal, in 1951. Here are some highlights:

"Today we have come to recognize that we have no knowledge of any Jesus of history other than the Christ to whom the writers of the New Testament bear united witness, that St. Paul made good his claim to have the mind of Christ and is in fact the greatest of all Christ's interpreters, and that St. Mark's Gospel is no less theological than that of St. John.

"Anyone who imagines that the contribution of critical scholarship to the study of the New Testament can be lightly brushed aside to allow for a return to the traditional orthodoxy must be totally ignorant of what he condemns.

"Sooner or later the demand was bound to be made for a new movement which should rediscover beneath the diversity the fundamental unity of the New Testament, which can be felt even by those unable to prove its existence. The prophet of the new movement was C H Dodd.

"We can still regard the Bible as the Word of God—a word communicated not by the automatic processes of verbal inspiration but through the fallible powers and kaleidoscopic variety of human speech and thought, yet a word unique in its authority and appeal.

"I propose to set before you in three illustrations a view of life which seems to me to be common to all the richly varied writings of the New Testament, and to be the peculiar contribution of those writings to the religious thought of mankind.

"The Sovereignty of God: God is the Lord of heaven and earth. It is he who makes his sun shine on the evil and the good. . . . The invisible nature of God is clearly seen in the things he has made. . . . Nowhere outside the Bible do we find such an exalted faith in the Living God. . .Only in the Bible and the religions derived from it do we find a belief in the sovereign purposes of God."

February 6

Exercise

In my junior year, spent abroad in Segovia, I had the good fortune to meet and friend. We climbed the mountains of Castile together, but I never saw her in church. Then the week before Lent in 1975, the last year of Franco's reign, we in the plaza. My friend was carrying, in good Castilian fashion, the Ejercicios Espirituales of Ignatius of Loyola. Surprised, I inquired about this reading for Lent, and participation in the visionary exercise of Loyola. "Siempre se saca algo bueno de estas cosas" said the confirmed agnostic: "ah, one always gets something good from these things," said the passionate climber of mountains. Another kind of mountain view . . .

February 7

Faith

Faith is the power to withstand what we cannot understand. Worship is the practice of faith by which we learn to withstand what we cannot understand. God is the presence, force, truth, and love Who alone deserves worship, and worship is the practice of the faith by which we learn to withstand what we cannot understand. Worship prepares us to resist. So we see Jesus again in the wilderness. To resist all that makes human life inhuman. So here you are, come lent, come Sunday, come this Sunday.

February 8

Grace

A scandalous universality is this—our shared dependence.

Bishop Solomon told a story about a dream of heaven, where entry required 100 pts. One man walked to St Peter, head bowed.

"What say you?" asked Cephas.

"Well, I once helped Habitat for Humanity."

"Good—one point. What else?"

"Well, I remember once I gave to my alumni fund."

"Good—one point. What else?"

"Uh, I was always kind to animals."

"Good—one point. What else?"

"Oh St Peter, I just do not have enough points! At this rate I would only get in by the grace of God."

"Grace of God—97 points! You're in!"

February 9

Ali

In May of 1992, in the middle of a big church meeting in Louisville, Kentucky, I got more than unusually lost, driving to church, an unfamiliar church, in that less than familiar city. I ended up somewhere I know not where on the other side of the wrong side of the tracks, driving on a peach of a spring Sunday morning, driving past row after row of terrible housing. Every city has such a neighborhood. Dirt where grass should have been. Rubble where porches should have been. Air where glass should have been. Peeling where paint should have been. And in front of this so-called housing, a range of quiet and taciturn children and grandparents. I guess this Louisville slum is not the poorest place I have seen but it stands out as the saddest poorest place, especially so on a sleeping city sidewalk, and Sunday morning (coming down). Nothing as lonesome as that sound.

Imagine my shock to turn a corner, still irretrievably lost, to meet this sign: "The birthplace of Cassius Clay, Mohammed Ali, heavyweight champion of the world." The prettiest, the greatest, the champion.

Bishop Robert Spain preached a wonderful sermon that morning, when I finally found my way. The music, teaching, fellowship and love of the suburban Methodist church were real and good. But God's Word, that Sunday, was in the drooping porches and rat infested squalor that somehow, miraculously, gave birth to a champion. How could such a voice, a face, a body, a spirit, an intellect, a will, a mind, a man ever, ever, ever have emerged from such abuse and neglect? Why, it would be like saying that the divine could emerge from cattle stalls, or over-packed inns, or Palestinian slums, or neglected religion. Change is possible, change for the better.

How does something good emerge from what is not good? How does healing come out of ill health? While we have our more modern ways of describing the mystery, the same mystery met those listening to Jesus as he began his ministry. An unclean spirit, of plural dimension ('us'), cries out. Jesus speaks: "Be silent. Come out." He speaks the same word still: be silent, come out. In apocalyptic mystery, "the unclean spirit, convulsing him and crying with a loud voice, came out of him." All that long winter of hurt, and there, just there, grace. Wasn't it Paul who claimed, 'where sin abounds, grace over-abounds'? A winter grace . . .

February 10

Huckleberry

My friend Jon Clinch, best man in our wedding and I in theirs, has a great new novel coming out this month. Titled, *Finn*, the book imagines the life of Huckleberry Finn's father, Pap. Pap's life is something to be mourned, though his death is not. In the course of writing this dark tale, the author has given us an insight, a novel reading of the greatest American novel, which no one, no one, for 120 years, had earlier seen! You read this book and sense that the author has found the key to pick the lock of Twain's mind! Do you know what a huckleberry is? What color it is? What hue? Twain hid his secret right in plain view, in the name, Huckleberry, whose mother, according to this newest fiction, was black.

Let us imagine in the form of the world to come.

February 11

John of the Cross

In the mountains northwest of Madrid, you will find nestled the little old Castilian village of Segovia. I spent only a year there. I walked its cobbled streets during the evening paseo. I was befriended by its teenagers. Adios Roberto. Adios Marie Carmen. Adios Celia. Adios Eduardo. I gazed out at the mountain range that had inspired Hemingway. I ate the baked lamb and drank the red wine of that region. I admired its aqueduct. I photographed its castle. I learned the language, the humor, the humors, the history, the heart, the soul of a noble people. I walked in the dark late night rain and greeted the town crier and constable: "Adios." Someday I hope to return. I find that Segovia appears with more regularity in my dreams now than it has for thirty years past.

I visited there the resting place of St. John of the Cross. I read and remembered his poetry: en una noche oscura, con ansias en amores inflamadas, o dichosa ventura!, sali sin ser notada, estando ya mi casa sosegada.

February 12

Kairos Moment

In December our granddaughter, our daughter, Jan and I rode the T to Haymarket Square. Our beloved's beloved baby gurgled past Boylston and Park. The Christmas lights glistened out from a soft Nevada. You could see your breath. Jan had seen advertised a free reading of love letters, from Abigail Adams to John Adams, and from John Adams to Abigail Adams, and offered in historic Faneuil Hall, and read by three couples named Patrick, Dukakis, and Kennedy.

There are kairos moments. Whether or not your earnest study of Oscar Cullman and Luke and Galatians convinces you, life will teach you. When Mrs. Duval read Abigail's letter following Bunker Hill, to a distant John in Washington, full of terror and wonder at whether she would live the week, the air went out of the room. When Governor Dukakis read later John's angry criticism of the laziness of the congress, and paused midsentence to look meaningfully at Senator Kennedy, no words were needed to bring the house to robust laughter. When Kitty Dukakis read slowly the long, love sentences, ripe and revealing, from wife to husband, from dearest friend to dearest friend, you wondered truly whether you could breathe again. When we heard the horrific sorrow of Abigail's mother's death, read out by Mrs. Kennedy, only a stone would not have cried. And I wonder about the stone. Every seat was full. As every heart. See how they loved each other!

Listen, for just a moment, Abigail to John:

"That your Sex are Naturally Tyrannical is a Truth so thoroughly established as to admit of no dispute, but such of you as wish to be happy willingly give up the harsh title of Master for the more tender and endearing on of Friend."[1]

Listen for just a moment, John to Abigail:

"It is a fortnight to day Since I had Letter from you but it Seems to me a month. I cannot blame you for one of yours is worth four of mine."[2]

February 13

---

1. Margaret A. Hogan and C. James Taylor, *My Dearest Friend: Letters of Abigail and John Adams* (Cambridge: Belknap, 2010), 110.

2. Hogan, 370.

Lake Placid

If the roads are clear this cold season is a fine time to travel in the mountains, north and west, and into Lake Placid NY. Near there you find a most exotically named preaching assignment, a four point charge: Owls Head, Chasm Falls, Mountainview, and Wolf Pond. You might pass through the strangely frightening prison town of Dannemora. I remember visiting near there the hunting lodge of a friend. He stood snow splattered in his meadow watching and listening to Nature in her farthest reach and said, "It's so wild up here."

Lake Placid itself seems like the top of the world, especially in the winter. Winter is our most visually beautiful season here in the north. We are in fact ice people, no bad thing. The world needs both fire and ice. Here is Mirror Lake. Here is the Olympic Pavilion. Here is the ski lift from which to view the grandeur of the mountains, the poverty of the north country, the stark serenity of Old Man Winter, a colossus striding upon the earth. You are on top of the world, or at least as far up as we get around here.

Before you go off to dinner or the hot tub, I propose a further little visit. Out behind the ski lift, a long way from the road and not overly well marked, there is a gravesite. Trudge a few paces into the snow and take a look. There, if you brush back the powder, you can make out the name and dates. Under mountain shadows, hidden in the ice box of the north, covered at least half the year with a beautiful white blanket of snow, there lies the body of John Brown, 1800–1859, whose flint like personality, bent to violence, and fiery rhetoric helped ignite the civil war, which began 150 years ago. His is a fitting rough grave lost in the outback of the Empire State. He lies just about as far from the Mason Dixon line as one go, and still stay within the country.

February 14

Manners

We will all do better if we watch our manners.

Listen before you speak. . . . Serve others then yourself. . . . Offer a prayer as you come to the meal. . . . Enjoy others, and let them enjoy you. . . . See if there is anything you can bring along. . . . Perhaps someone needs a ride. . . . You will no doubt send along some kind of thank you note. . . . Serve from the left, clear from the right. . . . Be sure to thank the host, and to bid farewell to the hostess. . . . Try not to eat and run. . . . Watch for those who are missing. . .Be grateful. . . . Give thanks. . . .

All these table manners, and personal graces, are ways of living out, and so remembering, our capacity to jostle, to bruise, to harm, to maim others. These table manners are ritual acts of kindness thrown up in the teeth of much unkindness. They have their root in a profound sense of dependence—on others, on God, on Pardon.

May I be excused? You may be excused. Pardon me. I beg your pardon.

February 15

Nine

The ninth commandment requires us not to bear false witness.

Some years ago the English translation of Victor Klemperer's two volume history, memoir, and diary of Germany in the 1920's and 1930's was published. "I Will Bear Witness," it is titled. I encourage you to read it. A Jewish man who became a liberal Protestant, a cultural and literary historian, an esteemed professor and writer, Klemperer applied himself to a humble daily task. He quietly recorded, in his diary, the clinking sounds of the Nazi shackles slowly, gradually tightening upon the German people, and, horrifically, with tragic weight upon those of Jewish ancestry. Including Klemperer.

Little things. Rationing. Distinctions in the process of rationing. Automobile registrations. Distinctions in the manner of registration. Little things. Slight, ever so subtle shifts in social behaviors. Invitations extended without response. Dinners offered but not reciprocated. Gradual transformations in daily language, in the language of the morning newspaper. Decisions about which words would be or would not be allowed, in the common spaces of life. Little things, really. Variations in the wording of classified ads. Glances, furtive looks across the street where before there was full eye to eye contact. Just little things. But seen, revealed, transfigured in the prescient, humble diary composition of one quiet teacher.

As you know, little things became big things. Family, friends and neighbors who decide to emigrate. Positions limited. Positions trimmed. Positions eliminated. The threat of confinement to town. Then confinement. To house. Then confinement. Marches in brown shirts. Yellow stars. Captivity. War. The unimaginable. The unspeakable. . . .

Klemperer recorded events and words both great and small, in order not to bear false witness.

February 16

O Canada

We are not alone,
we live in God's world.
We believe in God:
who has created and is creating,
who has come in Jesus,
the Word made flesh,
to reconcile and make new,
who works in us and others
by the Spirit.
We trust in God.
We are called to be the Church:
to celebrate God's presence,
to live with respect in Creation,
to love and serve others,
to seek justice and resist evil,
to proclaim Jesus, crucified and risen,
our judge and our hope.
In life, in death, in life beyond death,
God is with us.
We are not alone.
Thanks be to God.

February 17

Pasture View

A friend told me a story one winter. It is not a Groundhog Day story, nor a Valentine's Day story, nor a Presidents' Day story, but simply a winter story.

He has friends who live on a farm in Michigan. This is a multi-generational family farm. If you were to visit this week, you would find three generations working together. The grandfather died a few years ago, but his sons, grandsons and great grandsons still plow and harvest, milk and feed.

The matriarch of the family is now older and weaker. She was a typical farm wife of her generation, working alongside her children and husband. When plowing time came in the spring she would fix lunches for all hands, and deliver them into the fields. She delivered the meal, and while they ate, she would take over and plow. The same kinds of routines held for other seasons. The rhythms of seed and harvest, birth and decay set the beat for her life.

Now she is alone much of the time, in the old farm house. Her kids feed her breakfast in the morning and dinner at night. But every day, after breakfast, they settle her into a comfortable easy chair that rocks in front of an open bay window, from which she can look out onto the fields and forests and pastures of her home. Every day she watches, breakfast to dinner.

Now this is not an active scene. The barn and equipment are not in view. Most winter days there are no people to observe. A car on the road every half-hour is a lot of traffic. And snow lying on corn stubble looks about as exciting as it did one hundred years ago. Yet, she watches and looks. She seems to be deeply contented, as the late winter snow falls. She is eased and settled and comforted, looking out on a frosty field. There is something in that utterly ordinary scene that seizes her.

She has a sense, I think, of presence. Maybe she is weak and maybe she even has some mild dementia and maybe she dozes every now and then, rocking in front of the window. But this ordinary winter story captivates me, because I think she is enthralled by something not quite visible to the naked eye, yet present. There is something there, something alive, something at work, just beyond our comprehension. She rocks and stays alert to presence. She has a hard won trust in Presence, a kind of trust for which life is meant and for which with all our hearts we do passionately long and hunger.

February 18

Peace and War

Over 20 centuries, and speaking with unforgivable conciseness as one must in a twenty-two minute sermon, two basic understandings of war and peace have emerged in Christian thought. As you know, these roughly can be called the so-called pacifist and just war understandings.

Pacifism preceded its sibling, and infinitely extends to all times the interim ethic of the New Testament (which even here in Matthew, a late writing, expects that the coming of Christ will soon make moot our ethical dilemmas, and so tends to err on the side of quietism, or, in the case of arms, pacifism): "to him who strikes you on the cheek, offer the other also." Many utterly saintly Christian women and men have and do honor this understanding with their selfless commitment, including many in this congregation today. My own pulpit hero, Ernest Fremont Tittle, the best Methodist preacher of the 20th century, did so from his Chicago pulpit through the whole Second World War. Think about that for a minute. I did for more than a minute when I preached from that very pulpit last June. While personally I have not been able, to this date anyway, to agree with him, I never compose a sermon on this topic without wondering, and to some degree fearing, what his judgment might be.

The multiple theories of just war, or war as the least of all evil alternatives, have developed since the Fourth Century and the writing of St. Augustine. Here the command to "be merciful, even as God is merciful" is understood tragically to include times when mercy for the lamb means armed opposition to the wolf. The New Testament apocalyptic frame and its interim ethic are honored, to be sure, but supplemented with the historic experience of the church through the ages. Many utterly saintly Christian men and women have honored this understanding with their selfless commitment, including some present here today, and some who are not present because they gave their lives that others might live. Just war thought includes several serious caveats. We together need to know and recall these, in five forms: a just cause in response to serious evil, a just intention for restoration of peace with justice, an absence of self-enrichment or desire for devastation, a use as an utterly last resort, a claim of legitimate authority, and a reasonable hope of success, given the constraints of "discrimination" and "proportionality" (usually understood as protection of non-combatants). Response. Restoration. Restraint. Last resort. Common authority.

Prayerfully, we each and we all will want to consider our own understanding, our own ethic, our own choice and choices between these two basic alternatives.

February 19

Presence

Sometimes, as Ralph Harper taught us some years ago, we need the height of presence: "When I am moved by a painting or by music, by clouds passing in a clear night sky, by the soughing of pines in the early spring, I feel the distance between me and art and nature dissolve to some degree, and I feel at ease. I feel that what I know makes me more myself than I knew before. This is how the saints felt about God, and I see in my own experience elements that I share with the saints and prophets, the philosophers and priests."[1] Let us remember presence this Lent.

February 20

---

1. Ralph Harper, *On Presence* (Baltimore: Johns Hopkins Press, 2006), 6.

Refusal

Or, maybe you doubt that refusal takes a part of small stage play. Perhaps only the civil disobedience of Ghandi or the peaceful resistance of Martin Luther King or the risky French Resistance of Albert Camus stand out, great historic refusals, great moments of common endurance. But you would be wrong, I suggest, to think so. Most resistance is hidden, unheralded, unknown, unrewarded. Most principled refusal is known only to the one sagging against the ropes, the one catching the body blows. Most real principled resistance is very ordinary.

Tithing is primarily a form of spiritual refusal, refusal to accept the world's understanding of success and refusal to accept the implication that all that we have is ours alone. *Worship* is primarily a form of spiritual refusal, refusal to accept the world's time clock, where all time is meant for work or play. *Marriage* and *loyal friendship* are primarily forms of spiritual refusal, refusal to accept the world's low estimate of intimacy, refusal to accept the unholy as good. *Choosing carefully* is primarily a form of spiritual resistance.

You are a part of a tradition of principled resistance.

February 21

Relationship

What can prepare us for intimacy with the divine, if not human intimacy?
What can prepare us for covenant with the divine, if not human covenant?
What can prepare us for fellowship with the divine, if not human fellowship?
What can prepare us for love of the divine, if not human love?

Where else are we going to learn the rhythms of relationship that prepare a community and its individuals, an individual and his communities, for ultimate relationship?

No wonder Plato wrote so tenderly and toughly about friendship. No wonder John the Evangelist epitomized discipleship in the portrait of one 'beloved.' No wonder Bernard of Clairvaux wrote 86 sermons on the Song of Songs and never got past the second chapter! No wonder that John of the Cross and Teresa of Avila took Italian love poetry and formed their religious poetry on their models. No wonder that even today there is a returning interest in "nuptial mysticism," a recognition that love, friendship, partnership, marriage shape a soulful habit of living. It is in the relationship of lover and beloved that we plumb the depths of experience.

In relationship, we are addressed, truly, from beyond ourselves.

February 22

Routine

I remember the first time I was left alone with our first child, to give her mother a night out. She had been the most pleasant of children, happy and bright, sleeping through the night. She hardly cried. But that hot August night, at the very moment the door closed and the car drove off, she began to wail. Not to whimper or weep, but to wail and shriek and scream. Five, twenty five, fifty minutes. I was really shaken, terrified, angry and frustrated, at my wit's end, and probably at the edge of some irrational behavior. Over the din of the howling daughter, I heard the doorbell. In came our church's lay leader, Bernice Danks, a veteran nurse and teacher of nurses at Cornell who wordlessly took the child and somehow the howling ceased. "Oh, I like to make a few house visits a week. It's a little routine of mine. . . . You know I tell my nursing students that we call the things that are most important, 'routine' . . . and I came by the parsonage and for some reason I decided to stop. I hope you don't mind the intrusion. . . . What a pleasant baby she is!"

When we are helpless, insight can come.

Wesley is still with us to ask, "Will you visit from house to house?" Insight sees inside the closed door of personal need, and measures the distance between public appearance and private reality. We recognize personal need with every Sunday, at Marsh Chapel with gusto, in confession and kyrie, cry for forgiveness.

February 23

Royce

"Come let us reason together" says the Psalmist. God has entrusted us with freedom, and with minds to think through our use of freedom. While reason has its limits, it is reason, finally, that will help us learn the arts of disagreement—at home, at work, in church, in the community. We say, "Try to be reasonable." And reason often prevails. If you ever doubt the power of reason to bring insight, remember the words of the Psalmist, and the voices of great minds through the ages. Josiah Royce's Sources of Religious Insight, is itself a gem of such reasoned discourse. Come let us reason together. . . .

Now I submit to you that this meaning of the word reason is perfectly familiar to all of you. Reason, from this point of view, is the power to see widely and steadily and connectedly. Its true opponent is not intuition, but whatever makes us narrow in outlook, and consequently prey to our own caprices. The unreasonable person is the person who can see but one thing at a time, when he ought to see two or many things together; who can grasp but one idea, when a synthesis of ideas is required. The reasonable man is capable of synopsis, of viewing both or many sides of a question, of comparing various motives, of taking interest in a totality rather than in a scattered multiplicity.

You know, we recognize this chance for insight, this moment of clarity, every Sunday through a sermon, a word (we hope) fitly spoken.

February 24

Strange Bible

You will no doubt recognize the more apparent deterrents to worship, having weathered them over time. Empty sanctuaries deter worshippers as do cold ones. Empty sermons deter worshippers as do cold ones. Empty hearts deter worshippers as do cold ones. The ancient condition of buildings, the comparably ancient condition and average age of preachers, the ancient condition our condition is in has severed the head from the torso of northern historic Christianity. In some places we are dormant and convalescing, in others simply dead. Most parts of northeastern Protestantism have lost half their membership since 1977. There has been virtually no leadership acknowledgement of this deterioration and death. We remember William Tecumseh Sherman's quip about a soldier's death—"to die a hero's death and have one's name misspelled in the newspaper." Two centuries of toilsome (and some tiresome) preaching we have let go, with hardly an accurate report. Abuse, denial and neglect of the body by the head, of the church by the leadership of the church, have taken their toll.

There are other deterrents too.

Among the lesser impediments to church attendance are the Scriptures themselves, so wild and different in their variety. Our lectionary tries to corral this wildness with a set schedule for the readings. One wonders about this, this sort of quenching of Spirit. Maybe one reading, readily read, is sufficient. Kathleen Norris, author of Dakota: A Spiritual Geography, wrote recently of her own return to the cold, empty church of the Great Plains. She complained most about the words, the many, full, heavy, exacting words. As a poet, she would go home from a 50 minute service, three hymns, three readings, and a sermon, utterly exhausted, to nap all afternoon. The wild variety of words plum wore her out. Today, for instance, Isaiah, the Psalmist, and Luke–who have virtually nothing in common.

February 25

Terrier Fan

On Thursday Boston University gathered for the single biggest photograph ever. Students, faculty and staff filled out onto the basketball court at Agganis Arena, following the twilight victory, after sundown, of BU over Albany. One of the students was dressed as Jesus: long hair, full beard, white tunic, sandals. And a BU scarlet scarf. Who would have known that our Lord was a Terrier fan? Through the crowd I moved to greet him. I felt it was my duty, as Dean of the Chapel. At last the crowd parted, and before the sea of students moved again, I had the chance to stretch out my hand. My mind was blank, my lips were dry, and my voice quaked. At last, not knowing what to say, I gurgled, "I have always wanted to meet you. . . . " He lowered his chin, piercing me with his dark eyes, paused, and then said, simply, "I understand." We talk about Jesus every Sunday here in Marsh Chapel, but at the Athletic Department, you can shake his hand. We preach about him here, but there you can greet him. We sing his praise here, but there you can look him in the eye. Unfair competition. . . .

February 26

Time and Chance

For the race is not to the swift, nor the battle to the strong, nor bread to the wise, nor riches to the intelligent, nor favor to the men of skill, but time and chance happen to them all.

How well we remember the final game of the NCAA tournament in 1989, pitting Syracuse against Indiana. You remember the close finish, the wild crowd, the first place ranking at stake. Derek Coleman, then a freshman, somehow, inexplicably missed an easy shot at the end, and the player berating, chair kicking, opponent bedeviling Coach Knight went on victory. "O somewhere in this favored land the sun was shining bright, and somewhere children were singing, and somewhere hearts were light, but there was joy in upstate New York when mighty Derek struck out." The race is not always to the swift. . . .

On Monday the Rotary Club lunch began, in a deep and sorrowful reverie, broken only half-heartedly by the dejected President's call to order, the weekly off-key singing of the national anthem, and then, as usual, with the prayer, offered that day by county judge Jack Schultz. "Dear God, we know that we cannot always win. We know that we learn from our losses as well as our victories. We thank you for many blessings that have come our way, even though this inferior Indiana team, lead by a heartless and ruthless tyrant, has stolen our one chance in this generation for glory. Lord, we do not expect always to win . . . but, but, but . . . we do demand justice in the future! Amen." It still rings out as the most heartfelt public prayer I have heard.

No, the race is not always to the swift, nor the battle to the strong, nor bread to the wise, nor riches to the intelligent, nor favor to the men of skill, but time and chance happen to them all.

February 27

Trust

Is it that trust, that human response to the faith of Jesus Christ, that loving trust that "bears all things believes all things hopes all things and endures all things"? (1 Corinthians 13)

One early follower of Jesus said, "one thing I do, forgetting what lies behind and straining forward to what lies ahead, I press on toward the goal for the prize of the upward call of God in Christ Jesus?" (Paul of Tarsus).

An Irish man, Patrick, a killer of snakes and a lover of souls pronounced the same blessing, of "Christ before me Christ beneath?" (St. Patrick's breastplate)

Listen to that medieval convent maiden's prayer, "and all will be well and all will be well?" (Julian of Norwich).

As they sing at Taize, "ubi caritas, deus ibi est"?

There is something, Someone, there. Alive and untamed. Creating trust, trust, trust, deep in the heart.

Paul Lehmann taught us, "God is at work in the world to make and keep human life human."

Ralph Harper learned, "Presence suggests an alternate way of thinking about time and space."

In an early pastoral visit, I heard a homebound octogenarian, eyes gleaming, affirm: "I know whom I can trust."

David sang in the Psalms, "the Lord is my light and my salvation, whom shall I fear?"

And together, in fine four part harmony, we shall sing together this morning:

The soul that on Jesus still leans for repose

I will not, I will not desert to its foes

That soul though all hell should endeavor to shake

I will never, no never, no never forsake.

February 28

March

A Brief History of Christian Theology

Dawn: Jesus is Crucified and Risen. His Gospel is preached by Paul. The Synoptic Gospels are written to preach the same Gospel, with the aid of His story, teachings, deeds. Other letters are written to apply the Gospel to the growth of the church.

Morning: In response to the small Bible (Luke and the Letters of Paul) of Marcion, a Roman Gnostic, the Christian Bible (66 books) is assembled. John translates the preaching of the Gospel into the idiom of neo-platonic, gnostic thought.

Late Morning: Augustine of Hippo, converted from Manicheaism (an eastern Gnosticism), develops a full theological system, relying largely on Paul, in conflict with the British Monk Pelagius. Both Reformers and Counter Reformers rely later on him.

Noon: Thomas Aquinas in the 12th century constructs a medieval theological system, blending the basics of Aristotelian philosophy with the Scripture and tradition of the church.

Afternoon: The medieval synthesis begins to unravel under the influence of the early renaissance and pre-reformation.

Late Afternoon: The great reformers of Germany (Luther), France (Calvin) and England (H8 and later Wesley) shatter the Roman medieval synthesis on the basis of faith alone, Scripture alone, and a return to Augustine and Paul.

Evening: Post-Enlightenment modern theology reaches its zenith in the 19th\mid 20th century work of liberals (Schleiermacher), neo-orthodox thinkers (Barth) and culminates in the last full systematic theology to date (Tillich).

Dusk: Post-modern Christian theology, skeptical of universal systems, and indebted to particular, autobiographical witnesses, accentuates the varieties of religious experience and theological perspective (Black: Cone, Latino: Guttierez, Asian: Koyama, Feminist: Ruether, Canadian: Hall, other).

March 1

Best Foot Forward

I realize belatedly that the most lastingly formative aspect of my theological education, at Union Seminary in the City of New York, in the years of the Carter administration was the preaching of William Sloane Coffin. In his recent collection of wisdom sayings, Coffin has a typically urbane, piercing word to say about hypocrisy. It is as close to the mind of Jesus in John 4 as I think you can come: "Generally we try to pass ourselves off as something that is special in our hearts and minds, something we yearn for, something beyond us. That's rather touching."

We all have at least two life stories, the one we publicize and the one we privatize. They both have meaning. Nor should one be eliminated or the other. In this chapter, following on the opening given in our lesson today, Jesus addresses the two biographies of a woman from Samaria. . . . Go call your husband. . . . I have no husband. . . . You are right in saying you have no husband for you have had five husbands and he whom you now have is not your husband. . . . As people and as a culture, we have more than one story to tell, more than one biography. Two biographies, like the woman at the well. Our best foot and then the other foot. The gospel this morning, a saving and healing truth for you, is that Jesus the Christ knows both biographies, all our stories, and loves us still.

"We put our best foot forward, but it is the other one that needs the attention."

March 2

Changing Your Mind

Here stands Nicodemus, a man in full. A religious leader, really a representative of the best in spiritual inheritance. He ventures out at night, choking from the challenge of truth, new truth, full truth. Where he has been will not take him where he needs to go. He is a person on the edge of a great dislocation: he is about to make up his mind to change his mind about something that really matters.

Some years ago the Christian Century ran a series of articles by nominally great religious leaders, titled "How My Mind Has Changed." A disappointing series. One found really little significant change of mind in any of them. Typical of preachers—stubborn, self-assured; it takes one to know one.

But here stands Nicodemus, a courageous soul. He is facing the great heartache of maturity. You face it too. He is facing out over a great ravine, a great gorge, a great precipice. On a matter of mortal meaning, he is making up his mind whether to change his mind. That takes real courage.

Benjamin Franklin found this courage when he left behind his beloved Europe and his confidence in diplomacy to take up arms with his fellow colonists. Abraham Lincoln found this courage when he finally moved to side fully with the abolitionists. Robert F. Kennedy, then the junior Senator from the Empire State, found this same courage when he left the Cold War mind of his own past and of his dear brother to oppose the war in Vietnam. Sometimes you get to a point where you have to make up your mind whether to change your mind. To face facts, as Nicodemus courageously faced the works, signs, deeds of Jesus the Christ. It takes great courage to change your mind about something of mortal significance. In fact, it may not even be humanly possible, apart from grace.

It means admitting error. We would sooner be proven sinful than stupid. John takes us to higher ground. We have an easier time receiving forgiveness for sin than we do receiving grace for change.

Yet did not Samson finally see the error of his ways with Delilah? Did not David finally see his mistake with Bathsheba? Did not Peter break down and weep on understanding his betrayal? Did not Paul find the courage, in earshot of unmistakable evidence, to cease persecution, and in fact, to suffer it for Christ's sake? The Gospel of Jesus Christ is one of persistent failure, of persistence through failure, and of the grace to make up one's mind to change one's mind.

It takes more courage to lay down the broadsword of misjudgment than to cling to the spear of stubborn willfulness.

March 3

Christmas Eve

In 1989, three days before Christmas, our son Ben suddenly proclaimed a hankering for a train set. We had already bartered for the season's gifts, and Christmas being what Christmas is in a parsonage, we made a mental note for next year. Next year, a train, for Ben.

I remember that at our staff Christmas party on December 23 I had mentioned this desire of Ben's, as some sort of illustration of some now fully forgotten interpretation of the Incarnation. So it goes.

At 1 am on Christmas Eve, or rather morning, we return down the slope of Acorn Path and entered our garage, walking toward the backdoor. There on the steps we found a big box, wrapped in a red bow, "for Ben, from Santa." Ben loved his simple, new train. In January I spent many hours coaxing, cajoling, thanking, pressing my staff about who had given Ben the train. Our organist, former supervisor of music in Onondaga County, G. Frank Lapham—he loved kids, surely he had brought the train. My friend and student minister, now Bruce Lee-Clark, whose own train set covered his basement in full—he loved trains, surely he was the one. My dearest colleague, Al Childs, now 85 and four years from death—he was just the kind of guy to do such a thing. My sweet secretary Jo Stewart, then 80 and looking 55—she loved Ben liked the son she always wanted; it was she.

But they all denied it. To a man. Vociferously, they denied it. They seemed puzzled that I was sure it was they. I hate secrets and surprises, so I would not let it go. I was still at it the next Christmas. Finally, Al took me out to lunch and said, "Bob, drop it." So I did.

Until this summer. At a June graduation party in the old neighborhood, something marvelous happened. Marvelous like Spirit, full of surprise. Marvelous like real church, beyond any naming or denomination. Marvelous like life, true and good and present. Marvelous like love. I ran into Sue, who asked about Ben, and then said that Stan, her husband, a lawyer, a sometime Catholic, a quiet, quizzical guy, the last person on earth you would call religious, she said that Stan would like to know about Ben for a host of reasons, and, as she ended, "Well, all the way back, you know, to the train that Christmas. . . ." Stan was really angry with Sue for spilling the beans. I, though, was grateful.

This is what we are hoping for, what we imagine at our best: an experience of being alive, an experience of love, an experience of God.

The Gospel of John is not focused on ethics. There is only minimal ethical teaching here. One looks in vain for a Sermon on the Mount or Plain. One searches without result for a parable with a point. One hungers without satisfaction for a wisdom saying, an epigram, a teaching on virtue. In John we have the teleological suspension of the ethical. In John, only the command to love remains.

March 4

Colgate Alma Mater

At the very end of their years at Colgate, the commencement springtime circle of men would be formed around the swan pond. On a clear, warm spring evening. At dusk, at twilight. As they came to their moment of departure. It was unforgettable to hear those voices, and, even for those of us still on bicycles and in sneakers and blissfully unaware of what they were going through, there was a fine, haunting quality to the amateur three-hundred-voice male chorus. I remember they were dressed in graduation gowns. There was some speaking and some silence. They held torches around the lakeshore, and night fell, the same night regularly depicted in the Gospel of John: In the opening hymn, with Nicodemus, in the passion. Otherwise, too. And spectacularly in these five rare chapters, 13–17. There is nothing like these verses in all of literature, biblical or otherwise. They are dripping with the grief of loss, and teeming with the reception of love during departure. I suppose it might have been appropriate, one year or another, at Colgate, if John 15:12 and following had been read. It may have been read. Now in the full dark the torches burn out bright. You can feel their warmth even from the hiding place behind the willows. You can smell their birch bark scent. Night falls, and the men sing, "Colgate, alma mater. . . ." One by one they depart. One to work. One to marriage. One to teach. One to war. One to study. One to ministry. And all to the open, unforeseen future.

March 5

Dinner Conversation

Some years ago we sat at dinner with several other couples, in a beautiful home, over a majestic meal, graciously served. Because the couples knew each other well, and were in trust to each other, there was the chance for hard and serious conversation, consecrated conversation you might say. This evening the debate swirled around gay marriage.

There are tipping points in the way a culture moves. Some of them occur at dinner, in beautiful homes, over majestic meals, graciously served. The host was opposed, to gay marriage that is. The conversation widened, and then narrowed, and then widened again. We can surely agree that there are many ways of keeping faith, and many honest, different, points of view, on this and on many issues.

Across the table sat Carol, mother of two fine teenagers, married with joy to a business leader, baseball player, Red Sox fan. She had battled cancer once before, and now it returned, and she fought it again. We could not see it then, but in seven months she was gone.

Over some heat and some laughter, much disagreement but little discord, the conversation, consecrated you might say, moved on. Carol spoke fully, and at one point said: "You know, I have learned how precious life is, how fragile, what a gift every day is. Here is what I feel: if two people truly love each other, deeply commit to each other, and want to consecrate their vows, that is they want what Doug and I have, why would I ever want to stand in their way, why would I ever want to deprive them of that happiness that I know so well." I heard some minds changing as dessert came that night.

At a wedding dinner this month, in a beautiful room, with fine food and gracious hosts, gay and straight danced the night away together, gay and straight. It was right, normal, easy, organic, natural—the way things are meant to be. The embodiment of the embraceable variant.

March 6

Dietrich Bonhoeffer on Vulnerability:

"Nothing can make up for the absence of someone whom we love and it would be wrong to try to find a substitute: we must simply hold out and see it through. That sounds very hard at first, but at the same time it is a great consolation; for the gap, as long as it remains unfilled, preserves the bond between us. It is nonsense to say that God fills the gap: He does not fill it, but on the contrary, He keeps it empty, and so helps us to keep alive our former communion with each other, even at the cost of pain."

March 7

Gladys

Snow swirled that day, as the Nursing Home hove into view. Gladys deserved a call, on the line between life and death, and the preacher came prepared, or so he thought.

Would you like me to pray with you? Oh, it is not necessary. Of course I love all the prayers of the great church, particularly, now that I see little, those I carry in memory from our old liturgy. But I am fine.

Perhaps you would like to hear the Psalms? My grandmother appreciated them read as she, uh . . . You mean as she lay dying? . . . Yes. Oh, it is not necessary. I mean I do love the Psalms, and was lucky to have them taught rote to me at church camp so that they rest on my memory, like goodness and mercy, all the days of my life. But I am fine.

I know that you sang in our choir. Would you like some of the hymns recited for you? Oh, that is not necessary. I do so love music! I can sing the hymns from memory to myself at night! I found my faith singing, you know. It just seemed so real when we would sing, when we were younger, around the piano, around the campfire, around the church. I knew in my heart, I knew Whom I could trust. But I am fine.

I brought communion for you in this old traveling kit. Oh, that is not necessary. We can have communion if you like. It is so meaningful to me. I can feel my husband right at my side, knee to knee. After he died, I could not hear anything that was said in your fine sermons for so long, my heart hurt so loudly. But I still could get grace in communion. But I am fine.

Gladys, is there anything that I could bring you today? As a matter of fact, there is . . . Tell me about our church . . . I have been out of worship for so long. . . . How is the church doing this Christmas? . . . Are the children coming and being taught to give their money to others? And what of the youth? Are they in church and skating and sledding and hay-riding and falling in love? Tell me about the UMW and their mission goal. Did they make it? A dollar means so little to us and so much in Honduras and China. And tell me about the building. . . . Are the trustees preparing for another generation? It is so easy to defer maintenance. . . . What about the choir—are they singing from faith to faith? . . .Tell me about your preaching, and the DS, and our bishop. . . . What is going to happen with our little church? . . . Tell me, please, tell me about our church. . . . It is where I find meaning and depth and love. . . . That is what you can bring me today.

Jesus said, I am the resurrection and the life. She who believes in me, though she die, yet will she live. There are those places where what is beyond us enters among us. Where the line of death is smudged and crossed. Where it is not just so clear what is really death and what is really life. Worship, this hour, is such a moment, too. You can have an experience of God, right in church.

March 8

Tornado

My wife Jan drove home, that is, on July 8 at 7pm, heading to our summer house, coming with 7 miles of Peterboro at the tornado hour. She has never seen a darker sky, she says. And if she had not gotten home? That is, if our family were now living with the tornado tragedy and loss inflicted on others? On one hand, I would be of great gratitude, at a minimum, to find myself surrounded, as this morning, by a company of women and men, honest about hurt, graceful in grief, dignified in the hour of death, and loving in the face of meaningless, inexplicable, unintelligible laceration. But on the other, I know I would harbor, for the long stretch of healing it would take, a white hot anger at the injustice of such a loss.

We are left to wonder in conscience about "the things that are God's." What are they? Are they wonder and conscience—the starry heavens above and the moral law within? Wonder and conscience? Wonder and conscience, spirit and soul, things of God.

Jesus says—give to Caesar the things that are Caesar's, to God the things that are God's, to me the things that are mine, and to life a spirit of wonder and conscience. A life of wonder and conscience.

You can believe in God. You can believe in the creative divine power that unleashed the universe. You can believe that no one has ever seen God. You can believe in the potential for a purposeful existence by faith, the faithfulness of God in Christ in my case. You can believe that even the darkest moment and harshest experience is held, included, embraced and redeemed in love, as a mystery and as a hope.

You can believe in freedom. You do not need to believe that God has a plan for every single life, free of human freedom, nor that God has a map quest route for your life, nor that God sends tornados to chew up poor towns with rich histories, nor that God brutally executes young mothers and little children living in mobile home, nor that everything has a purpose, that everything is beautiful in its own way, that we will understand it better by and by, or that all experience is directly, divinely, precisely ordered.

You can believe in love. The gospel is the gospel of freedom, of grace, of love, of pardon, of forgiveness, of acceptance, of healing, and of hope. I believe all of us are better when we are loved by others and when we connect in faith with divine love. The statement, God is Love, is more about the second than the first person of the Trinity. For those looking today for a more formally exacting or exacting theological position—good. Come along with us next week and on future Sundays.

Do you believe in God, in freedom and in love?

Are you leading the kind of life you most want, need, and deserve?

Will you join me, and others, day by day, seeking the things that are God's?

March 9

Last Things

We lived for some years right across from a large cemetery which also hides a back entrance to the Carrier Dome. I used to keep count of how many friends, real friends, I had, and how many were on one side of Comstock and how many were on the other.

One late autumn Saturday, a football game day, our kids parked cars for five dollars a piece in the backyard. Then all became quiet in the neighborhood, except for the strong wind of the day and an occasional muffled shout, like heaven's trumpet, from the dome behind the cemetery.

I had determined, wind or no, to rake, and so with my ears muffled, I set out to rake the front lawn. So quiet, so empty, that street, during a football game. Back to the cemetery I raked and raked, wind rearranging all my art and labor. Back again, and raking again. I was lost in worries about Sunday to come, or some other bother. I raked and mused.

Suddenly, I turned for once to face the graves across the street. There, standing shoulder to shoulder was an army of men and women, a great sea of orange, now in the wind ready to cross at me, hundreds, more, coming, streaming out of the graveyard, walking at me with no more warning than Lazarus gave his sisters. Lost as I was in reverie, I really did not know for sure, whether the resurrection of the dead was upon us, or more simply whether the game had ended early. The resurrection at the last day.

March 10

Leap of Faith

On Friday I was brought to heel sitting at a red light. At the corner a man was being tutored in the use of a seeing-eye dog. The old black lab, harnessed and steady, was ready to guide him across the street, and his care-giver, a strong woman, held in at the shoulder from the back. Green came for him and the dog pulled forward. But the noise was great, and the wind was blowing, and the traffic was heavy, very heavy, and drivers were zinging left and right, all in the shadow of the Lutheran Church. And this dear young man held fast in fright. He could not move. The dog pulled and the woman pushed and he froze. At last, she saw that he was not ready. And her arms went around him to a great hug from the back, and she pulled him back toward the safety of the sidewalk. I had no right to see the utter disappointment on his face and covering hers too. Yet I see there an autumnal holiness, a real freedom, a love. Her hands moving from his shoulders to his cover his chest and enfold him told me, somehow, that one day, one day, one fine day, he would muster the courage to shake free of disappointment. I cannot even begin to imagine what it must take to trust a mute animal, a dog, amid the cacophony of urban traffic. But I know he will find it. Why, I bet by today he has done so. Sometimes you just have to jump, you know: when you learn to swim, and let the water hold you. When you take a leap and take a new job. When you ask someone to marry you. When you decide to leave a relationship or a friendship. When you retire. When you join or leave a church.

March 11

Light

Looking out over sixty years of theological imagination in this country and abroad, speaking now both of, and to, the liberal Protestant communities, it will have been in retrospect rather a disappointment to see that we have not moved beyond Genesis 9, and in particular that we have not made our way out six more chapters to Genesis 15, in these sixty years. It is Noah who receives the rainbow, the covenant of color; but it is Abraham who receives the firmament, the covenant of light!

Jesus says, I am the light of the world.

I love the rainbow too. I love what Bishop Roy Nichols used to preach, that the world needs a spiritual rainbow. We can sing a rainbow. And we have. But Jesus here does not say I am the color of the world. He says light. John reminds us of the light from which all colors are refracted. And for the twenty-first century, we will need more light than color. W.E.B. Dubois was right that the issue of the twentieth century would be the color line. The issue of the twenty-first century is light.

I like color. Indigo and yellow, great colors. Orange, a personal favorite. You like blue, he likes red. Good for you. It is not easy being green, I know. Color is great, as long as color remembers the light from which it is refracted. We are all far more human and far more alike than we have recently envisioned. It is John who fills our existential disappointment with a great, universal hope! That this world can work! That in Christ there is no east or west! That God is at work in the world to make and keep human life human!

It can be dangerous to focus too much on difference. Friends, we are all more human and more alike than we regularly affirm, all of us on this great globe.

We all survive the birth canal, and so have a native survivors' guilt. All six billion.

We all need daily two things, bread and a name. (One does not live by bread alone.) All six billion.

We all grow to a point of separation, a leaving home, a second identity. All six billion.

We all love our families, love our children, love our homes, love our grandchildren. All six billion.

We all age, and after forty, it's maintenance, maintenance, maintenance. All six billion.

We all shuffle off this mortal coil en route to that undiscovered country from whose bourn no traveler returns. All six billion.

And in the light of the light of the world, what of all our colorful difference? It is the covenant of the rainbow that fascinates us still. We have not yet opened our eyes, or had our eyes opened, to the awesome bounty and beauty of the covenant of Abraham, the promise of firmament. We need to leave the rainbow and gaze at the firmament, to leave the fretting about color coordination for the joy, the expansive great joy of welcoming the fifty percent of this county that has had no first helping of faith, no first exposure to the light. That is where the fun is.

Here is one great, freeing hope for the twenty-first century, that we will move from Noah to Abraham, from rainbow to firmament, from difference to grace.

March 12

Loaves and Fishes

I turn again to Marcel Proust, whose thousands of print pages burst forth from the memory of a long lost moment of tea and Madeleine cakes, the cakes swirling dreamily in the tea. Meal and memory.

The other day, because I had some coupons, I stopped at the Subway to by sandwiches for my class lunch. Fewer came to lunch than I had thought, so, later in the afternoon, the extra tuna sub did beckon sufficiently to be consumed. Somewhere in the late afternoon of a non-descript autumn Monday, I found myself slowly and a little guiltily enjoying an extra sandwich.

Did you ever find yourself just sort of in a strange reverie, carried along by an avalanche of physical memory, occasioned in a simple meal?

When I was 16, in the middle of the autumn we were dislocated or relocated to a new home by the remarkable ministrations of the Methodist church. It was November, and we all suddenly had a new house, a new neighborhood, a new room, a new city, a new school, a new church, and not a single friend. The school was a large urban school which was in the throes of serious unrest, some chaos and violence, and yet still with a fine building, faculty, and program. I have not thought, or felt, clearly about those November days of 1970 in a long, long, time. Maybe I have never done so.

For some reason the humble tuna-fish and bread carried me fully back. . .

There is a teenager alone in the cafeteria. For some days he goes alone to lunch, after trigonometry and before chemistry. He is not very artfully dressed. Some of that is the culture of the day and some is just who he is. He knows really no one. He is white in largely black school, overtall and awkward, hoping in vain against hope to make the basketball team, bright but not too eager to show it, curiously glad for a new and strange city environment and deeply lonely at the dislocation of the move. You can see him on these many days at the first lunch period. He sits with his back to the wall, close enough to some others not to appear solo. The school—and by extension the world around—run quite well without any recognition of his being there. He feels something that is hard and throat-lodged and aching and chilling and strange. He is homesick for a home that no longer exists. He hurts too much to laugh and he is too tall and adult-looking to cry.

In a month or so a group of other young men, Chris Bennett and Joel Burdick and Chris Heimbach, will somehow oddly include him in lunch, as if he had been there for the previous ten years, which he had not. But right now he is out on the boat, and shore is a long way off. And a shared meal seems like it will never come and if it did it might just be too awesome and too wonderful to receive. So he leans the chair against the wall. He watches the racial tensions and hatreds. He memorizes the periodic table. He tries not to look conspicuous in any single way. He looks at the girls and wonders what he could possibly say to any of them. He looks forward to basketball. He feels what it takes a young heart really to feel.

Every day he carries to his back table a brown sack. This is a full meal, fairly hastily but utterly lovingly prepared in the earlier morning before the two mile walk to school. It is the same lunch every day. Bread and fish. Two full sandwiches. Some chips. Carrots. Cookies, sometimes made at home. And it will take another thirty-five years for him to fully appreciate—to taste—what he could already feel against the cafeteria wall. At least here, in this meal, for all the depressing dislocation and frightening foreignness and leavened loneliness all around, here was something to eat. Prepared with love. As reliable as the sunrise and the seasons. Grace, in the midst of dislocation. The sandwiches come slowly out of their tight wrap. They taste the same, reassuringly the same. Maybe, day by day, this is really all we get, a taste.

March 13

Mary Pipher

When you carry the faithful anxiety of serious parenting, and you grieve over a youth culture that seems heavily material and falsely physical, You ought to give Iowa a try. Listen again to the voice of Mary Pipher, who spoke right in this nave last year. Her *Reviving Ophelia* is still on the money, and on the market, when it comes to reminding us of the challenges of growing up female in America. The Spirit of Truth is alive and well and abides and allows us, however stumblingly, to move forward as a people, to learn, from one generation to another, to grow, to do better. She says:

> I was a teenager in Beaver City, Nebraska, a town of about 400 people. My mom was a doctor in that town. I knew everybody, and I knew the name of every dog in that town. And so when I walked around that world, I was moving among people who I knew well, and who knew me well. Increasingly, that's not the experience of children. They aren't growing up in communities of adults who care about them. They're constantly meeting strangers, and they've been socialized to be frightened of strangers. So they're moving among people they have some reason to fear. They don't get nurtured the way children were nurtured thirty years ago. And they don't get corrected and informed about their behavior the way I did. Now, some of the rules I learned were silly. Some of the rules I learned, I could hardly wait to cast off when I left home. But the fact of the matter is, there were a lot of adults deeply invested in my becoming a well-behaved civic citizen. And that's something children don't experience as much. So loss of community is one thing.

March 14

Parker Palmer

A new commandment I give you, that you love one another. Even as I have loved you, so you also ought to love one another. This is my commandment, that you love one another.

One example. Parker Palmer writes movingly of his salvation from depression in *Let Your Life Speak*. I thank my colleagues for identifying this book in connection to the footwashing. Palmer painfully records those many attempts to help that were not helpful. Well meaning but ineffective. Sympathy that only led to greater sadness. Positive advice that made him more depressed. Reminders of his many talents, which left him in greater malaise. Those who said they knew what he was going through, which, of course, no one ever does. He concludes:

> Having not only been "comforted" by friends, but having tried to comfort others in the same way, I think I understand what the syndrome is about: avoidance and denial. One of the hardest things we must do sometimes is to be present to another person's pain without trying to "fix" it, to simply stand respectfully at the edge of that person's mystery and misery. . . . Blessedly there were several people, family and friends, who had the courage to stand with me in a simple and healing way. One of them was a friend named Bill who, having asked my permission to do so, stopped by my home every afternoon, sat me down in a chair, knelt in front of me, removed my shoes and socks, and for half an hour simply massaged my feet. He found the one place in my body where I could still experience feeling—and feel somewhat reconnected with the human race. Bill rarely spoke a word. When he did, he never gave advice but simply mirrored my condition. He would say, "I can sense your struggle today," or, "It feels like you are getting stronger." I could not always respond, but his words were deeply helpful: they reassured me that I could still be seen by someone—life giving knowledge in the midst of an experience that makes one feel annihilated and invisible. It is impossible to put into words what my friend's ministry meant to me. Perhaps it is enough to say that I now have deep appreciation for the biblical story of Jesus and the washing of the feet.[1]

A new commandment I give you, that you love one another. Even as I have loved you, so you also ought to love one another. This is my commandment, that you love one another.

March 15

---

1. Parker Palmer, *Let Your Life Speak: Listening for the Voice of Vocation* (San Francisco: Jossey-Bass, 2000), 63.

Pasternak Sings Shakespeare

Pasternak loved Shakespeare's Sonnett 66. It is said that whenever he read aloud the crowd would not let him leave until he had rehearsed it for them. "Give us the 66th . . ." Its evocation of daily anxiety bears remembering. The poem is unequaled in its announcement of trouble. When life gives you the 66th remember Shakespeare, but especially his last couplet.

Tired with all these, for restful death I cry,
As to behold desert a beggar born,
And needy nothing trimm'd in jollity,
And purest faith unhappily forsworn,
And gilded honour shamefully misplac'd,
And maiden virtue rudely strumpeted,
And right perfection wrongfully disgrac'd,
And strength by limping sway disabled
And art made tongue-tied by authority,
And folly—doctor-like—controlling skill,
And simple truth miscall'd simplicity,
And captive good attending captain ill:
Tir'd with all these, from these would I be gone,
Save that, to die, I leave my love alone.

"Captive good attending captain ill . . ." Can you hear that? It begs to be heard. Stand with your people in tragedy, honest and kind in word and deed.

March 16

Read Headed John

We are four siblings in my family of origin. The older three have brown hair. The youngest is a redhead, whose name is John. John's bright red locks are unlike, quite unlike, the less remarkable curls of Bob, Cathy and Cynthia. He stands apart, does John. It makes you wonder where he came from, with such a distinctive aspect. John is like his Gospel namesake, the Fourth Gospel. The youngest of the four, he stands out, so different from his synoptic siblings Matthew, Mark and Luke. They with their shared brown hair, their shared parables and teachings, their shared emphasis on the humanity of Jesus, their shared trips from Galilee to Jerusalem, they just don't look at all like their younger redheaded brother.

In the summer, it happens, as it may in your family, there is a family reunion for one part of our tribe. Occasionally, we would go, growing up. Like yours, ours is something of standard reunion. It is held on a farm near Albany, which has been in the family since before George Washington rode a horse. After the usual light meal of beef, corn, potatoes, bread, sausage, pies, and pickles and so on, the extended family (or those who having eaten heavily but can still move) will sometimes stand for a photograph on the long farm house veranda. I ask you to look at the photo. I am holding it here. Can you see it? Well, even if you cannot see it across the radio waves, you can probably guess what it shows. Of these eighty people, do you see how many have red hair? About 60—young or old, tall or short, heavy or slight, male or female, they mostly have red hair, like John. 75% are redheads. In fact, in the photo, it looks like a sea of red hair. Maybe a red heads convention out in the farm fields of Cooperstown, NY. John isn't the odd ball. His siblings are.

John is not the second century Greco Roman odd ball. His synoptic siblings are. When you put the Fourth Gospel, with all its red haired radical difference, on the farm house veranda of second century religious family literature, he fits right in. He stands shoulder to shoulder with all the Gnostic writings that are so like him, especially in these late chapters. It looks like a redheads convention. He looks and sounds quite like the rest of his second and third cousins, once or twice removed: The Paraphrase of Shem, the Treatise on the Resurrection, the Odes of Solomon, the Apocryphon of John, the Gospel of Peter, the Gospel of Mary. How else will we ever hear this voice of Jesus from John 17?

And this is eternal life, that they may know you, the only true God, and Jesus Christ whom though hast sent.

Six Synoptic differences! Eternal life, not kingdom of heaven. Know, not believe. The only true God, not Abba. Jesus Christ, not Rabbi or Master. Sent, not begotten.

This voice is *nothing* like that of the Sermon on the Mount, or that of the parable of the Good Samaritan, or that of the cry from Psalm 22 on the cross. Not human, but divine, here. Not earthly, but heavenly, here. Not low, but high, here. Not immanent, but transcendent, here.

March 17

Rich Man Poor Man

A poor man went to a Methodist church for worship. The congregation welcomed him and he returned week by week. After a while the women's circle took up a collection and bought him a nice new suit, with a blue tie. He happily received the gift, but they never saw him in church again.

A while later, on the street, one of church members saw him and asked what had happened. Did he not like the suit? Did it not fit? Was he afraid to wear it?

"Oh no, I love the suit. I look great in it. When I saw myself in the mirror, I looked so good I thought, 'I look like a million bucks. I look too good to go just to the Methodist church. I think I'm dressed well enough to go the Episcopal church. I think I will go there. And that is what I did."

Sometimes a dose of realized eschatology can clear the mind and strengthen the soul. In a way, every day is our last. In a way, heaven and hell are here and now. In a way, the end time is all of time. John puts it this way: "the hour is coming *and now is.*"

The freedom of the gospel has gradually embraced multiple variants. The poor. The immigrant. People of color. Those once enslaved. Women. Gay people. Others. The Other. In fact, the lesson of the gospel of freedom enshrined in John is the spiritual expansion of freedom found in the embrace of the embraceable variant.

March 18

Sex Ed

What are we teaching our children about sex? Do we happily and strongly affirm the covenant of marriage? Do our sentiments and advisements short of marriage lead, for the most part, to preparation for healthy marriage? Across the gender divides, can we still be responsible not only *to* but also *for* one another, without yet patronizing or prevaricating? Why are young men so largely absent from our churches?

I have no word of the Lord on this, but what insight I have I share.

You are a grandfather or grandmother. With rosy cheeks and a smile, before dinner, you may recall a harvest moon, an evening of affection, with gentle hints at what chivalry can mean, did mean, will mean.

You are a mom or dad. Books with information can be bought and shared. But priceless and purchasing power is what comes next. Your sense of gratitude for life. Your honest joy, happiness, and pleasure in intimacy. Your witness to the vulnerabilities of such closeness. Your conviction that God made humans as sexual beings and means to help us as sexual beings to become as humane as possible. Then stop. Look. Listen. Listen. Listen.

You are an aunt, uncle, teacher, neighbor, youth counselor. Bless you. Do you realize that you are, in trust, safe space and trusted freedom for younger person who may need to rely on you?

You are such a youth. Remember these five things: You are made in the image and likeness of God. You are precious. You know the difference between loving someone and using someone. You need not be afraid to stand apart from the crowd. You have right to sense how you are feeling, what you are thinking. Does this seem right to me? Does this feel right for me? If you make a mistake, well, remember forgiveness, consider what you have learned, shake the dust from your feet and move ahead. And you can also, if the moment is right, quote Anne Lamott: "No is a complete sentence."

You are a church on East Avenue. Say this: "Jesus is among us, speaking and healing. His grace tells us that the Word became flesh, that we are made in God's image, that physical pleasure and sexual intimacy are God's good gifts, that we can live with integrity, that we can become self-aware, that we can learn from but not be defined by our mistakes, that the covenant of marriage provides the best and surest and healthiest and safest location for sex amid the great dislocations of our time."

Life is good. The Word became flesh and dwelt among us. This is the ringing affirmation of the Fourth Gospel. Physical life, in all its panoply of intimacy and estrangement, is good.

March 19

Spirit of Truth

You shall know the truth, and the truth shall set you free. To be set free. By knowing. Truth.

Know the world. Know God. Know others. Know thyself. All these are overshadowed in John by knowing the Spirit of Truth, which liberates, heals, saves, and makes new.

The divine spirit captures our fullest selves, our heads, our hands, our hearts. This is the spirit, the advocate, whom Jesus here introduces, through the preaching of the early church, to the wounded needs of the early church. "I am going away." That, in retrospect, the Johannine Christians could interpret. We get it, too. This is the hour, the moment, the glory, the cross. It is the other phrase that may have puzzled. "And I am coming to you," Jesus said. Here is the hard Scriptural evidence of truth, sent, truth, coming, truth, expanding, truth in the spirit, truth on the move. Jesus makes way for the rest of the truth. The Holy Spirit will (future tense) teach you (plural) everything (boundless expanse). Our imaginations may be kindled today. Our hands may become instruments of love today. Our hearts may be inspired today, all through the same Truth, known in this chapter through ongoing conversation.

John replaces Armageddon with Truth. Here, just where veteran readers of other Gospels would have come to expect apocalypse, after the ministry and before the passion, John affirms the Spirit of Truth. Mark 13 and the wars and rumors of wars are gone. Matthew 25 and the future judgment of sheep and goats are gone. Luke 26 and the children snatched from the rooftops are gone. The earliest hope of the primitive church came a cropper. The apocalypse never lypsed. The end did not come, not after two, three, four generations. And so, dear John.

In place of Armageddon, he puts the artistry of the spirit. In place of eschaton he places the ecclesia. In place of apocalypse, truth. The world is going on for a while, maybe even an eternity. And what we once thought has more depth than once we thought! Heaven is not a matter of the last day but of every day! Hell is not a matter of the last day but of every day! Judgment is not a matter of the last day but of every day! The last day is today—live every one as if it were your last because it is. As Walter Rauschenbusch wrote, "What is more demanding, to believe that on the last day we will stand in the presence of the Lord, or to believe that every day is lived in the presence of the Lord?"

March 20

Struggle with Church

For nine years we have moved heaven and earth to reconnect our congregation to the connection of the United Methodist Church. In our church life, at the same time, the Risen Christ is healing our blindness in stewardship and evangelism. We are learning to share our money and we are learning to share our faith, and the mud and spittle of the Savior's hand are bathing our spiritual eyes in sight. Our new sight is somehow a troubling condition to our mother religion. We have paid massive apportionments, and yet relationally we are shunned in our conference. We have instituted a connectional Sunday, sponsored a pulpit exchange, participated in youth ministries, and yet our voice is not heard for the future of the denomination. We have sent our clergy now every year to conference, and have taken our places, hours on end, in the Visioning Committee, on the Board of Ministry, on the Finance Committee, in teaching and preaching across the area, yet we are "put out of the synagogue" when the voting occurs. We have hosted the meeting of the conference, even, and yet in the gathering we are distant cousins. Why is it that this moment for us, this epoch of new sight, of beggars finding sight and bread, of health and growth, in spite of all our effort, becomes an occasion for emotional and relational contention with our beloved denomination, our community of origin?

John's gospel can really help us, here and now. We are not the first to know the endless contention and intractable difference that is a part of all institutional life. There will be grace enough and to spare in this period of turbulence. We can be kind without being dishonest. We can be honest without being unkind. And we can say to the mother religion, our inherited tradition, "Let me find a way to help you get down off my back without hurting yourself."

Here, just here, right here in our communal need stands the Gospel of John, a moment in the Day of God and the Gospel of Christ: you will find grace for every time of need. In the supreme dislocation, the movement from dysfunction to well-being, from addiction to sobriety, you will sense and you will know real grace.

March 21

The Last Word in John

These things are spoken that you may believe that Jesus is the Christ, the Son of God, and that believing you may have life in his name.

This week you can choose to grow in faith, and so find a fuller part of your second identity. This week you can choose to grow in love, and so open a fuller part of the world's imagination.

Faith is personal commitment to an unverifiable truth. It involves a leap.

Faith is an objective uncertainty grasped with subjective certainty. It involves a leap.

Faith is the way to salvation, a real identity and a rich imagination. But it does involve a leap.

Now is the time to jump.

All of us are better when we are loved.

March 22

Theological Courage

I believe it is very difficult for us to appreciate the courage in John, the theological courage of this writing. One of the most precious beliefs of the earliest Christians resided in the confidence that very soon the world would come to an end and the Lord would return for his people. This expectation of the end governs the letters of Paul and the first three Gospels. It was, if you will, the bedrock belief of the primitive church. Had not Jesus preached, "There are some standing here who will not taste death until they see the Son of Man coming on the clouds of heaven"? Yes he had. And he was wrong. Had not Peter left nets, family, homeland, and life itself on the expectation of the apocalypse? Yes he had. And he was wrong. Had not Paul predicted, "We the living, the remaining, will be caught up together with him in the clouds"? Yes he had. And he was wrong.

Only John faces this grave disappointment with utter honesty. The others hold onto the old religion, the expected return. John admits delay. John has the guts to say to his people: "What we once believed is clearly not true. Let us look about us and see what this means." And behold! In place of parousia, we find paraclete. In place of cataclysm, we find church. In place of speculation, we find spirit. In place of Armageddon we find artistry and imagination! When finally we stop chasing what is not to be, and wake up to what is, we may be utterly amazed.

Seasoned Religion said that the end was near. John says the beginning is here.

Old Time Religion saw the end of the world. John preached the light of the world.

Inherited spirituality waited for the coming of the Lord. John celebrated the Word among us, full of grace and truth.

Old Time Religion feared death, judgment, heaven, and hell. John faced them all every day.

Traditional Religion clung fiercely to an ancient untruth. John let go, and accepted a modern new truth, and hugged grace and freedom.

Our inheritance, and Matthew and Mark and Luke and Paul all looked toward the End, soon to come. John looked up at the beginning, already here. They said with Shakespeare, "All's well that ends well." John replied, "*Gut begonnen, halb gewonnen!*" (Well begun is half done.)

John alone had the full courage to face spiritual disappointment and move ahead. So we memorize John 8:32: "You shall know the truth and the truth shall set you free!" Copernicus knew that truth. Galileo knew that truth. Darwin knew that truth. And Robert Lee caught that truth on the lips of Clarence Darrow: "The Bible is a book. It is a good book. It is not the only book." All faced the need to change from inherited untruth to new insight and imagination.

March 23

Thurman's Favorite Psalm: 139

1 O LORD, thou hast searched me and known me!

2 Thou knowest when I sit down and when I rise up; thou discernest my thoughts from afar.

3 Thou searchest out my path and my lying down, and art acquainted with all my ways.

4 Even before a word is on my tongue, lo, O LORD, thou knowest it altogether.

5 Thou dost beset me behind and before, and layest thy hand upon me.

6 Such knowledge is too wonderful for me; it is high, I cannot attain it.

7 Whither shall I go from thy Spirit? Or whither shall I flee from thy presence?

8 If I ascend to heaven, thou art there! If I make my bed in Sheol, thou art there!

9 If I take the wings of the morning and dwell in the uttermost parts of the sea,

10 even there thy hand shall lead me, and thy right hand shall hold me.

11 If I say, "Let only darkness cover me, and the light about me be night,"

12 even the darkness is not dark to thee, the night is bright as the day; for darkness is as light with Thee

March 24

Two Basic Problems

The two basic historical problems of the New Testament are ancient cousins, first cousins to our two fundamental issues, the two existential battles in your salvation today.

The first historical problem behind our 27 books, and pre- eminently embedded in John, is the movement away from Judaism. How did a religious movement founded by a Jew, born in Judea, embraced by 12 and 500 within Judaism, expanded by a Jewish Christian missionary, become--within 100 years--entirely Greek? The books of the New Testament record in excruciating detail the development of this second identity, this coming of age, that came with the separation from mother religion.

The second historical problem underneath the Newer Testament is disappointment, the despair that gradually accompanied the delay, finally the cancellation, of Christ's return, the delay of the parousia. Jesus was an apocalyptic prophet. Paul expected to be alive to see the advent of Christ. Gradually, though, the church confessed disappointment in its greatest immediate hope, the sudden cataclysm of the end.

These two problems, historical and fascinating, create our New Testament: the separation from Judaism and the delay of the parousia. In the fourth Gospel the two come together with great ferocity. What makes this matter so urgent for us is that these very two existential dilemmas—one of identity and one of imagination—are before every generation, including and especially our own.

How do I become a real person? How do we weather lasting disappointment? How do I grow up? How do we become mature? What insight do I need, amid the truly harrowing struggles over identity, to become the woman or man I was meant to become? What imagination—what hope molded by courage—do we need to face down the profound despair of nuclear twilight and break free into a loving global future?

Dislocation and disappointment. More than any other document in ancient Christianity, John explored the first of these great dilemmas. More than any other document in Christianity, John faced the second.

March 25

Vernon Jordan

Vernon Jordan stood surrounded by suitcases, on the steps of Depauw University. He was 19. He watched his mother and father and many siblings depart, driving an old station wagon out the drive in Greencastle, Indiana. He was weeping. Moments before, his father had said, through his own tears: "Son, we are going now. We won't be coming back. You know how much we love you. But now it is up to you. Read, Vernon, read. When others are playing, you read. When others are drinking, you read. When others are partying, you read. This is your life now. We will be back when you are finished." Did that feel good? No. Was it good? Yes. It was love in an hour of departure.

March 26

Women's Liberation

The most pervasive social change of the last thirty years, across our culture, lies in the rearrangements related to gender and to sexuality. The social distance between me and my grandfather is dwarfed by that between my grandmother and my daughter. My grandmother learned to drive using a buggy whip and sitting behind a team of horses. My daughter flies across the continent week by week. Elsie was born thirty years before she gained the right to vote. Emily rocks the vote. Gramma was one of a very small percentage of women to graduate from college. Emily runs the place. Elsie raised children, cooked meals, supported the church, and listened. My daughter works, leads, earns, and speaks. Women are still undergoing the tears and strains of pervasive social dislocation. Nor is feminism finished. Nor is equality achieved. Nor does freedom fully ring, not for women in America nor certainly for women around the globe.

March 27

World Truth Center

Perhaps our greatest present disappointment is 9/11. We face new truth: The world is smaller and starker than we wanted to believe. We have not yet found our way out of the psychic rubble of that dreadful day. We are trying, and we are moving, but the almost unspeakable disappointment of that moment remains. Here is why: We have to change our understanding, our philosophy, our theology even. We have to face the hard fact, that the future is open, freely open, both to terror and to tenderness. And here is John. He who wrote in the ancient rubble of dislocation and disappointment, telling us something wonderful and good: The Word became flesh and dwelt among us. It is in the spirit of the Fourth Gospel that we affirmed three years ago on this Sunday: "Terror may topple the World Trade Center, but no terror can topple the World Truth Center, Jesus the Christ."

The World Trade Center, hub of global economies may fall, the economy of grace still stands in the World Truth Center, Jesus the Christ.

The World Trade Center, communications nexus for many may fall, but the communication of the gospel stands, the World Truth Center, Jesus Christ.

The World Trade Center, symbol of national pride may fall, but divine humility stands, through the World Truth Center, Jesus the Christ.

The World Trade Center, legal library for the country may fall, but grace and truth stand, through the World Truth Center, Jesus the Christ.

March 28

Senior Breakfast Invocation 2011

Boats on Charles, wind in sails, at back, through all
Studying, doing, being: learning, virtue, piety
Conger a prayer for the same wind in sail, at back, through all
Including a spirit of generosity
Gratitude for what we are given, grace to share with others
Magnanimous generosity, liberality
Like that of the religious tradition, Methodism, which gave birth to BU, and its founder,
John Wesley, who adorns the doorway of Marsh Chapel, and who memorably said:
Do all the good you can. . .times, ways, people, as long as ever. . .
And who gave us our now tradition senior breakfast prayer
I need your help, and want to hear your voices, so that when your voices are raised in influ-
ence for generosity many years from now I can lean forward in my barcolounger and say
I have heard that voice
You have?
Yes, many years ago.
When did you hear that voice?
Over breakfast, May 6, 2011, we had eggs together, and they prayed with me.
What did they pray?
It went like this
(repeat after me)
Gracious giver . . .

March 29

Senior Breakfast 2013

13 Prayers for the Class of '13

May you finish your papers, wake up for your finals, and pass your courses

May you find a job when you are hunting for one, and be found by a calling when you are not (hunting for one)

May you remember your mom on Mothers' Day, nine days from today

May our recall that there are two ways to be wealthy: have a lot of money, or, have very few needs.

May you honestly face death, as we have done this spring, and so discover the precious value of every breath, as we also have done this spring.

May you, with the Greeks, see in tragedy the seedbed of nobility.

May you bring a sense of purpose to days and events which lack both (sense and purpose).

May your return your overdue library books. May you find your overdue library books.

May you with Samuel Johnson keep your friendships in good repair, with John Wesley and Mother Theresa remember the poor, with Lord Baden Powell do a good turn daily, and with Bill Coffin take yourself lightly so that you may fly, like the angels.

May you as a generation find the wisdom to design a better world, acquire the power to build a better world, and have the goodness to want a better world.

May you have a life long, rapturous, torrid love affair—with Boston, dear old Boston, the home of the bean and the cod, and take your first born to Fenway Park, and remember the radiant, sun-dappled happiness of this morning all your days.

May life be good to you, and may you be good to life.

My dear ones, my dear friends, who so resemble my own dear children, may you be safe, may you be well, may you be happy.

May it be so.

March 30

Senior Breakfast 2008

Friends
A long, long time ago . . .
Before Dr Robert Brown became President of BU
Before Provost Jean Morrison had chaired a single dean's council
Before Vice President Joe Mercurio had built a single building
Long ago . . .
Before Dean Elmore had perfected his renowned jump shot
Before Dean Sapiro had left Wisconsin fresh water for Boston salt sea air
Before Dean Hill had preached even one soporific sermon
Before there were Yankees or Red Sox or even baseball
(Before rivalry that is)
Before there was Starbucks or Taco Bell
(Before calories that is)
Before beanpot or slapshot or softspot or Lancelot
A long time ago—I mean a very long time ago!
Before any of us were born, or any of our great, great grandparents, or their parents
Before male and female, animals and birds, before trees and fish, before morning and evening, even
Before anybody had ever eaten any breakfast
Before there was anybody to cook and eat breakfast
Before there was anybody
A long time ago, long ago
There was light, light, sunlight, morning light:
Light!
Let us bask in the light of this one day in the great Day of God and offer our breakfast prayer:
Thou in whose light we see light:
Fall upon our hopes for tomorrow to illumine and guide
Warm our selves and souls as we hold memories dear
Shine on our learning, our virtue, our piety
To grow us into all that is true and good and beautiful
May we receive with happy hearts the gifts of this hour—nourishment, enjoyment, compliment
As the grateful, good, giving people we were born to be.

March 31

April

After 20 Years: A Fictional Account of 2020 from 2000

Looking back over the last twenty years of ministry, it is heartwarming to feel the new freedom that is pulsing through the body of Northeastern United Methodism. By God's grace, our churches and leaders have recovered our joy in faith and our confidence in Christ.

Since the turn of the millennium, we have walked together toward our own "North Star," Jesus Christ, who sets us free. Like Harriet Tubman and others who hiked the underground railroad, walking north, at night, toward freedom ("following the drinking gourd"), we too have kept our eyes lifted due north, walking toward Christ. We remember that "where the Spirit of the Lord is, there is freedom." It has been quite a journey, this night march, for twenty years, due north toward freedom. But look at the ground we have covered! Jesus is our saving, freeing "North Star."

As the century ended, women were finding full voice and place in our pulpits and pews, on the way "north." Remember Cleveland in '00? We found the freedom, there, to agree to disagree (agreeably!) about homosexuality, on the way north. Then over a decade we loosened the shackles of excessive, outdated apportioned overhead, and so freed our churches to run again, and move again, and grow again, headed due north. That combined growth in body and frugality of budget opened up the space we needed, in the conferences, to do the one thing needful—to develop leadership. We invested in preventive and physical health care for our leaders. Why, I was trying to explain to a new young DS last week that there was a time when we didn't even have dental care for clergy—hard to believe isn't it! We focused on continuous education, for lay leadership. We improved our remuneration and housing for clergy. A sense of self-respect returned, and helped us restore our noble preaching tradition, so hobbled for so long. Today in our pulpits, there is weekly fire and consistent excellence, and dependable depth, as our preachers point to the "North Star" of freedom. Through the long night trek since 2000, we learned again that the Bible is, first, a book about freedom, that is to be read and interpreted, first, with "the glorious liberty of the children of God." The Bible is freedom's book, the pulpit is freedom's voice, the connection is freedom's defense. We remembered that, as we walked north.

Yes, I know, we suffered, too. At least in the short run. It cost us to speak of a straight moral life, in a crooked world, especially when we emphasized tithing and hospitality. It cost us to champion children—expensive, expensive. It cost us to make space for gays. I particularly recall the courage of those moderate and conservative men who found a way, back then, in conscience to accept what in conscience they could not easily recommend. It cost us to temper our freedom to abort with a responsible regard for potential life at 23 weeks. I particularly recall the courage of those moderate and liberal women, back then, who helped us learn from our experience. Yes, it hurt us to continue to fund clergy health care and to hold onto a guaranteed appointment, through all those rebuilding years. And it hurt us to keep churches open, to stay present, with the poor—in the mountains and downtown. It hurt to walk into the open space, the northern exposure, of freedom. It hurt us to agree to disagree, when some wanted a killing frost to fall on difference. But "suffering produces endurance and endurance character." We got by, and came through, and walked due north. Thank God for Jesus Christ, our North Star!

Last night, in a clear spring sky, after reading again from Kasemann's old book, *Jesus Means Freedom,* I gazed at Polaris. I thought about those heroes of liberty who had endured their own northern exposure. Jesus in Galilee. Paul in Galatia. Augustine in Hippo. John of the Cross in Segovia. Luther in Wittenberg. Wesley in Bristol. Frederick Douglass in Rochester. John Brown in North Elba. Handsome Lake in Geneva. Susan B Anthony in Seneca Falls. John Humphrey Noyes in Oneida. Mother Ann Lee in New Lebanon. And then faces of colleagues in the ministry came to mind. Next month I retire, and with the doctor's last not so cheery diagnosis, this will probably be both my last active and last earthly annual conference at which to preside. I leave happy. I give thanks that in the new millenium, over twenty years, we have walked due north. We have followed the North Star, Jesus Christ, and we have joy and confidence in ministry, hearts again strangely warmed beneath the night sky: "Warmth! Warmth! Warmth! We are dying of cold, not of darkness. It is not the night that kills, but the frost." (Unamuno).

April 1

Benson Ordination: A Sketched Homily and Charge

Risk, go to high wire, we will be there to catch you if you fall

Listen. In love. Minister—to be with her people. To visit. In the homes. Two dozen calls of various forms every week. Let the church be the church together. Flee the office. Ministry centered office not vice versa. Flee the office. Visit. Listen. Amy Whetzel. Father a long time dying. Lot didn't help. Every Friday. Smoked a cigar for an hour. My father slept well one night each week. Wesley, movable feast. Watch over one another in love.

Speak. If you have faithfully made those 2 dozen visits each week you will have no shortage of things to say that are not innocuous on Sunday morning. Your people are hungry for a word of truth. Death of Salesman, Phillips Brooks, I Shall Bear Witness. Romans 10;; How shall they. Numbers 11: 29—all prophets. Star for your people. They want a word of relevant saving truth. To lean, to speak in a certain time. 90's—everything negotiable. Now—nothing negotiable. You want to lean in the other direction, give your people some height. Star. 1961. JFK oath. "Pay any price. . .let us never negotiate out of fear, but never fear to negotiate"—star. Balance, to stay our minds on.

Be well. Healthy, happy, pastor, christian, human . . . be healthy. Church is not responsible for your health, happiness. Evenings, weekend, holidays, 9–5 in office. It takes a chunk out. 1 hour day, day week, quarter year, summer. Travel. Live well. Family. Wallet: inside in one year: liberary card, athletic club, no credit debt, symphony tickets. We care about you , we are proud of you. . . .

April 2

Conflict

Some conflicts in church life have no resolution. No forgiveness, nor reconciliation, nor resolution. When the stakes involve income and employment, on the one hand, or honor and shame, on the other, there often is no early or short term resolution. Disdainfully, almost thirty years ago, I took a book from a larger church pastor whose secretary he had fired, and whose secretary now sat in my pews. He asked that I give her the book, his greetings, and his affection. I thought: you low life pervert. How could you possibly resort to such an indirect, passive, easy attempt at reconciliation. Now, having terminated two secretaries on unfriendly terms, I understand. People are not happy or reasonable when someone moves their cheese, particularly a Pastor. 'Pastoral administration' is an oxymoron. These things are driven out only by prayer and fasting. Thus, they really have no place in the sermon.

Other typically church conflicts may be avoided or avoided and ameliorated, 'finessed,' by wise, sensitive, and politically savvy pastoral conniving. People usually back off if they feel they have been heard, truly heard. Hence the need for a 'cast iron fundament' on which pastorally to sit through many useless meetings, useful only to air the grievance of the aggrieved. 'Up in the Old Hotel' includes a story of a man who allegedly spends thirty years writing 100 or more books of history about New York City. He leaves them in packages around town—with a bartender, in the library, under a friend's porch. At his death they are collected and found to be thousands of repetitions of a single grief: the author's piteous relationship with his dad.

April 3

A Spoof: Father of the Bride Wedding Recipe (the way Dad would do it)

Invitations: Post Card, Office Computer, Phone RSVP

Shower Themes: Presidents (Thomas Jefferson, Andrew Jackson, Theodore Roosevelt)—New Crisp Bills Only Please

Dress: Use Mom's

Photography: Single Use Cameras for Wedding Party

Flowers: Sunday's

Tuxedo: Purchase, but not shoes

Reception: Back Yard Pig Roast, Keg

Gift Registration Options: Key Bank, Chase Bank, MT Bank (Certificates of Deposit)

April 4

Generosity

You may believe that generosity is a façade and that givers have ulterior motives. We in fact knew a Cornell post-graduate Ph.D. who studied habits of giving. Ithaca is fifteen square miles of unique life surrounded by reality.

You may assert that one generation gives out of guilt to assuage and another gives out of greed to receive. There have been wise and well-known writers who have published impressive and earnest books to argue so. The older give from guilt, the younger give to get. So the great pundits assert.

It is interesting to me that those who argue so, in the main, have no pastoral experience. They may write book in Ohio or run seminaries in New Jersey, but they have no significant pastoral experience.

In 20 years, I have yet to see any significant giving, any lasting, ample generosity, that comes from guilt or greed. People so motivated soon stop giving. Giving out of a lurking fear rooted in a haunted past, or giving to receive some supposed programmatic blessing in the present—it burns away with the midday sun. In my experience, it is simply not the case.

Why do people give? Whence generosity?

Real giving is from the heart. Real giving wells up from a deep desire. Real giving along the blue highways comes from pain, from the awareness of lack and then an urgent craving to fill up what is lacking. Poor—economically hurt. Widow—relationally hurt. Real giving, generosity, comes from a change that God works in the heart. Guilt and greed won't get you very far on the blue highways. Real giving comes from "self-denying love" (Wesley), which is the meaning of life.

There are many ways of keeping faith, many travelers along the blue highways. You are one.

Are you generous?

Are you a generous traveler?

Are you a living testimony to generosity along the blue highways of life?

April 5

Gordon's Pastor: written by the Rev. G. W. Knapp

The Seminary and The Board of Ordained Ministry May Not Tell You That To Be A Faithful Pastor . . .

1. You must be willing to place yourself at the disposal of others. Not everyone has this temperament.

2. You must make the pastoral task the central focus of your life, with the conviction that no other job is any more important than yours.

3. You must not expect to find any relationship between your work in ministry and the compensation you receive for performing that work.

4. You must be a "self-starter" to avoid the sloth that largely unsupervised work makes a possibility and a temptation for some clergy.

5. You must have no delusions of grandeur. You are a pastor, not a minor league CEO . . . as if any intelligent person would want to be CEO of a volunteer organization.

6. You must be interested enough in your people to go out and get to know them "on their own turf."

7. You must strive to be "no respecter of persons." The pastorate needs even handed persons who neither "kiss up" at superiors nor "spit down" at subordinates.

8. You must not only be well read in all areas of ministry, but also in disciplines apart from ministry so that you can relate to as many people as possible.

9. You must be more interested in people than either process or academics.

10. You must have such a keen appreciation for life's incongruities that you laugh often. . . especially at yourself.

11. You must have an ego strong enough to endure criticism, rejection and abuse from both parishioners and ecclesiastical superiors.

12. You must approach life with realistic expectations; dealing with life's circumstances for what they are, rather than wailing about what they ought to be.

13. You must be gracious, even when you really don't feel like it . . . a pastor to all your parishioners, not just those whom you like.

14. You must be able to suffer fools, if not gladly, then at least patiently. The world will provide an ample supply.

15. You must learn that "freedom of the pulpit" is not a right, but a privilege earned by service as a caring pastor.

16. You must measure success in your life by what you are able to give rather than what you are fortunate enough to get.

April 6

Highlights and New Sights in Ministry

Every so often someone will stop me, as happened the other day, to say a word of thanks for our worship service that is now broadcast on the radio—neighbors, shut-in members, older adults in our community, and one letter from the Livonia prison. One of the happiest hours this summer I spent driving the Thruway and listening to two of our broadcast tapes—brilliant organ, fine prayer, clear and solid sermon, great choral music. What an offering to God and neighbor!

It is amazing how the summer heat of two months broke on the last evening of July, making August 1, our Summerfest Sunday, a clear and beautiful day. It is moving to hear people speak about this new, annual summer offering—the good attendance under the tent, the extended hymn singing, the meaningful message, and the real fellowship, during service, and at the picnic. An offering to God and neighbor!

Clad in hardhats and wearing tool belts, several of our congregation's men—dads, uncles, friends—helped several of our talented women to design and operate this summer's Vacation Bible School. Over 150 teachers and students participated in this highly creative, attentively detailed, musically spiced educational ministry. "This is the best VBS I've ever seen!" said one parent.

Through the summer of 1999, Asbury First continued to provide a full and varied ministry—from Annual Conference, to the Antique Sale, to the Strawberry Social, to the Confirmation City Mission Trip, to the UMYF mission trip "Y2K" to Kentucky, to the New Horizons Evening of Music and Ice Cream, to the enhanced 8:30 Sunday Worship Service, to Sunday Morning Bible Study, to Women's Softball, to Methodist Summer Camp, to our third Summerfest Weekend (Saturday program, Sunday worship and picnic under the tent, Sunday evening Gap Mangione), to various Adult Class picnics and trips, to Vacation Bible School, to the Jubilee Women's Retreat. Summer is a different season, but the life of faith rolls on!

Our Storehouse ministry is taking a new direction, and moving toward opening both for service and for volunteer help on Saturday! Our daycare center recently received a grant of $20,000 from Xerox for playground improvement. The AFUMC nursery school ended their spring term with a wonderful evening program—one of the finest secrets of AFUMC today! Every week the dining\caring center serves food to the hungry, and is moving now into providing computer training. Our resident Rochester Oratorio Society performed at Chautauqua Institute this summer, with outstanding reviews.

These are examples of some of our newer initiatives in this calendar year. Our "core" or maintenance financial plan for 2000 projects an increase of 4–5%, in order simply to maintain our current work. If we were able to stretch together, and increase our giving 8–9%, new ventures like these would be possible, especially in new *worship* opportunities, in *building* care and maintenance, in better and finer *communications* both internal and external, and in various initiatives with *children*.

April 7

Meditation in Transition

Let us center ourselves in a moment of silence . . .

What are the best, good things that come to mind about change?

What are some harder feelings and memories of change?

Are there two or three hymns that have been meaningful to you in times of transition?

And do certain passages from the Scripture stand out in such times?

What do we best learn from change?

Let us center ourselves in quiet and ask ourselves silently: What is the most dramatic change I have experienced in my life?

April 8

Men's Fellowship

Last Tuesday morning at 6am, a dozen men came together from all over the county, for our weekly Men's Fellowship. We stood around the piano and sang several hymns. A man waiting for breakfast at the dining center came in from the cold and joined us. We then sat in a circle, in the warmth and light indoors, watching the snow fall outside in the dark. One of our members led us in a probing study and conversation about fathers and sons. He is a tenderhearted physician, and with his gentle, but insightful, guidance, we were able to be honest about some of our hurts, and some of our hopes. All around us, far more than we knew that morning, our lives were being influenced by the calamities of life. Job loss, care of parents and children, physical health, relational struggle. In one case, the following days included unforeseeable tragedy.

I realize looking back a few days that there was something moving among us. There was an interpersonal, intertextual, interpsychic something among us. It was almost as if, out from underneath the cold and snow and anonymity and fear and uncertainty of life, some gracious Hand was enfolding us and trying to mold us, and use us.

April 9

Notes on Hospitality

I agree that grace (and freedom) are at the heart of historic Methodism. . . . That self-absorption blinds us to God. . . . That disciple making is only a fraction of life, love, Christian life, and hence is a procrustean bed mission statement. . . . That we should not fear the culture but transform it by living in it. . . . That the post modern moment particularly should not frighten us but arouse us. . . . That our current mission statement is fear in a handful of dusty hymnals. . . . That hospitality, or radical hospitality, or living well for others, is much truer to our faith. . . . That ministry discussions quickly depend on theology and ecclesiology.

I think the fear about, and concern for, the body of the church are legitimate and healthy. These numbers are all people—malnourished babies, children home alone, teenagers immersed in internet sex, couples battling crack addiction, pastors crucified, church roofs caving in, systemic addiction in conferences, bishops using their freedom for sexual predation, in short, the ruins of the church. I do not think that lament, grief, and combative resistance to bodily death, as with any death, is a bad thing. Death is the enemy, in all its forms. I suspect you agree with this, but how to work this into your larger argument is food for further talk.

I'm not sure I share the assumption that the amputation of deacon's orders from elder's preparation and orders was necessarily an entirely good thing. I want to think about this further. Do we really ever want elders who are not deacons at heart? We may have made a mistake at this point in 1996.

I puzzle over the word holiness, and my own and other current uses of it. Not your use of it but other possible uses of it. Any active preacher will say that the main religious divide today is between holiness and compassion. Both are crucial, but compassion is more important than holiness. Again, fodder for further conversation.

April 10

Pastor's Reflection

This note is for those women and men who are suffering, little or much, on your own. Loneliness compounds all hurt. It has been on my mind and heart to write you a note, all who labor and are heavy laden. These two poems, one a remembrance of childhood hurt and the other a reflection of mature hurt, are radiant—are they not?—with awareness of another reality. As alone as we are, we are not ultimately alone.

Here is a poem written by a man of color, remembering his youth and his father. One of our church members gave it to me last spring:

Sundays too my father got up early
And put his clothes on in the blueblack cold,
Then with cracked hands that ached
From labor in the weekday weather made
Banked fires blaze. No one ever thanked him.
I'd wake and hear the cold splintering, breaking.
When the rooms were warm, he'd call,
And slowly I would rise and dress
Fearing the chronic angers of that house,
Speaking indifferently to him,
Who had driven out the cold
And polished my good shoes as well.
What did I know of love's austere and lonely offices?
(By Robert Hayden)

Here is a poem written by the greatest of English poets, amid the pain of near blindness and lonely ache.

When I consider how my light is spent
Ere half my days in this dark world and wide,
And that one talent which is death to hide
Lodged with me useless, though my soul more bent
To serve therewith my Maker, and present
My true account, lest He returning chide.
"Doth God exact day labor light denied?"
I fondly ask. But Patience, to prevent
That murmur, soon replies, "God doth not need
Either man's work or his own gifts. Who best
Bear his mild yoke, they serve him best. His state
Is kingly: thousands at his bidding speed,
And post o'er land and ocean without rest;

They also serve who only stand and wait.
(John Milton)
Jesus said, "Come to me all who labor and are heavy laden. I will give you rest."

April 11

Sixth Grade Teacher

Instead, jog for a moment along a familiar village green. For there is a second persistent woman today, not of Scripture but of experience. It is largely in the interplay between these two women, Scripture and Experience, that we discover truth. You can see her in your own past, your own gallery of saints. Name the most persistent woman you ever met. Bella Abzug. Betty Bone Scheiss. Florence Nightengale. Elizabeth Cady Stanton. Eleanor Roosevelt. Esther. Barbara Streisand. That uppity Syropheonician woman. Harriet Tubman. Sojourner Truth. Susanna Wesley. Your grandmother. Whomever. I was thinking of one such persistent woman on a 90 degree day in the summer. For that summer day, hot and humid and happy, I took the car into Hamilton for repair. They needed much skill and two hours and some money to do the job. So in the great heat I was free to run through a familiar village, and across a village green, where long ago I was raised in a patchwork complex of relationships, durable and healthy.

Running along, with no deeds to do no promises to keep, I recalled an earlier age. . . . There is a lanky Baptist preacher, heralding the promise of truth; and a musician on the bandstand, singing for justice; and a postmaster protecting communications; and a library, awaiting the emergence of justice; and a church and a store, and a graveyard with night falling. All in the mind's eye.

Through the familiar streets I ran thinking, steadily and especially, of my teacher, Marjorie Shafer. In the sixth grade she opened the world to us—by teaching us to read. As a teacher, she used the resources she had available, namely, her time and her voice. She persisted, through those years, prayerfully using the common resources of time and voice. You have time and you have a voice, too. You have need of persistent prayer, too. You have a desire not to lose heart, too. I was impressed, with the dogs barking in the summer heat, by the persistent memory of her persistence. It was a good to remember the time given and the voice lifted, in 1966 in the 6th grade—SRA reading, sock hop, changes in classmates, baseball—Sandy Kofax and Orlando Cepeda, the Beatles, James Bond, memorizing the map of Africa, a mock debate about Vietnam, and the long great story of Bilbo Baggins. And, suddenly, girls.

Three things I do not understand
Four are too wonderful for me
The way of a ship on the high sea
The way of an eagle in the sky
The way of the serpent on the rock
And the way of a man with a woman
So continued this reverie, in a summer run, on a hot day, along a village green.

April 12

On Ferguson: A Marsh Chapel Reflection

In a pastoral mode, let me offer three overtures in reflection upon the events in Ferguson, MO this week. These brief thoughts follow on sermons delivered this fall at Marsh Chapel, which already have addressed the tragedy in Ferguson (8/24, 9/7, 10/12, 10/26, 11/23, 11/30), and on the Marsh Chapel forum held here on 9/3, and on several other group and individual conversations.

First, it may help us most, and this counter-intuitively, to place ourselves sub specie aeternitatis, under the gaze of God, and approach this particular but revelatory event from a spiritual, and theological perspective. In prayer. In thought. In worship. In gathering. In conversation. To remember that we and all whom we encounter are children of the living God. We are not economic engines, solely, nor political operatives, mainly, nor cultural agents, centrally, nor partisan players, primarily. We are angels in waiting. And those whom we greet and consider are so, too. As children of the living God, grounded in grace, sustained by spirit, we may have food for the work and bread for the journey. General calls for ongoing conversation are well meaning but misdirected without daily rations. Theologically then we will again brood over sin, death, meaninglessness. Theologically then we will confess pride, sloth, falsehood, hypocrisy, sloth and idolatry. Theologically then we will return to admission of evil, both banal and horrific, to admission of the enduring hardness and hardship of injustice, to admission of our complicity, hate to say so as we do, in the gone wrong part of life. Isaiah Berlin would agree. If nothing else, a spiritual, theological perspective will perhaps improve our capacity to listen.

Second, it surely will help us, and this more obviously, to read some history, some good, probing history. Ferguson comes 200 years or so after much of our American economy, politics, culture and struggle were forged in cotton. You can read Edward Baptist's The Half Has Never Been Told: Slavery and the Making of American Capitalism. But the calculation is closer to home. 30% or 40% of slavery is still with us today—in economy, culture, politics, and struggle. From 1810 to 1860 a quarter-million slaves from the Old South were re-sold into the New South (Florida, Alabama, Mississippi, Louisiana, Arkansas, Texas, and, yes, Missouri). Mothers had their babies torn from their arms on the now beautiful Baltimore harbor. Husbands were whipped away from wives, and marched to Birmingham. Children were held up like pumpkins and sold to the highest bidder, then sailed down to New Orleans. They were herded into what had been Indian land (the Native Americans having been either slaughtered or 're-located' to Oklahoma). With cost free land and cost free labor trees were cut, fields were plowed, cotton was planted and harvested, mills in the north were set to work, all or almost all funded by a tsunami of credit, legitimated by the US government and various banks. You know, you, even you, I, even I, can make money if you pay nothing for land and pay nothing for labor. But the bills do accrue into the future, not just for the enslaved, but also for the enslaver, and for all those, both north and south of the Mason Dixon line, who benefitted from slavery and the torture it took to keep people chained. The sky-line of Boston, dear old Boston, old money Boston, is so beautiful, especially if you don't look too closely at where all that 200 year old money came from. If nothing else, a historical perspective will perhaps improve our capacity to lament.

Third, we need to act. I do not mean re-act. To act we need a moral compass. To find a moral compass you need a community of faithful women and some men, acquainted with wonder, vulnerability, and self-mockery, with mystery, generosity, and, yes, morality. You need a church. I am glad to host a vigil, as we will do Tuesday night. Please come. Please do. But my interest in your presence will be quickened, made real, if I see you in church, praying, tithing, teaching children, visiting the sick, studying the Gospels, singing hymns, living a life in which you are really alive before you die. I have less interest in, less compassion for, people who descend for a moment from the heavenly clouds of utter self-centeredness to attend a vigil or watch a car burning on TV, only to return later to a lonely, greedy, narrowly immoral life. I don't care that you come to Marsh, or not. I am glad to greet you here, or not. But. Go somewhere once a week to gather with others, admit your mortality and fragility, and grow up, Sunday by Sunday. The kinds of labor that it will take in this country for us to live down chattel slavery will require a moral compass rooted in ancient faithfulness. Over time, then, you with others, over much time, will gain the footing, find the leverage, provide the strength to make real change in real time.

How shall you respond to Ferguson? Spiritually, historically, and morally.

April 13

Ernest Fremont Tittle on Prayer

"There is special need for persistence in prayer when the object sought is the redressing of social wrongs. God will see justice done if the human instruments of his justice to not give way to weariness, impatience, or discouragement, but persevere in prayer and labor for the improvement of world conditions. Here we can learn from the scientist. Medical research is a prayer for the relief of suffering, the abolition of disease, the conservation of life—a prayer in which the scientist perseveres in the face of whatever odds, whatever darkness and delay. More especially we can learn from great religious leader like Luther, Wesley, Wilberforce, Shaftsbury, who year upon year prayed and fought for the causes to which they dedicated their lives. The need for persistence in prayer arises not only from the intransigence of the oppressor, but also from the immaturity and imperfection of the would-be reformer. We have a lot to learn and much in ourselves to overcome before we can be used of God as instruments of his justice. Recognizing this, Gandhi spent hours each day in prayer and meditation, and maintained a weekly day of silence."

April 14

Village Green

November 20, 2001, a sparkling and crisply brilliant autumn day in Rochester, became the occasion for the latest surprise apocalypse of a "village green" moment along East Avenue.

The great modern architect 'Le Corbusier' taught that "architecture is the will of an epoch translated into space: living, changing, new." Gracious, open, free space is the heart's desire of the community of faith. We long for space and time to "meet and greet and watch our children grow." So much of our life becomes a struggle to do what we must do: we become "human doings" rather than "human beings." Imagine the sheer delight of arriving at Asbury First on a Saturday morning and seeing for several hours a community of people simply enjoying the open space of this church and the chance to be together. Whatever was done (and it was much) was merely an excuse for the main point: being human together.

One group was cooking in the dining caring center. The altar guild was busy with the construction of the Thanksgiving Altar (to many the most beautiful of the year). A group of younger men were painting a second floor room, with only a few "runs, drips and errors." Behind 1010, a solitary figure was seen, alone, planting ferns to beautify our backyard. Volunteers were working steadily in the Storehouse, while a volunteered husband repaired the lock on the Storehouse chute. But outside, along the village green, many hands made light and short work of raking the whole lawn. What a day on which to work a little, talk a little, play a little, and pause now and then to be inspired by the magnificent spire of our church. A street person whom we know peddled up, took a rake and said: "I suppose this is like Tom Sawyer and the fence." Indeed.

At noon, the whistle blew. A feast was spread before rakers, fern planters, painters, clothiers, street people and florists alike. A prayer was offered: "Lord, make us human beings, shaped again in your image. Love us so that we can love others. Free us so that we can set others free. And bless these hot dogs. In Jesus name." One had to notice, as the mustard was applied, the various ages, stages, ethnicities, backgrounds, zipcodes, professions, and raking styles represented. It was quite an assortment.

Corbusier also said: "the great problem of America is the suburb." He said its solution is found in urban space, gardens, roof decks, green lawns that allow people to come together and have communion "along a village green" where we can meet and greet and watch our children grow.

We owe the gift of November 20 to Heath Rist, our Campus Care Coordinator, whose ministry of presence and hospitality is just now emerging to our communal benefit and delight! Maybe Heath has been reading Corbusier: "what makes our dreams so daring is that they can be realized."

Like many good things, it also was so simple. A rake, a grill, a morning. As our 19th century Albany neighbors sang: "in truth, simplicity is gain. To bow and to bend we shan't be ashamed. . . . And when we find ourselves in the place just right, it will be in the valley of love and delight."

April 15

What is in a Name

As Methodism continues to shrink and diversify, we may need to look at the coura-geous examples of those who gave up their denominational names for the sake of a healthier future. As a cradle Methodist, and one who loves to tell these stories, this is a difficult admis-sion for me. Yet, particularly in the Northeast, we may need to remember, sometime, the willingness others found to leave older names behind. Two nearby examples come to mind.

The United Church of Canada was born out of the willingness among Methodists to leave their name behind for the sake of a greater good. Some of the best people I have known have come out of this tradition, like Douglass John Hall.

The Evangelical and United Brethren church gave up its own name to become a part of a larger whole, the United Methodist Church. Pastors and lay leaders lost traditions, hymns, campgrounds, influence, and the various other intangible but significant relations that go into extended family life. They did so happily, to a great degree. Some of the most caring pastors I have known have come out of this tradition, like Joe Yeakel and David Lubba.

April 16

Women Need Men Like Fish Need Bicycles

The remains of the 1960's clog and block renewal in ministry today. Ideas, currents, clergy, patterns, habits, language, assumptions that had a moment of importance, back then, linger in our pews, classrooms, denominational offices and pulpits. Some clergy came along to the church in opposition to war or to the war, or in pursuit of a way to avoid the draft for the war. Few remain, but there are a few. Their general sentiment is not overly affirmative of institutional life. Likewise, the free ride feminism that brought and kept a tide of talented and other women in the ministry continues to lap at the shoreline of church life. The civil rights movement did not bring racial integration to the churches. Oppositions to war and other political actions did not bring us justice either. But feminism came, made camp, and has stayed. It is really feminism that has remained abroad in the church for 40 years, continuing in ways both healthy and unhealthy to influence Christian life.

I remember deciding to recruit female ushers for our Syracuse congregation. Ushering had been an all male activity. We found two women to usher. The head usher fumed. Why, I asked? "It is the only thing we can still get the men to do around here!" he said. Of course we needed to have female ushers, as we need to have female leaders, finance chairs, trustees, pastors, teachers, clergy, superintendents, bishops and professors of New Testament. But as the women have come, the men have left. They have left the seminaries and pulpits. They have left the pews and Sunday schools. They have left the church. Where are the men, especially the young men? The feminization of American culture has progressed for two centuries, as Ann Douglass so well documented in her book of that title. But the feminization of the church has become, in some quarters, so extreme that the UMC has become an enlarged UMW.

Cleaning up after the sixties will take yet another generation. Here is our lesson. Women do need men, and so does the church, not only, for sure, in the positions of power, but also, for sure, in those positions. The truth that has no name in our time is that the northern church has lost half its membership in the decades in which women have taken over half its pulpits. The latter did not cause the former, of course. But the two phenomena occurred at the same time and were conditions, if not causes, for each other. Here is our other lesson. Carrying women along, as ineffective clergy, simply because they are able to ride the free ride of the feminist wave is a danger, a peril, an exhausting expense.

April 17

SMG Invocation

Gracious God, our source, our guide, our deep resting place,

This is a day of new beginnings, a time to remember and a time to move on

In this commencement hour we pause, with reverence, to seek your blessing and to invoke your presence.

Rest upon us, upon our minds and hearts, we ask, with a real spirit of gratitude, for all of the good we have known.

Today we thank you for the inspiration of creative teachers, for the insight of careful administrators, for the imagination of diligent and earnest students.

We wear robes upon our bodies, but on our hearts we wear a suit of thanksgiving for what we have learned, and a vestment of gratitude for what we have been given.

We carry away diplomas in our hands, but in our memories we carry the remembrance of things past, which we will know, for their truest sense, many days into the future.

We offer and accept honors and accolades—from summa to thank ya, but we take away not a set of promises, but a set of challenges, not a set of gifts but a set of dreams for a new day, a better world, a finer future.

Bless us and our time in commencement we pray.

Amen.

April 18

Ten-Year Luncheon

Gracious God,

We lift our hearts in thanks, for being, for being here, for being here together.

We honor all being present whose work supports the work of learning. Help us to be mindful, daily, of the shaping of young minds.

We hold up the challenge and privilege of being here, over a decade, engaged in the swirl of a University community, ever growing we hope in virtue. Help us to mindful, daily, of the beating of young hearts all about us.

We celebrate this moment, being here together, in the common piety of a shared meal, to mark ten years of labor, in these hours of fellowship. Help us to be mindful, daily, of the growth of young souls.

We lift our hearts in thanks, for being, for being here, for being here together, in the nourishment of this table and meal.

Amen.

April 19

Recipe for a Sermon: Research

1. What do the Greek\Hebrew text, commentaries, translations, parallels offer?
2. How did 'the Fathers' read the text or handle the theme?
3. What do Luther, Calvin, Wesley, Barth, and Tillich do with the text or theme?
4. What does your favorite journal offer (Christian Century, NTS, Interpretation)?
5. What recent pastoral conversations come easily to mind?

April 20

Recipe for a Sermon: Writing

1. What is the whole gospel for this sermon ('diamond point') in a sentence?
2. What three part division will be used (abc, a1b1c1, e/e/e, s.s.s., verses, moments)?
3. What practical suggestions has the sermon for personal life?
4. What references has the sermon to social life?
5. At what points does the sermon use appropriate humor?
6. What can children understand in the sermon?
7. Is the mortality of the preacher and congregation clear?
8. Is the gospel preached, clearly and forcefully?
9. Do you believe what you are about to say?

April 21

Recipe for a Sermon: Delivery

1. Is the sermon written, rewritten, memorized and practiced?

2. Are silence, dynamics, singing, emotion, body language considered?

3. Is it under twenty minutes?

April 22

Christian Atheism: One

Religion on campus has a theological chance, a spiritual opening, the opportunity and freedom to dream, both regarding creation and regarding redemption.

That is, the remaining significant campus pulpits (Marsh, Harvard, Duke, and just a few others) have the spiritual opportunity to challenge and engage thought forms in college and culture, including some forms of popular atheism and agnosticism, and introduce them, for example, to some religious forms of atheism and agnosticism. Leslie Weatherhead did this already sixty years ago with sermons collected as *The Christian Agnostic*. Edward O. Wilson this fall wrote: "Faith is the one thing that makes otherwise good people do bad things." But the contrary is true as well: "Love is the one thing that makes otherwise bad people do good things."

The asperity with which the Holy Scripture summarizes creation is only matched by the asperity which the creeds of the Church summarize creation. "In the beginning God created the heavens and the earth." Period. "I believe in God the Father Almighty, maker of heaven and earth." Period. Scripture and creed say what reason and experience know: we have the brute fact of the brute creation. Period. The rest of the Holy Scripture, all 65.9 other books, and the rest of the creed, the long second paragraph and the shorter third, go on from there. The love of God comes accompanied by faith and hope. Creation is the occasion of love but does not occasion love, does not occasion faith in love, and does not occasion a hope for a loving future. God is Love is more about the second person of the Trinity, the Christ of God, than about the first person of the Trinity, the creation of God, more Fairest Lord Jesus than For the Beauty of the Earth. Love is in the Second Person of the Trinity.

April 23

Christian Atheism: Two

When invited to come to Marsh Chapel, I looked back on the great dreamers, the voices, influential and real, that had formed me. My father-in-law, who built a Wesley Foundation from the ground up in the 1960's in Oswego, NY. My dad, who served a college town church and helped create an ecumenical form of college ministry, UMHE, in the same decade. My mother and mother in law, who in those years hosted and graced endless fellowship meals for nervous pre-seminarians, bruised freedom riders, troubled conscientious objectors, chastened veterans, and their various boyfriends and girlfriends. Our friend, the Chaplain at Colgate, RV Smith, whose presence and courage, in hard years, were sustained by MOTIVE magazine. William Sloane Coffin, chaplain at Williams, and then at Yale, before becoming our pastor at Riverside Church in NYC in the 1970's. Coffin's preaching ministry, in New York and at Columbia and through Union, continues to be a large part of my model for work here at Marsh, in Boston and at Boston University and through the School of Theology. Peter Gomes, both colleague and mentor, who succeeded at Harvard, as he famously said, by being 'ubiquitous.' The years and losses have mounted up in equal measure for religion on campus. There are but 1 for every 5 to 10 pulpits now on campus that there were 50 years ago. But we are here. You are here. Where there is life there is hope.

All of these fine ministers, for all of their substantial theological differences, when it came to spiritual theology, shared a freedom to dream. In fact, far beyond their own limited spheres, they kept dreams alive, in decades of confusion, and kept preaching alive, in years when across the land there was, in Amos's fine phrase, "a famine of the word." They read Paul Tillich and made his 'depth' available to others. We can do the same, here, with the great theological minds of our time, some of whom are close at hand.

The Nobel Laureate Patrick Modiano said recently, "I have always felt like I've been writing the same book for the past 45 years." And I have felt the same, preaching or trying to preach the same sermon for the past 45 years. I preach love. God's love. Love is God. All of us are better when we are loved. Love divine, all loves excelling, joy of heaven to earth come down. Love God, love neighbor—so the Bible says, today.

Religion on campus can give future leaders, secular and religious, a sense of possibility, imagination, freedom and breadth in the theopoetics of God talk. Those who attend worship at Marsh Chapel over four years as undergraduates, that is, will have also virtually acquired much of the vocabulary and content of the first year of graduate study in theology—biblical, historical, philosophical, and pastoral theology. At no extra charge! What a bargain!

April 24

King

"Agape is more than romantic love, agape is more than friendship. Agape is understanding, creative, redemptive, good will to all men. It is an overflowing love which seeks nothing in return. . . . When one rises to love on this level, he loves men not because he likes them, not because their ways appeal to him, but he loves every man because God loves him. And he rises to the point of loving the person who does an evil deed while hating the deed that the person does. I think this is what Jesus meant when he said 'love your enemies.' I'm very happy that he didn't say like your enemies, because it is pretty difficult to like some people. Like is sentimental, and it is pretty difficult to like someone bombing your home; it is pretty difficult to like somebody threatening your children; it is difficult to like congressmen who spend all of their time trying to defeat civil rights. But Jesus says love them, and love is greater than like."[1]

April 25

---

1. Martin Luther King, Jr., "Love, Law, and Civil Disobedience," in *A Testament of Hope*, ed. James Melvin Washington (San Francisco: Harper, 1991), pp. 46–7. Washington notes how King relies expressly on Nygren in his depiction of agape and also amplifies what he finds, p. 16. For an interpretation of King's account of love, see James H. Cone, *Martin & Malcolm and America: A Dream or a Nightmare* ((Maryknoll: Orbis, 1991), e.g., pp. 120–150.

Ecclesiology: One

Religion on campus has an opportunity with regard to religion off campus, an ecclesiological rather than a sociological responsibility, one of church rather than college. That is, the voices of religion on campus can provide a hopefully humble but also historically nuanced counterbalance to contemporary church vision and leadership.

For instance, as only one example, and turning to our own situation and heritage here at Marsh Chapel, there has been an historic, creative tension between the preaching leadership and the administrative management of the Methodist church, dating back at least to Peter Cartwright and his tangles with various presiding elders. Both are important, both spirit and structure. Our ministry at Marsh this year emphasizes spirit, but structure has its role, importance and place. Today, however, with most of the preachers in many Methodist conferences now lacking full education, and lacking ordination with consequent guarantee of appointment, the balance of power has shifted dramatically in the last generation. Those whose primary weekly commitment is to interpreting the scripture are outweighed by those whose primary annual commitment is to upholding the discipline. The gospel trumpeted in Scripture and tradition, freedom and grace and love, for all, including especially those in minority, including sexual minorities, is overshadowed by the rules and constraints re-voted every four years. University pulpits, the few that remain, bear a significant responsibility to model dimensions of humility, integrity and courage (along with those healthy, strong churches whose northeastern voices you heard a summer ago, from New York, Washington, Rochester, and Boston). As Lou Martyn said, we are free here to set heaven is a little higher. So we need to take responsibility to lead, along the fewer strong, stable pulpits across the land. We have the advantage of resources in interpretation, in memory, in thought, and in reflection that can be of some use, in this particular time.

April 26

Ecclesiology: Two

One illustration. Ministry is now denied to gay people in Methodism. Ordination, that is. But think about this for a minute, in a University chapel. We have spent more than a generation re-learning that ministry belongs not to the ordained, alone, but to the baptized. Entrance into ministry does not begin with the bishop laying on hands, at ordination. Entrance into ministry begins with the pastor laying on hands, in baptism. 99% of ministry is conferred in the sacrament of baptism, and 1% in the sacramental rite of ordination. Those who really would consistently exclude gay women and men from ministry *should never have allowed the church to baptize or confirm or commune gay people.* That would have been more fully effective and consistent bigotry. But in baptism—the barn door has been opened, and no amount of shutting it will ever work! Gay people are baptized, and therefore are already in ministry! It is a short way from denying orders to denying baptism.

April 27

Ecclesiology: Three

Christopher Morse, my theology professor, and a Methodist minister from Virginia, told us once at dinner about a humorous baptismal moment. Forty years ago you baptized every infant in the northern half of the county, no matter what county, on Palm Sunday. 38 baptisms in a row. He moved down the line, seizing the children one at a time. "What name shall be given this child?" John. Mary. George. Pinundress. A French couple, just learning English, presented the child. So, "Pinundress, I baptize . . ." A distraught father came up later to show Christopher the pin on the dress, on which the name had been clearly written, 'pin on dress!' We are not so hasty now. We have spent a good deal of time on the prevenient, justifying, sanctifying grace of God in baptism. All the baptized are all in ministry. Jew or Greek, slave or free, male or female, gay or straight. But it is our religious opportunity, on campus, freely and safely to think about these things, with humility but also with honesty.

April 28

Ecclesiology: Four

Another illustration. The rules in Methodism explicitly state that the pastor alone is to decide whose marriage will be solemnized, "in accordance with the laws of the state and the rules of the church." No local committee decides. No vote of session. No poll of the community or neighborhood. No family habit of a patriarchal auction of a daughter to an opposing family. No. The pastor shall decide. There is an accrued wisdom in this, the leaving of these lasting decisions to those in the local situations, in the contexts in which they are to be lived out. Would you want a General Conference every four years voting on a list of those to be married in Boston, those to be allowed to marry in Los Angeles, those types of people fit for matrimony in Wisconsin? Surely not. That is why the primary directive in the discipline leaves such to the discretion of the pastor.

In ecclesiology, Jesus is our beacon not our boundary.

April 29

Marriage

Marriage: UMCBOD Para. 340 2.a.3.a. *(Duties of pastor) To perform the marriage ceremony after due counsel with the parties involved and in accordance with the laws of the state and the rules of the United Methodist Church. The decision to perform the ceremony shall be the right and responsibility of the pastor.* So. Do we mean this? Are we going to 'enforce' as one general superintendent in the book, *Finding Our Way,* "enforce the discipline?" Here the burden of responsibility is clearly, unequivocally placed upon the pastor whose "right responsibility" it is to decide to marry a couple. There is no shading here, no hem or haw. The pastor decides. After due counsel (pastoral care) and in accordance with *state law* and church rules. No comment here is offered to the situation when state law and church rules, both of which are to be upheld, are different. State law 50 years ago to prohibit interracial marriage was widely ignored by Methodist clergy, who performed interracial marriages in states prohibiting such. Not to marry a gay couple is now to contradict the laws of 30+ states who protect the right of gay people to marry. Rightly, the BOD leaves these difficult (pastoral) decisions in the hands of the minister. "The decision to perform the ceremony shall be the right and responsibility of the pastor." Not the General Conference. Not the General Superintendent. Not the District Superintendent. Not the Charge Conference. The pastor. And that is as it should be. Thanks be to God.

April 30

May

2013 Commencement Benediction

Boston University

Spirit of Life and Love
Prayerfully we thank you
For the hands that carried our clothes into the freshman dorm
For the voices over the phone that encouraged us when we were low
For the arms that reached forward in embrace when we came home
For the friends that kept us from hurting ourselves
For the teachers who listened and spoke formative words
For moments of wonder:
Snow on the Public Garden
Sails on the River Charles
Wind to chill and cheer on the Esplanade
Light at twilight, light at dawn, light in cloud, light in sun
For thy light in which we see light
Spirit of Life and Love
In Benediction we thank you.
Amen

May 1

Basketball Team

Spirit of Life and Love
Prayerfully we thank you
For the hands that carried our clothes into the freshman dorm
For the voices over the phone that encouraged us when we were low
For the arms that reached forward in embrace when we came home
For the friends that kept us from hurting ourselves
For the teachers who listened and spoke formative words
For moments of wonder:
Snow on the Public Garden
Sails on the River Charles
Wind to chill and cheer on the Esplanade
Light at twilight, light at dawn, light in cloud, light in sun
For thy light in which we see light
Spirit of Life and Love
In Benediction we thank you.
Amen

May 2

Benediction SMG

As we go, Dear God, we pray:
Remind us that we do not go alone.
We are a part of working fellowship, a spirited community.
The voices of our teacher here go with us.
The voices of future teachers will accompany us.
Our family and friends have not forgotten us.
Our community of fellow workers surrounds and watches over us.
Our closest friends, partners, lovers and spouses attend us.
Wonder, Generosity, Goodness, Kindess are present and Presence among us.
We commence, but not alone.
Send us forth with thy blessing we ask.
Amen

May 3

Commencement Convocation 2012

Boston University

Gracious God

Holy and Just,

Thou who art loving us into love and freeing us into freedom,

We gather today as a University community,

One BU both in mourning and celebration.

Grant us we pray the spiritual balance in this hour both to rejoice with those who rejoice

and to weep with those who weep.

Dear God

Our spirits and souls are overcast today with a sense of loss

Be with the parents, families, loved ones, friends, teachers and colleagues, of these four we pray,

And give us all we ask the faith

To face loss with love,

To face grief with grace,

To face disappointment with honesty,

To face death with dignity.

Give us the apostle's courage to say, 'when I am weak, then I am strong.'

Oh Thou who overshadows all that is overcast,

Grant us thy blessing and peace.

Dear God

Our souls and spirits are illumined today with a sense of celebration as we honor our graduates.

Be with their parents, families, loved ones, friends, teachers and colleagues we pray.

Give us radiant hearts truly to celebrate

With grandparents who have come to honor another generation,

With parents who sacrificed in time and treasure and tutelage to make a way for their children,

With graduates of keen mind, good conscience and strong will, who will make this world a better place, in heart and service,

With professors and administrators who in unsung ways and in quiet hours provoked learning, inspired virtue, and practiced piety,

With leaders of our beloved University who have gone the second mile in their labors on behalf of this entire community.

Give us the psalmist's heart, 'that weeping may tarry for the night, but joy comes with the morning'

O thou who is the light in every light, the light in which we see light

Grant us thy blessing and peace.

Gracious God

Thou who gives us the soulful ambidexterity both to rejoice and to weep in this hour,

We invoke thy presence, spirit, blessing and peace on this Commencement Sunday.

May 4

Autumn Retreat

Erazim Kohak: Wonder

"The ageless boulders of the long abandoned dam, the maple and the great birch by twilight, the chipmunk in the busyness of his days and of his dying, even I, making my dwelling place among them, are not only right in our season. We also have our value in eternity, as witnesses to the audacious miracle of being rather than nothing. Ultimately, that is the moral sense of nature, infinitely to be cherished: that there is something. That is the eternal wonder articulated in the rightness and rhythm of time which humans honor in their commandments, the wonder of being. . . . There are humans . . . who become blind to goodness, to truth and beauty, who drink wine without pausing to cherish it, who pluck flowers without pausing to give thanks, who accept joy and grief as all in a day's work, to be enjoyed or managed, without ever seeing the presence of eternity in them. But that is not the point. What is crucial is that humans, whether they do so or not, are capable of encountering a moment not simply as a transition between a before and an after but as the miracle of eternity ingressing into time. That, rather than the ability to fashion tools, stands out as the distinctive human calling."

May 5

Opening a Prayer

When our fine university leadership asked whether I could bring an invocation for this evening's inception of our campaign I thought of the minister who, asked to do something similar, was overtaken by an honest anxiety and replied, "Yes. Sure. I will. It would be my pressure—I mean, my pleasure!" So, in life, so tonight, we live day by day amid pressures and pleasures. That makes this moment ideal for prayer, a word of thanks and blessing. Let us pray.

May 6

Commencement 2007

Let us pray.

Gracious God, Holy and Just,

We fold our hands in solemn gratitude on this Sunday morning.

We are grateful for these 4000 young lives. We take not one of them for granted.

We are proud of them, and we love them.

As we extend our hands to theirs, in the giving of diplomas, we thankfully remember other hands.

We are thankful for the skilled hands that delivered them at birth, and washed them on the way to life.

We are thankful for the gentle hands that fed them, and rocked them, and comforted them.

We are thankful for the stern hands that brought discipline, in early forms of learning, virtue and piety.

We are thankful for guiding hands, who taught that community is the native soil of the human spirit.

We are thankful for old hands, worn hands, folded in prayer this morning, whose veins and muscles and sinews have been spent in the raising of another generation.

Especially we are thankful for unseen hands—of Spirit, Presence, Truth, Love—invisible hands of goodness, loose in the universe.

As the fingers of one generation receive the blessing of another this day, we are thankful.

Now with folded hands we invoke your blessing: For those whom we have lost, and for those who have suffered loss this year. Quietly, for a moment, we remember them this morning. For those who have known trial this year. For those who have borne disappointments this year. Our hearts and hands go out to them. With folded hands we ask your blessing.

With lifted hands we offer our thanks. For what education, and wisdom, we have acquired. For what virtue, and courage, we have developed. For what piety, and humility, we have attained. With lifted hands we offer our thanks.

Make of our hands instruments of peace, now and always, we pray.

May 7

Commencement 2012

Call to Worship

Here and Now
Where the Dawn of the East
Meets the Twilight of the West
And the Cool of the North
Touches the Calm of the South
Where the Transcendent Grace of God
Touches Ground in the Humility of Christ
In the Spirit—Right Here, Just Now
At Marsh Chapel, Boston University
Where the Head of the Charles meets the Heart of the Country
In this Holy Place, at this Sacred Time
We Assemble to Worship Almighty God
To Illumine the Imagination by the Beauty of God
To Quicken the Conscience by the Holiness of God
To Warm the Heart by the Love of God
To Devote the Will to the Purposes of God
We Gather to Worship Almighty God
We welcome to our service today all visitors
We welcome President Robert A Brown
We welcome Provost David K Campbell
We welcome our Baccalaureate Speaker Dr. William H. Hayling
We bask in the light of this sun drenched, sun blanched, sun baked, sun dappled, sun spanked day
As an addressable congregation in this nave of Marsh Chapel: a heart for the heart of the city, and a service for the service of the city
As a radio congregation through WBUR FM across New England
As a virtual congregation around the country—Illinois, Kansas, Ohio, New York and the District of Columbia included
As those who are absent this week, yet may choose to be present next week
It is the embrace of Love Divine that gathers us
Here and Now
As we are able, may we stand in the praise of God

Benediction

May the sun show warm and bright on you
Your darkest night a star shine through
Your dullest morn a radiance brew
And when dusk comes God's hand to you.

May 8

Commencement 2011

Let us pray.

Gracious God, Holy and Just,

We fold our hands in solemn gratitude on this Sunday afternoon.

We are grateful for these 4000 and more young lives. We take not one of them for granted.

We are proud of them, and we love them.

As we extend our hands to theirs, in the giving of diplomas, we thankfully remember other hands.

We are thankful for the skilled hands that delivered them at birth, and washed them on the way to life.

We are thankful for the gentle hands that fed them, and rocked them, and comforted them.

We are thankful for the stern hands that brought discipline, in early forms of learning, virtue and piety.

We are thankful for guiding hands, who taught that "community is the native soil of the human spirit" (H Thurman).

We are thankful for old hands, worn hands, folded in prayer this morning, whose veins and muscles and sinews have been spent in the raising of another generation.

Especially we are thankful for unseen hands—of Spirit, Presence, Truth, Love—invisible hands of goodness, loose in the universe.

As the fingers of one generation receive the blessing of another this day, we are thankful.

With lifted hands we offer our thanks. For what education, and wisdom, we have acquired. For what virtue, and courage, we have developed. For what piety, and humility, we have attained. With lifted hands we offer our thanks.

Make of our hands instruments of peace, now and always, we pray.

May 9

Prayer

Dear God,

We pause in prayer to place before you all the past four years have taught.

Our learning from these years we present to you. We bundle together what we have known and the ways we have grown in tasks partly completed, in challenges met, in losses unexpected and foreseen, in spurts of creative energy, in disappointments, in surprises, in changed relationships. All this past experience we give over to your care and keeping.

Together we seek your blessing for what is yet to be. We seek your blessings of imagination and insight for the learning in the years to come. For keen eyes to sense unexpected opportunity. For faithful ears to hear a call to speak truth. For steady obedience to the way of love, in teaching, in healing, in community, in spirit. For curiosity to discern the odd joys embedded in trials. O Lord, we pray, make of all that will come toward us a pattern of meaningful learning and growth.

For all that has been, we offer Thanks

For all that will be, we say Yes.

Amen.

May 10

Commencement Prayer 2008

With congratulations to our graduates, and with respect for those who have come before us, from Augustine of Hippo to Niebuhr of New York, we pause for prayer.

Great art thou O Lord and greatly to be praised. Great is thy power and thy wisdom is infinite. Thee would we praise without ceasing. For our hearts are restless until they find their rest in thee.

As we celebrate the achievement of today and the beckoning challenge of tomorrow, we bow to receive the blessings of patience, courage and wisdom.

Grant us the patience to do justice, the courage to love mercy, and the wisdom to walk in humility as doers and lovers.

Grant us the patience to be quiet when speaking would lack faith, the courage to speak up when silence would be failure, and the wisdom to know the difference between faithful quiet and useless speech, faithful speech and cowardly quiet.

Grant us the patience to endure healthy stresses, the courage to resist unhealthy abuses, and the wisdom to know the difference between faithful endurance and false self-abnegation, between courageous resistance and selfish contention.

Grant us the patience to accept human failure, the courage to aspire to human greatness, the wisdom, as we straddle the two, of sure footed balance and adult maturity.

As we leave these hallowed halls of Boston University, grant us a lifetime of learning, virtue and piety, patience to know the right, courage to do the right, and wisdom to become the people we were born to be.

Great art thou O Lord and greatly to be praised. Great is thy power and thy wisdom is infinite. Thee would we praise without ceasing. For our hearts are restless until they find their rest in thee.

Amen.

May 11

Pauline Thirteen

Let love be genuine
Hate what is evil
Hold fast to what is good
Love one another with mutual affection
Outdo one another in showing honor
Never lag in zeal
Be ardent in spirit
Serve the Lord
Rejoice in your hope
Be patient in tribulation
Be constant in prayer
Contribute to the needs of others
Practice hospitality

May 12

Faculty Retirement Invocation

Three blessings, O Lord, we ask of Thee
    We ask thy blessing for our memory.
    We ask thy blessing for all we have yet to see.
    We ask thy blessing and return thanks to Thee.
Three blessings, O Lord, we ask of Thee.
    A blessing on yesterday
    A blessing for tomorrow
    A blessing in this present hour.
Three blessings, O Lord, we ask of Thee.

May 13

Forecourt Blessing

In the accuracy of your choices through life may you blessed with the precision of a Jimmer Freddette.

In your attitude and temperament may be blessed with the happy heart of a Carmelo Anthony (and salary too!)

In your style, your way of walking and being, may you be blessed with the sartorial creativity, the wardrobe, the grace of a Walt Frazier. Cut your own fashion edge!

In your habits of being may you be blessed with the earnest diligence, the attention to detail of a John Havlicek.

In your leadership may you be blessed with the maturity of a Bill Russell.

In your endurance of difficulty may you blessed with the longsuffering of a Bill Russell.

In your team spirit may you be blessed with the capacity for comraderie of a Bill Russell.

And may the joy and success of this season continue to reverberate in your memory all your life long.

May 14

Grace for Alumni Awards Dinner

Dear God,

We pause in this hour of memory and celebration

To give thanks to thee, thou God of every time and season

In the quiet of winter we give thanks for moments of reflection,

hours of recollection, hints of happiness remembered and expected

In the vesper stillness of the evening, we offer grateful thanks for careful friends,

caring companions, care continued, pardon and rest

In this minute of grace before dinner, we pray your blessing for Boston University with its storied past and its exciting future, for our President and Provost and all university leaders, for our alumni and alumni leaders, for our students, faculty and staff, for our community, city, nation and world. We are truly thankful for those whose wise, steady, and inventive leadership has and does guide us into the open future.

On this occasion of honor, we give thanks for heart and voice, for those who heal the body and for those who share the arts of communication

The gentle arts of healing and the artful gentleness of speech do us honor tonight

We are thankful for such human gifts and graces.

We pray both for the wisdom to avoid the dangers of a graceless perfection and the insight to appreciate the powers of a graceful imperfection.

May the poet's words be our own:

Ring the bells that still can ring

Forget your perfect offering

There is a crack in everything

That's how the light gets in

Now as we receive the nourishment of food and fellowship, we do so with happy hearts, remembering those who have labored to prepare it, as we are nourished by spirit, grace and presence.

Amen.

May 15

Greeting for Lu Lingzi Memorial (the student killed in the Marathon Bombing)

Good Friends All,

We are gathered in community tonight, mourning our shared loss of Lu Lingzi, and present to honor and remember the gifts and graces of her life.

Our verbal and musical remembrances flow out in concentric circles of love and affection.

Lingzi's family is graciously present with us, the first circle of memory and care. Her friends, fellow students, and colleagues form another wider circle, embracing and holding her family. The Boston University leadership and community—President, Professor, Chaplains, all—configure yet another, bigger, circle. But her life and loss also have gathered even larger circles, too, present or listening tonight: the citizens of Boston, the commonwealth of Massachusetts, the people of the United States, and well wishers and sympathizers from around the globe. Circle enfolds circle in concentric compassion this evening, finally stretching out to include the *oikumene*, the whole inhabited earth.

Tonight, as we grieve and remember, we are mindful of those who have been hurt, in China, in the 7.0 Richter Scale earthquake in Sichuan Province: 156 dead and thousands injured. Their own families and loved ones we recall as well this evening.

All of my chaplains are present this evening (Fr. McLaughlin, Rev Yoon, Rabbi Beyo, Mr Aberrazaq, Rev Partridge, Rev. Olson, Rev. Gaskell, and Br. Whitney), to honor and support the family. Br. Whitney will briefly introduce each speaker and musician, as the service progresses.

Boston University is a caring community. Boston University has a long tradition of honoring persons and personality. Boston University has arms broad enough to embrace the whole globe, but a heart close enough to feel heartfelt pain in the loss of one young woman, Lingzi Lu. You all, every one of you present and listening, are a part of that heart. Your presence matters.

Tonight we hold one another in just such a *natural embrace.*

May 16

10 Years of Service

Dear God,

We are glad to stop for a minute and listen.

We hear a feeling of gratitude for work to do, important work for a good cause.

We hear the willingess of others to be thankful for our work.

We hear the longing of others, near and far, who yet hope to find good work.

Before lunch, we listen.

We hear the rumbling reminders of ten years past, of a decade gone by.

Our ears fill with a decade of new words and phrases, from Y2K to tweet, from dangling chads to Katrina, from WMD to housing bubble, from nineleven to tea party.

We listen, in memory, in this moment of quiet.

Our ears fill with words that have helped us in our work: thank you, you are welcome, well done, you taught me something, its something to work on.

Help us we pray to honor work and those who work. Help us not to take work for granted or those who work for granted, for any profession is great when greatly pursued.

As we receive the gifts of this meal and this time, we do remember those in the far east suffering from earthquake and tsunami, and those in the middle east suffering from conflict and war.

Bless this food to our use and us to thy service

Amen.

May17

Invocation Retirement

After all the spring events, Alumni Awards, 10 year recognition, 25 year recognition, Senior Breakfast, Baccalaureate, Commencement, Hoodings, BU Academy: this is the gateway to summer. I love this lunch!

Your President and I spoke at the Service of Remembrance in Marsh Chapel last Saturday, for the class of 1970. It was quite a moment. The article in Monday's New York times captures the experience. And mentions my wife, the pianist, by name!

Thou Gracious Spirit of Life and Love

We pause to mindful. We pause to be grateful.

Of the challenges in our time, we are mindful.

For the simple gifts of breath and life, we are thankful.

Of the memories and hopes we share, we are mindful.

For the chance, about these tables, to share them, we are grateful.

Of the many, far and near, whose backs are against the wall, we are mindful.

For the nourishment of this fine, well served, beautifully presented meal, we are grateful.

Thou Gracious Spirit of Life and Love

We pause to mindful. We pause to be grateful.

Amen.

May 18

Invocation SMG

Thou source of every gift and grace, from whom we come and unto whom our spirits return

Together we invoke thy blessing for this hour as we give thanks for gift and grace

We are thankful for individual persons, from whose every gift arise goodness and newness

From individuals come insights, imagination, creative invention, discoveries, new ideas

For the gift of personal creativity, and individual achievement, including such gifts found in today's graduates and in tomorrow's work, we are thankful.

We are thankful also and more so for communal support and compassion, the grace to watch over one another in love.

From community come care and support of those in need, nurture and education of the young, challenge and responsibility for the well and wealthy, and the wisdom of generations passed on, in special moments, like this very hour.

For the grace of the common good, the commonwealth, including such grace as we have known here in this school and university, founded expressly for such common good, and located along an avenue of commonwealth, we are thankful.

Grant us in commencement, in commencement, in graduation, a divine dialectical capacity to be thankful both for personal gifts and for communal graces.

Amen.

May 19

Invocation 2007

Gracious God,

We pause at this evening hour to offer our thanks.

We are grateful for the good gifts of life: freedom and safety in which to gather, shelter and raiment to protect us from the cold, friendship and fellowship to keep us from loneliness, and the nourishment of a fine meal, carefully prepared, diligently served.

We are grateful for women and men who have committed themselves, in time and treasure, to this University: women who have provided new directions in learning through generous giving; men who have embodied new dimensions of virtue, through thoughtful giving; women who have shown a creative piety, through disciplined giving.

For the breath of life, for the nourishment of these hours, for the good examples of others, we are most grateful.

May the sense of meaning, the feeling of belonging, and the experience of empowerment we know here this evening, be fully shared with generations to come.

With happy and thankful hearts we do pray . . .

Amen.

May 20

Marsh Spirit

Come Sunday, every Sunday, here at Marsh Chapel:

The Chapel's gothic nave, built to lift the spirit, welcomes you

The Chapel's sixty year history, at the heart of Boston University, welcomes you

The Chapel's regard for persons and personality, both in its Connick stained glass windows and in its current ministry, welcomes you

The Chapel's familiar love of music, weekday and Sunday, welcomes you

The Chapel's congregation of caring, loving souls, in this sanctuary, welcomes you in spirit.

Welcome today as we enhance our endowment.

Endowment.

Yes, a word brings a lift to the decanal eyebrow, a stirring to the Episcopal soul, a tingle to the Provostial spirit, a warming to the Presidential heart.

Now, endowments are crucial for chapel, for school, for university. We shall other days on which to build such.

But today we celebrate the endowment we already have. It is a rich and treasure.

It is an endowment vocal not visible, audible not audited, psychic not physical, moral not material.

Listen for its echoes. . .listen. . .listen to the voices of Boston University and of Marsh Chapel . . .

All the good you can . . .

The two so long disjoined . . .

Heart of the city, service of the city . . .

Learning, virtue, piety . . .

Good friends all . . .

Hope of the world . . .

Last Week: Are ye able, still the Master, whispers down eternity . . .

Common ground . . .

Content of character . . .

May 21

Gaston Bachelard: Self-Awareness

"Words—I often imagine this—are little houses, each with its cellar and garret. Common sense lives on the ground floor, always ready to engage in 'foreign commerce,' on the same level as the others, as the passers-by, who are never dreamers. To go upstairs in the word house, is to withdraw, step by step; while to go down to the cellar is to dream, it is losing oneself in the distant corridors of an obscure etymology, looking for treasures that cannot be found in words. To mount and descend in the words themselves—this is the poet's life. . .*Yet listen well. Not to my words, but to the tumult that rages in your body when you listen to yourself.* . .And why should the actions of the imagination not be as real as those of the perception?"

May 22

Service Recognition

Gracious God, Holy and Loving,
Before Thee at this evening hour we pause to bow, to listen, to pray
With head and hand and heart we place ourselves in Thy care
Mortals all, we bow before Eternity
Frail and fallible all, we pause before Love Divine
Tonight we are especially thankful for years of service
We are grateful those who went the second mile, and so gave life to the common good
We are thankful for those who silently carried coat and cloak as well, as so gave life to community
We are thankful for those who served without public acclaim, without regular notice, without visibility, and yet did so with grace and care
We are thankful for examples of others by which to measure our own days and so gain hearts of wisdom
With head and hand and hear we pause to bow and listen and pray
Even as we offer our thanks for this hour, this place and this meal
Amen.

May 23

Matriculation

Gracious God, Holy and Just
Thou Silent Mystery, beckoning deep
In whom we live and move and have our being
Grant us peace, we pray
Give us grace, we pray
In the eyeblink of these four years
Give us peace to resist what we would regret
Give us grace to receive what will make us rejoice
Four years hence, diplomas in hand
May we be heavy with joy and free of regret
Help us to avoid the regret that follows abuse of ourselves,
Of our environment, of substances, and of others.
Warn us away from what, lastingly we will regret.
Fill us with a daily sense of adventure to embrace
What lastingly we will enjoy:
Friendship, discovery, reading, effort, achievement, accomplishment,
Self-giving, devotion, and love.
Grant us peace to resist what we would regret and grace to receive what
Causes us to rejoice.
Amen

May 24

New England Retired Preachers Invocation

2012

Gracious God, Holy and Just,

We lift our hearts in thanksgiving

For the partnership of the Gospel in which we have labored and shared.

For the privilege of ministry at birth, in crisis, over time, at death.

For the withering challenge of preaching a gospel of truth that is both gospel and truth

For the adventure of pastoral leadership, the thrill of community life and the joy of transformative service

We are grateful to have shared in the covenant of the clergy in conference, in the discipline of the itinerancy, and in the responsibility for the freedom of the pulpit.

We are thankful for those superannuated preachers who have borne the heat of the day

Who have waited by the bedside, and listened in the kitchen, and prayed over the open grave

Who graciously have blessed marriages and brides and their mothers

Who have organized two car and two hundred car funerals

Who have weathered leaky parsonage roofs and cranky parsonage committees

Who have been appointed and disappointed by Bishops

Who have known when to pack their books and shake dust from their feet, and done so with a humble courage, in grace and freedom

Who have heard the cry of need, and responded, in season and out

We are grateful for this precious, noble calling to ministry which in Christ we have shared

With those dear friends who know rest in greater light on a farther shore

Gracious God, Holy and Just

We lift our hearts in thanksgiving as we break bread together

Grateful for the partnership of the Gospel in which we have labored and shared.

Amen.

May 25

One Sentence

Reverence for Life is the beginning of wisdom.

May 26

Table Grace

Dear God,

Tonight we are thankful for this meal in this setting at this hour.

As we honor those who have labored faithfully over many years, we also give thanks for work itself.

We are thankful for work to do, for people with whom to work, for a place in which to work, for a project and institution more than worthy of labor and effort.

We remember those hunting for work, and hope for a day when all who can work and want to work will have a chance to find meaningful work.

Especially we are happy for those who mark a quarter of a century in service to this great University, committed to learning, virtue and piety.

Tireless Guardian on our way

Thou hast kept us well this day

While we thank thee we request

Care continued, pardon, rest.

Amen.

May 27

A Thought or Two on Matthew

Ignatius would love the star, but Luther would mark the voice, the sound, the birdsong of searching, inquiring, wise, questing, serious, real faith: "Where is he, who has been born king of the Jews?"

The first to find Him are not Jews at all. Gentiles, they. Some of our most natural gospel hearers and speakers today are atheists.

Matthew, though usually (mis)understood otherwise, is a Gentile gospel. The magi come first. Light centrally shines, chapter by chapter. The book is written in Greek. Its mound sermon celebrates greek wisdom and greek discipline. The wise man built his house on rock. A ruler's daughter is healed. The Sabbath is overrated. The only sign the natives deserve is that of Jonah. The disciples dish traditions of elders. The greatest faith is the gentile woman willing to take the dog crumbs that the table guests despise. The faithful followers will judge the 12 tribes. And, by the way, make sure to render your taxes to Caesar Matthew's endless explanation of kosher requirements is made for greek ears. I will not even pause to recite the damnation of woe given to scribes and Pharisees. Its concluding universalism would make Plato blush. Matthew? Jewish?

May 28

ROTC Benediction

Gracious God, Holy and Just,

Upon the completion of our vigil we pray thy benediction.

Send us forth, from this place, with thy blessing, we pray.

As we have watched, day and night, make us watchful, night and day.

As we have walked, day and night, walk with us night and day.

As we have remembered, day and night, remember us, night and day.

We honor the service of those present, and their future leadership.

We pray thy comfort and care for in service who have suffered, in these very hours of our vigil.

As those who have received the gift of freedom, prepare us to be vigilant in freedom's defense.

Amen.

May 29

ROTC Invocation

All things blessed come from Thee.

In this hour of consecrated commitment, we ask to sense Thy blessing.

Bless our country with a hunger for liberty and justice.

Bless our leaders with courage and patience.

Bless our people with a new rebirth of wonder.

Bless the parents here today with a feeling of your embrace.

Bless those to be commissioned here today with a confidence born of obedience.

Bless, O Lord, these young women and men with the graces of safety and courage.

And bless us who rely on their sacrificial service, with a deeper, truer admiration for them and for that service.

All things blessed come from Thee.

Grant us thy peace.

May 30

Senior Breakfast

We thank thee God for this most amazing, most beautiful day.
For the promise of this day
For the hope of this day
For the possibilities in this day
For the urgent challenges of this day
We thank thee God for this most amazing, most beautiful day.
Bless our gathering, we pray
Bless our graduates, now alumni, we ask
Bless our fellowship and meal, we pray
Holy Presence, we invoke thy blessing.
For all that has been, we say thank you. For all that is to be, we say yes.
Amen.

May 31

June

A City in Sorrow: Sunday Following Marathon Bombing

We are a city drenched in sorrow.

Our good words about resilience, rightly spoken, as our honest first reaction to neighborhood terrorism, the middleeastification of the globe, do not displace our sorrow. The best of days, the highest of moments, the most charmingly gracious of cityscapes, the culmination of the American experiment in PatriotsDayMarathonDaySpringHolidayBostonGlobeDay—all trashed by senseless, needless, heedless, injurious, intentional, hateful, killing violence. When another takes what you hold dear, count precious, think lovely, and rapes it, you cannot avoid anger, and the sorrow at the heart of anger.

Out there in listenerland there are still some wise, sensitive hearts, minds, souls, who are trying to come to firm grips with random death in the wake of intentional terror. Every little neighborhood, now, anywhere, has curbs and sidewalks where blood may drip, streetlamps that may be shot out, houses and shops whose glass may shatter and maim. We have known this. Since before. Since Oklahoma City. Since Columbine. Since nineleven. Since Virginia Tech. Since Newtown. Now the angel of hurt has come near, here. Some of the sensitive in listenerland wonder whether anything religiously cast, any preachment, can carry any truth, any good.

In the first place, sin is utterly personal. This we understand. The covenantal commands of the decalogue have a personal consequence (Exodus 20). For we confess, too a personal dimension to the apocalyptic sway of sin. The angels in heaven—and perhaps a few others—may "need no repentance." As grace touches ground in Jesus Christ, sin touches sand in personal confessions. We get lost. It is our nature, east of eden. We get lost in sex without love: lust. We get lost in consumption without nourishment: gluttony. We get lost in accumulation without investment: avarice. We get lost in rest without weariness, in happiness without struggle: sloth. We get lost in righteousness without restraint: anger. We get lost in desire without ration or respect: envy. And most regularly, we get lost in integrity without humility: pride. If you have never known lust, gluttony, avarice, sloth, anger, envy or pride you are not a sinner, you are outside the cloud of sin, and you need no repentance. (You also may not be quite human).

June 1

A Pastoral Prayer

Dear God:

We pause in prayer to place before you all the past year has taught.

Our learning from this year we present to you. We bundle together what we have known and the ways we have grown in tasks partly completed, in challenges met, in losses unexpected and foreseen, in spurts of creative energy, in disappointments, in surprises, in changed relationships. All this past experience we give over to your care and keeping.

Together we seek your blessing for what is yet to be. We seek your blessings of imagination and insight for the learning in the year to come. For keen eyes to sense unexpected opportunity. For faithful ears to hear a call to speak truth. For steady obedience to Christ Jesus, his teaching, his healing, his church, his spirit. For curiosity to discern the odd joys embedded in trials. O Lord, we pray, make of all that will come toward us a pattern of meaningful learning and growth.

For all that has been, we offer Thanks

For all that will be, we say Yes.

Through the same Jesus Christ our Lord.

Amen

June 2

Dinner Prayer

Dear God:

Holy and loving

We pause in this evening hour to offer our thanks and praise.

For the very gifts of life and faith, of community and work, of safe space and gracious time, we are deeply thankful.

Bless our time together in this place, we pray.

For the daily chances to encourage one another, to give another generation a place to grow in learning and virtue and piety, we are truly thankful.

Bless our work together on this campus, we pray.

For the example of those honored tonight, whose steady service, valued loyalty, and hard work we celebrate here, we are happy and thankful.

Bless our life together across this great University, we pray.

Spirit of Life: Thou our source of meaning and hope,

Before we break bread together, we pause to be thankful for bread to break together, remembering those, far and near, who are in need.

Now on land and sea descending brings the night its peace profound.

Let our vesper prayer be blending with the holy calm around.

We invoke thy blessing in this hour.

Amen.

June 3

Generosity

We offer our prayers to thee, O Lord, thou source of life and refreshment, of spiritual irrigation.

In the quiet of this hour, and the beauty of this space, with the meditation of music to guide us, we remember and are refreshed.

We remember a moment of generosity in our youth.

We recall an act of generosity which impressed us.

We uncover a reminder of generosity in our hearts.

Thou whom we have loved, even when loving thee late.

June 4

Ground Hog Day: Five Reflections

I have this response to those of you who will not abate the ongoing contention related to my claim that Ground Hog Day is the best of all holidays:

In the ministry you surrender to God and neighbor all weekends, most evenings and holidays, and then work 9–5, Monday to Friday. All this takes a chunk out of the year. Holidays, in particular, carry, shall we say, some stress. Christmas, for an example. There are expectations. Special services. People. Doings.

Behold the blessing of February 2! An utterly ordinary day, and a holiday to boot! No expectations. No special services. No people. No Doings. Just the blessing of a single, average, wintry, bereft of expectation day. Ground Hog Day. It doesn't get better than Ground Hog Day. A quiet, ordinary, no frills day.

What is ordinary about any day, anyway?

Every one of them is a gem.

Monday's child is fair of face
Tuesday's child is full of grace
Wednesday's child is full of woe
Thursday's child has far to go
Friday's child is loving and giving
Saturday's child works hard for a living
But the child that is born on the Sabbath Day
Is happy, witty, bright and gay!

Every day is a chance to do a good turn. Do one daily. Be:

Trustworthy
Loyal
Helpful
Friendly
Courteous
Kind
Obedient
Cheerful
Thrifty
Brave
Clean
Reverent

The 111th Psalm was meant for use on a holiday, a festival. It is set out in an acrostic format. There are 22 lines, each beginning with a letter of the alphabet. "This is an arrangement that makes for considerable artificiality." Well yes. And some fun! Look what daily, ordinary gifts are celebrated: community, observation, memory, food, history, wisdom.

Reverence for God is the beginning of wisdom. What a remarkable phrase, the beginning of wisdom. A hopeful phrase, too, that wisdom grows. We all have wisdom sayings with which we have grown.

Some are cultural:

A stitch in time saves nine

An ounce of prevention is worth a pound of cure

Look before you leap

Some are personal and familial. In my family:

You would complain if you were to be hung with a new

Never try to teach a pig to sing. It wastes your time. And it annoys the pig.

Are you a journalist or are you writing a book?

Where were you before you were born? Down in Canada boiling soap.

There are no ordinary days, no insignificant holidays.

June 5

Haiti and King Pastoral Prayer

We invite you to enter a time of quiet, meditation, reflection and prayer.
Stand, kneel, sit as you are accustomed.
As se sense again the deep, subterranean rivers of our common life
We lift our hearts, as they are
    Our hearts teem with sorrow
        Sorrow for life lost in natural violence
        Sorrow for young life maimed and lost
        Sorrow for sudden, tragic, lasting separation
        Sorrow for all, far or near, who have suffered, and do suffer, through
            The Haitian earthquake
    Our hearts bear witness to anger
        Anger at disordered mayhem in creation
        Anger at random injustice among the least and the last
        Anger at surges of violent power we neither
            Understand, affirm, or accept.
        Anger at crippling pain

    Our hearts seek peace
        Peace built on an infrastructure of justice
        Peace sought in an infrastructure of trust
        Peace shared in an infrastructure of humility
        Peace, like a river, to mend and heal.
    Our hearts hold a gratitude for love
        Love in hand and cup, to soothe and save
        Love in service to another
        Love to remind us of who we can be
        Love seen and sensed in adult responsibility.
In quiet we know sorrow
In meditation we feel anger
In reflection we want peace
In prayer we honor love
Amen.

June 6

Matriculation 2006

Gracious God:

Holy and Just:

Thou who hast safely brought us to this new, beautiful day, and this new season of learning, and this new year of adventure.

Watch over us we pray by thy grace.

That we may fall into no harm no run into danger.

But that all our doing and speaking may be attentive to Thy presence.

We honor in memory those who have stood in this space before us.

We honor in hope those who will follow us here.

In our time, help us not to miss this moment, this one year.

But to meet this moment, to master it, and to be mastered its good gifts.

To those who will study, give energy heart.

To those who will teach, give the courage to seek and speak Truth without fear or favor.

To those who will lead, give the imagination and insight to create community.

To all of us, we pray, grant a measure of grace to watch over one another in love.

Together we do pray.

Amen.

June 7

Matriculation 2007

Gracious God:

Upon this brilliant morning, brimming with possibility, and with the holy energy of 4000 young hearts, we pause in silence.

(Silence)

We pray a blessing upon Boston University throughout this coming year.

(Silence)

We pray for safety, for vocation, and for wonder.

(Silence)

Inspire us, we ask, as we rise to meet each new day, with a full feeling of gratitude.

May this gratitude make us attentive to what makes for health, attentive to what protects against harm, attentive to ways that we may watch over one another in love. May our morning prayer of gratitude provoke a daily attention to safety.

(Silence)

Inspire us, we ask, as we rise to meet each new day, with a full feeling of gratitude. May this gratitude make us curious about our place in the world, curious about our emerging vocations, curious about where our passion meets the world's need. May our morning prayer of gratitude provoke a daily curiosity about calling.

(Silence)

Inspire us, we ask, as we rise to meet each new day, with a full feeling of gratitude. May this gratitude make us sensitive to the delight of each day, sensitive to the wonder of life, sensitive to the sheer joy of being alive. May our morning prayer of gratitude provoke a daily sensitivity to wonder.

(Silence)

Spirit of Life, guide, we pray, the journey of this great sailing vessel, Boston University, to the far off shore of springtime 2008. Bless those on the bridge, and those in the brig, and all of us in between. Bring us to that sunny far off springtime, safe and secure, curious and confident, delighted and sensitive, a people attentive to safety, insightful about calling, and capable of wonder.

Amen.

June 8

Matriculation 2008

Dear God:

Before you we place by imagination all of the next four years.

Bless our *friendships* these four years, we ask.

Help us to grow in kindness.

Help us to listen in silence.

Help us to acquire the gentle arts of camaraderie.

Teach us to speak heart to heart, soul to soul, I to Thou.

That when we leave we may have befriended and been befriended.

And so have found our own identity, our second identity, our selves.

Bless our *decisions* these four years, we ask.

Help us to grow in confidence.

Help us to weigh consequences.

Help us to learn to choose and to choose to learn.

Teach us to decide with grace, with passion, with humility.

And so by choosing to find our own identity, our second identity, our selves.

Bless our *intuitions* these four years, we ask:

Help us to acquire a vocational tongue, to learn the language of calling.

Help us to honor what lasts, matters, counts.

Help us to have courage to become who we are.

Teach us not to cut against the grain of our own wood.

And so by hearing our calling to find our own identity, our second identity, our selves.

For all that has been we say thank you. For all that will be we say yes.

June 9

Matriculation 2010

Gracious God:

We summon the better angels of our nature to sit quietly before you in gratitude.

For the gift of your love to inspire us in our freshman year, to quicken us to try, to join, to sign up, to get out, we are peacefully thankful.

For the gift of your presence to sustain us in our sophomore year, to strengthen us to continue, to persevere, to stay up, to move on, we are simply thankful.

For the gift or your power to embolden us in our junior year, to encourage us to achieve, to give, to change, to travel, to grow, we are spiritually thankful.

For the gift of your peace to illumine us in our senior year, to steady us to plan, to finish, to complete, to leave, we are personally thankful.

Help us to love what is lovely, to be present to what is real, to find strength in what lasts, and to know peace in what honors, but surpasses, understanding.

Inspired by your love, sustained by your presence, encouraged by your power, confirmed by your peace, our life before you flows on in endless song.

For the privilege of these few days, these fast four years, we are thankful.

Amen.

June 10

Matriculation 2011

We bring forward our thanks today.
For the study of medicine, dentistry, physical therapy.
Whose fruit is public health.
For the study of law.
Whose fruit is justice.
For the study of management, business and economics.
Whose fruit is community.
For the study of art—music, dance, drama, all.
Whose fruit is beauty.
For the study of communication.
Whose fruit is truth.
For the study of engineering.
Whose fruit is expanding safety.
For the liberal, metropolitan and general study of art and science.
Whose fruit is freedom.
For the study of hospitality.
Whose fruit is conviviality.
For the study of education.
Whose fruit is memory and hope.
For the study of military and physical education.
Whose fruit are security and strength.
For the study of social work.
Whose fruit is compassion.
For the study of theology.
Whose fruit is meaning.

In this year may the 40,000 member city of Boston University—students, faculty, administrators, staff, alumni, neighbors all—become, by grace: healthier, more just, more connected, fairer, truer, sturdier, freer, gentler, deeper, safer, more compassionate, and more aware.

O Thou who loves us into love and frees us into freedom.
Amen.

June 11

Matriculation 2012

Gracious God, Holy and Just
    Thou Silent Mystery, beckoning deep
    In whom we live and move and have our being
Grant us peace, we pray
Give us grace, we pray
In the eyeblink of these four years
    Give us peace to resist what we would regret
    Give us grace to receive what will make us rejoice
Four years hence, diplomas in hand
    May we be heavy with joy and free of regret
Help us to avoid the regret that follows abuse of ourselves,
Of our environment, of substances, and of others.
Warn us away from what, lastingly we will regret.
Fill us with a daily sense of adventure to embrace
What lastingly we will enjoy:
Friendship, discovery, reading, effort, achievement, accomplishment,
Self-giving, devotion, and love.
Grant us peace to resist what we would regret and grace to receive what
Causes us to rejoice.
Amen

June 12

Military Prayers: Book of Common Prayer

Almighty God, who hast given us this good land for our heritage: We humbly beseech thee that we may always proveourselves a people mindful of thy favor and glad to do thy will. Bless our land with honorable industry, sound learning, and pure manners. Save us from violence, discord, and confusion; from pride and arrogance, and from every evil way. Defend

our liberties, and fashion into one united people the multitudes brought hither out of many kindreds and tongues. Endue with the spirit of wisdom those to whom in thy Name we entrust the authority of government, that there may be justice and peace at home, and that, through obedience to thy law, we may show forth thy praise among the nations of the earth. In the time of prosperity, fill our hearts with thankfulness, and in the day of trouble, suffer not our trust in thee to fail; all which we ask through Jesus Christ our Lord. Amen.

Almighty God, we commend to your gracious care and keeping all the men and women of our armed forces at home and abroad. Defend them day by day with your heavenly grace; strengthen them in their trials and temptations; give them courage to face the perils which beset them; and grant them a sense of your abiding presence wherever they may be; through Jesus Christ our Lord. Amen.

Almighty God, giver of all good things: We thank you for the natural majesty and beauty of this land. They restore us, though we often destroy them. *Heal us.*

We thank you for the great resources of this nation. They make us rich, though we often exploit them. *Forgive us.*

We thank you for the men and women who have made this country strong. They are models for us, though we often fall short of them. *Inspire us.*

We thank you for the torch of liberty which has been lit in this land. It has drawn people from every nation, though we have often hidden from its light. *Enlighten us.*

We thank you for the faith we have inherited in all its rich variety. It sustains our life, though we have been faithless again and again. *Renew us.*

Help us, O Lord, to finish the good work here begun. Strengthen our efforts to blot out ignorance and prejudice, and to abolish poverty and crime. And hasten the day when all our people, with many voices in one united chorus, will glorify your holy Name. Amen.

O Judge of the nations, we remember before you with grateful hearts the men and women of our country who in the day of decision ventured much for the liberties we now enjoy. Grant that we may not rest until all the people of this land share the benefits of true freedom and gladly accept its disciplines. This we ask in the Name of Jesus Christ our Lord. Amen.

June 13

MLK Day Prayer

Gracious God:

God of Moses and David and Matthew and Peter:

Thou by whose power Moses did split the rock, and by whose grace David did fell the giant with five smooth stones and by whose spirit Matthew did teach us about a house well founded, and by whose wisdom was the church built upon Peter, Cephas.

Thou Rock of Ages: Come Sunday we lift our hearts to thee: Help us we pray.

When a man in middle age breaks the commandments of Moses, or better said, is broken by them, bring a stream of remembrance of mercy, thou whose property it is always to have mercy.

When a student hunting for a manifest destiny wonders whether one person can make any difference, conjure for us again the story of David, an unknown shepherd, one boy with five stones, and remind us of what we have to offer—our five fingers on each hand, our five senses head to toe, very blessed pentagonal promise of potential to strike a blow for freedom, somehow.

When a child learns the faith, its hymns and psalms and words, may they become, today as they long have been, for that seven year old, a sure foundation, against which the rain may fall, the flood may come, and the wind may blow, but will not prevail.

When a community of faith, this morning, gathers to worship, help us to remember those who came before, on whom the church was built, and help us resolve in their shadow, to offer something to those who have not yet had a first serving of faith—a prayer, an encouragement, an invitation, a ride to church.

God of Moses, David, Matthew, Peter

We long for thy mercy, thy power, thy wisdom, they love

God of our weary years

God of our silent tears

Thou who has brought us far on the way

Thou who has by thy might

Led us into the light

Keep us forever in the path we pray

In the name of Christ, who taught us to pray.

June 14

Morning Prayers

Invocation

Gracious God, loving and holy and just,
We lift our hearts in thanks and praise this morning.
We come to this sanctuary ready again to live as glad hearted women and men.
With glad hearts, curious minds, and eager spirits we offer ourselves in worship. Bless us, we pray, by thy presence, which we invoke in the name of Jesus Christ our Lord. Amen.

Call to Confession

Are we as ready to receive the gifts of grace as we should be?

Have we been prepared, in these days, to notice the bountiful goodness by which Divine Love has touched us?

Do we need to confess a little slowness, a little occasional lack of perception, shortness of spiritual breath, a slight or not so slight disregard for what we have been given?

O Lord, as a people of glad heart, we confess that we have not always been fully a people of open hands. Open us in these moments of silence, to a new rebirth of wonder.

June 15

Seasons of Change

Pastoral Prayer

In a season of change, may we embrace what lasts.
In a time of loss, may we hug the new.
In an era of decrease, may we find the unexpected.
In an epoch of debt, may we (sacrificially) endow the future.
In a day of disappointment, may we savor simple gifts.
In a month of worry, may we undress our anxiety.
In a year of decline, may we again see winter's gifts.
In an hour of depression, may we, with effort, accept kindness.
In a moment of fear, may we grasp the gift of faith.
In a morning of acedia, may we enter our prayer closet.
In an afternoon of besetting sin, may we recognize, humbly, our humanity.
In an evening of loneliness, may we experience graceful solitude.
As dusk comes, gracious God, help us walk in newness of life.

June 16

The Samaritan: Part One

To the faithful, honest, prayerful agnostic, to the various goods and various Samaritans around about, we offer, in brisk and brilliant revelation, come Transfiguration, a way of thinking and feeling, a thought feeling, a felt thought, a form of faith where there is no faith.

Our experience of the Samaritan, as his gift of love attends us, is the faithfulness of God. Where others profess too much and too quickly, where others believe blindly and shallowly, where others pronounce themselves holier, humbler, more religious than thou, where others rush in where angels fear to tread, behold the goodness of the northern Samaritan. His life, in loving and giving, in knowing and loving, in giving and knowing, has become his faith, a faith that has no name. Yesterday he shoveled the widow neighbor's walk, uncovered a neighbor student's car, brought milk and eggs to a homebound neighbor's kitchen, chipped ice from an elderly neighbor's roof, included in family sledding a busy neighbor's son. Come blizzard weekend, a faith with no name may be the truest faith of all. Is that faith yours?

June 17

The Samaritan: Part Two

A generation ago, our dear teacher Paul Tillich called such faith the state of being ultimately concerned. Are you deeply concerned? Do things concern you? When we come upon a man whom bandits have stripped and beaten and left by the side of the road for dead, does your heart quicken? You see this victim of violence, harmed by others who have since disappeared, as with wily politicians who are "eager to dominate but reluctant to offend" (so, FDR, NYRB, 1/13). Before gun violence, or unfettered drone flight, or children untutored, or wayward greed, or amoral sexuality, or steady drunkenness, or moral indiscretion—somewhere the road from religion to life, from Jerusalem to Jericho—are you concerned? Your concern is your faith. In deep concern you discover grace and freedom and love. Your concern is your faith.

But now Tillich is long dead, and his concern may not fit twenty year olds. In our generation, then, we might call such a state of faith the state of being ultimately connected. Are you deeply connected? Does life connect you to others? When you come upon a man whom bandits have stripped and beaten and left by the side of the road for dead, does your heart quicken? When a fog surrounds you brought on the collision of the warm winds of love and frosty glacier of wrong—what? Do you connect? Do you text, then, or tweet, then, or post, then, or email, then, or call, then, or write, then, or visit, then? Does the plight of another move you toward others? Along the road then from religion to life, from Jerusalem to Jericho—are you connected? Your connection is your faith. In your deep connection you discover grace and freedom and love. Your connection is your faith.

Live your faith. Live your faith.
No other God, no graven image, no name in vain.
Remember Sabbath, honor father and mother.
Do not kill, commit adultery, steal, witness falsely or covet
Live your faith. Live your faith.
Thou shalt love the Lord thy God with all thy heart, soul, mind and strength.
And thou shalt love thy neighbor as thyself.
As did the Samaritan.

June 18

The Shepherd: Preface

The Shepherd is present and loving and good.

But today we are city, and a world around, drenched in sorrow. Some of that sorrow lies at the feet of those killed, Martin and Lingzi and Krystle and Sean. Some of that sorrow arises from the thought of those physically injured. Some of that sorrow dimly recognizes the many others, near and far, harmed in other less visible ways. Some of that sorrow kindles anger at the video image of assassins who lingered to view the potential effects of unspeakable actions on fellow humans. This weekend we are a people drenched in sorrow.

We are also a University working through sorrow. Monday began with brunch and celebration, and ended with terror. Our staff opened the chapel later for the throngs walking, T-less, by. Water, refreshment, prayer, counsel, they gave. One runner came very cold and was shrouded with a clergy gown, all we had to offer, a shepherd's outfit. Tuesday brought us to the plaza, come evening, in vigil, to honor and reflect. Wednesday, in this chapel, and also at other hours in other settings, gathered us for ordered worship, prayer, music, liturgy, Eucharist and sermon. Thursday we heard the President, on a familiar theme, 'running the race set before us.' Friday at home we watched televised news. Saturday we listened for the musical succor of Handel's beautiful *Messiah*, right here. Tomorrow we will again gather for a memorial service, for our deceased BU student, Lu Lingzi. But today is Sunday, when we come to church, to pray, sing, and hear the Word. Quietly, now, as a visible congregation in the pews and as a virtual congregation in the region, we might want to allow our Gospel to help us, to speak a pastoral word to us, to live in us, in three ways.

June 19

The Shepherd: Here

The Gospel of John, more than any other ancient Christian writing, and in odd contrast to its prevalent misunderstanding across the continent today, knew the necessity of nimble engagement of current experience, and the saving capacity to change, in the face of new circumstances. The community of this Gospel could do so because they had experienced the Shepherd, present, 'here,' hic et nunc. In distress, we hold onto divine presence, on word, the Shepherd—*here*.

Two BU students were maimed on Monday. One survived, in part because an Iraqi war veteran ran to her, held her, acknowledged her shock, staunched her bleeding, kept her from focusing on the carnage at hand, and made it his business to be present to her, on Boylston street. His experienced prediction later that evening, that she would "make it," proved true. The Shepherd is here, present, in the shepherding acts of people like him who put on the equivalent of a pastor's robe, to aid others.

It is not trite and not redundant repeatedly to honor the first responders, those first present. It is faith, good faith, and theology, good theology. God has no hands but yours.

In quieter hours, we may simple say, "God is here," "the Shepherd is here," referring only to the brute, undeniable experience of breathing, of life, of something, of something not nothing. But in sorrow, and in the distress causing sorrow, we know presence through the Shepherd. Next to us, it may be, we hear a voice: "Hold my hand. Look down not out. Focus on my eyes. That pain in your leg is a good sign. Breathe in and out. I am here."

We are a community devoted in witness to the One in the stained glass behind you, the Shepherd. It is a good and healthy thing to enter a gothic nave whose form is a thousand years old, an Indiana limestone chapel built to last another thousand years, with a form of worship as ancient and historic as it is beautiful and true, and music from the ages, and readings 2000 years in use, all in a place of graceful space. A physical recollection that we are not the first, nor will we be the last, to face inexplicable horror. I do not know of a week when one does not need that, but this week, in particular, we do. John's community had none of that in Ephesus in 90ad. They had only voice. Speaking, and hearing. They found that in speaking of the Shepherd: 'he is here.' 'I am . . . ' That is all, still, we have, the voice. Utterance. 'I am . . .' The 'here' is in the hearing. Can you hear that? It begs to be heard, here.

It is an old word. The Shepherd is here.

June 20

The Shepherd: Love

The Gospel brings a second old word. One writer said he used the old short words. 'I know the other ones, the big words, but the short ones say it better.' Love. God so loved the world, to give God's only Son. I try to remember that when a boy who looks like my son did at age 8 is taken. It is as if God walked over, and put a hand on my shoulder, and said, 'You know, I do understand. Yes. I had a son once, too.' The reason the community of faith, John's church, could hear the 'here' of the Shepherd is that they had experienced his love. With them, I am a Christian more for the cross than for the empty tomb. The Gospel of John knew the reality of love, and called love God. Love is God, said the later letter bearing the name of John.

But it is a strange, somewhat unfamiliar kind of love. (The gospel makes the familiar strange, and the strange familiar.) Not the love of family or kindred, those with whom you watched TV on Friday. Not the love of lover and beloved, to whom you rightly repaired on Monday. Not even the religiously frequent reference, across the globe, to a principle, idea or virtue. Ours today is rather a love that *gives, and gives of self,* which they knew in Ephesus, and we know today, in loving hands. God has no hands, none, but yours. We all need loving hands.

To recall love, when you see others, in brutality, shredded by insidious evil, you will need to pronounce love in life. It is also repeatedly said, not tritely, that the only thing evil needs to succeed is the inattention and inaction of good people. This passage, 'the Father and I are one,' created a new religion—in love. The verse is usually thought to convey a heightened Christology, the raising of Jesus to divine status. But for the first century Christians it arguably may have meant the very opposite, the lowering of God to human status. It meant the lowering of the Father, not the raising of the Son. It meant, well, love. The Shepherd loves, is loving, is love.

Love is God. That is all we have of God, as we breathe and listen and live. Love means love of self, family, kin, but also of neighbor, other, friend, but also, remarkably, of enemy. Now John does not get quite that far. I am not sure that I have. But the Christian Gospel as a whole does, and more. I will try to remember that when I feel my anger welling up, or when I am tempted to disparage groups for the behavior of individuals, or when I want a faster solution to a thorny problem.

That is why you come to church every week, to be prepared for love. You cannot develop a worldview, a religious perspective, a depth of faith, or a disciplined life, in the 3 minutes following a bombing. You have to get started a lot earlier in order to have, in crisis, the nourishment, the power, you will need, really to live. Love means taking responsibility. Love means taking responsibility. And taking responsibility means finding, *soon,* a community wherein you can know and show meaning, belonging, empowerment, where you can learn from others to pray, to tithe, to keep faith.

I encourage you to continue in ways many have already begun, to find effective modes of help for those well beyond our community who have been hurt, one way or another. A card, a note, a check, a gift, a prayer—we all have things we can do to lean forward and help those harmed. One of our students is active in bringing a blood bank to campus in the next few days. It is healthy and it is helpful, in many directions, to find one thing or two things creatively to do, to bring some good to bear in the face of tragic violence. So you will don a shepherd's gown, hoist a shepherd's crook, live a shepherd's life, for the moment, in love.

It is an old word. The Shepherd is love.

June 21

The Shepherd: Good

Here is one other old word. Good. The Shepherd is good.

But, let us be frank. There is a kind of nihilism abroad today, which is not good. You can hear it, in the word 'whatever': and see it in inebriation, in amoral sexual practice, in materialism, in incapacity for human communication, in incapacity for moral discernment. These features of current life, exploding all about us on a daily basis, are just not good.

As our fellow preacher the Rev. John Holt, of Osterville, wrote two weeks ago:

"I'm troubled. Really troubled. Disturbed because compassion is scarce. Too often, we live in a "what's in it for me" world."

You remember, from last Sunday, my friend describing life, in one word as 'good,' and in two words as 'not good.' Well, no early Christian document surpasses John in plumbing the depths of that duality. A bright Monday, bombs. A sunny Patriots Day, carnage. A glorious marathon, death. As my teacher Robert McAfee Brown said, "This is God's world. But is a crummy one. We have to live with both realities." I remember Anglican Bishop Hapgood, circa 1975, facing a group of idealists and saying, "Go ahead, keep your dreams, be dreamers. Just remember that others dream, too, of gulags, and genocide, and terror."

From this pulpit four years ago, (Nov 29, 2009), we tried to be alert to the probability that, at some point, another nine-eleven would befall us. How little we knew how close it would be, both in time and in space.

The best of days, the highest of moments, the most charmingly gracious of cityscapes, the culmination of the American experiment on Patriots Day—trashed by hateful, killing violence. When another takes what you hold dear, count precious, think lovely, and bombs it, you cannot avoid anger, and the sorrow at the heart of anger.

Some may wonder whether anything religiously cast, any preachment, can carry any truth, any good. Religion, like the weather, is just so mixed—good and bad and other.

One response: Do you have good religion, or bad, asked the spiritual? Are you putting on that shepherding robe, that pastoral gown, to fend off the cold?

Unamuno wrote, " Warmth, warmth, warmth. We are dying of cold, not of darkness. It is the night that kills, it is the frost."

Religion that brings good relationships can bring much good. You can see and hear that right here in the pews of Marsh Chapel. Come and join us!

Our passage about the Shepherd shepherded into experience something new, over time, the relational community of God. Yes, we are monotheists, but not really fully so. God is not One, for us. God is Three, or, at least, Three in One. That is, the good Shepherd, is good— *in relationship*. God is in *relationship*, with God. We might want to think about that, as we measure our relationships into the future. 'The Father and I are One' was step toward Chapter 14 and the Spirit, and beyond that to Nicaea. Ours are the hands with which to touch, hold, greet and honor.

By the way. I do not believe in a God who wills that some are hurt and others spared. Who would worship such a God? I see rather random chance in life, both freedom to will and the freeing of the will, to be present, *to love, and to do the good.* Jan and I did not turn left on Boylston, Monday at 2:30, we went around the back way. Not because we are more beloved, smarter, or more faithful. No, random, just random. Rain falls on the just and unjust. But through it all: There is good, there is good, there is good in every day. Part of that good is found in relationship, blessed by the relational God of John 10. Some of that good is right here in Boston, 'the Hub'—in relationship. Hugs in cold of First Night, cheers for the music come July 4, waves to the rowers come Head of the Charles, and, yes, next year, celebration come Patriots Day. Connected in relationship.

It is an old word. The Shepherd is good.

June 22

The Shepherd: Coda

How then will you live?

Will you find your way, through the crowd and the rubble, to the Shepherd—who is here, who is love, who is good?

We will want to live with presence, love and goodness. Thankfully, from Monday itself, we have a shining example of people modeling dimensions of healthy spirituality, of the runners and the race (a metaphor not unknown to the biblical mind by the way—Psalm 19, 1 Cor 9, Hebrews 12). I picture all the runners practicing months and weeks. I see the lacing of the running shoes. I hear the starting whistle and the throng surging forward. We saw at Kenmore, the brightly attired elderly man, the young guy with blue hair, the student running in a tuxedo, the troop from a nearby college ROTC program, the woman running—as so many—in memory, the folks in wheel chairs, the straining forward, by mile 25, of striving, disciplined energy. They all are models for us of running the spiritual race and finishing the spiritual course. We can lace up and run, too, in our own ways. God's goodness, love and presence beckon us onward.

June 23

Deliverance from Evil

The teacher implores his student to make God his place of dwelling, his home. To rest in God, so that all else is secondary. Evil will not befall, or at least will not define, such an one. How can someone escape all evil? We know better. We know that evil touches us all. But this misses the meaning of the poem. The writer is praying! In the same way we pray, every Sunday. Deliver him from evil! Not from some, or most, almost all evil, but from evil! Religion is a matter of the heart before it is a matter of the head. As Wesley said, the mind is the bit and bridle, but the heart is the great horse, the mighty steed of faith. "He will give his angels charge of you to guard you in all your ways. On their hands they will bear you up, lest you dash your foot against a stone."

June 24

Psalm 91: Deliverance from Night Terror

Our psalmist is speaking just here to our immediate need. Fear not the terror of the night. Go about your discipleship: pray, study, learn, make peace, love your neighbor, agree to disagree agreeably, every one be convinced in his own mind. The night is not as terrifying as you fear. . . . "You will not fear the terror of the night."

June 25

Call to Confession

Are we as ready to receive the gifts of grace as we should be?

Have we been prepared, in these days, to notice the bountiful goodness by which Divine Love has touched us?

Do we need to confess a little slowness, a little occasional lack of perception, shortness of spiritual breath, a slight or not so slight disregard for what we have been given?

O Lord, as a people of glad heart, we confess that we have not always been fully a people of open hands. Open us in these moments of silence, to a new rebirth of wonder.

June 26

Pastoral Prayer

Great art thou, O Lord our God, and fully to be praised, morning by morning.

We pray for thy blessing in this our, thy gifts of confidence, certainty and sureness for the days to come.

Help us to receive, with confidence, the many surprising gifts embedded in our personal lives. Help us to notice the unexpected possibility, the new friend, the unusual word, the strange connection. Help us to see more than we plan to see, to receive more than we expect to receive, with the confidence born of obedience.

Teach us to claim some certainty in the midst of uncertainty, as a church and and as a congregation. Teach us we pray the path we best should trod into the unforeseeable future. Teach us rightly to connect yesterday with tomorrow, in the light of thy certain love.

Shower with cool saving rain and moist power the leaders of this world, with sureness to seek justice and peace. Help those in the torn out conflicts of our day to continue daily, surely, to seek the promise of the Prince of peace. Kindle daily in the hearts of great leaders an even greater desire for peace, with a sense that surely goodness and mercy shall follow.

Through Jesus Christ our Lord.

June 27

Christian Century: Theological Temptations

Your love of Christ shapes your love of Scripture and tradition and reason and experience. You are lovers and knowers too. We are ever in peril of loving what we should use and using what we should love, to paraphrase Augustine. In particular we sometimes come perilously close to the kind of idolatry that uses what we love. We are tempted, for our love Christ, to force a kind of certainty upon what we love, to use what is meant to give confidence as a force and form of certainty. It is tempting to substitute the security and protection of certainty for the freedom and grace of confidence. But faith is about confidence not certainty. If we had certainty we would not need faith.

June 28

Errancy

Your love for Christ shapes your love of Scripture. You love the Bible. You love its psalmic depths. #130 comes to mind. You love its stories and their strange names. Obed-edom comes to mind. You love proverbial wisdom. One sharpens another comes to mind. You love its freedom, its account of the career of freedom. The exodus comes to mind. You love its memory of Jesus. His holding children comes to mind. You love its honesty about religious life. Galatians comes to mind. You love its strangeness. John comes to mind. You love the Bible like Rudolph Bultmann loved it, enough to know it through and through.

You rely on the Holy Scripture to learn to speak of faith, and as a medium of truth for the practice of faith. Around our common table today in worship, we share this reliance and this love. The fascinating multiplicity of hearings, here, and the interplay of congregations present, absent, near, far, known, unknown, religious and unreligious, have a common ground in regard for the Scripture. A preacher descending into her automobile in Boston, after an earlier service, listens to this service to hear the interpretation of the gospel. A homebound woman in Newton listens for the musical offerings and for the reading of scripture. On the other side of the globe, way down in Sydney, Australia, a student listens in, come Sunday, out of a love of Christ that embraces a love of Scripture. Here in the Chapel nave, on the Lord's Day, scholars and teachers and students have in common, by their love for Christ, a love for the Scripture, too. In this way, we may all affirm Mr. Wesley's motto: *homo unius libri*, to be a person of one book.

But the Bible is errant. It is theologically tempting for us to go on preaching as if the last 250 years of study just did not happen. They did. That does not mean that we should deconstruct the Bible to avoid allowing the Bible to deconstruct us, or that we should study the Bible in order to avoid allowing the Bible to study us. In fact, after demythologizing the Bible we may need to remythologize the Bible too. It is the confidence born of obedience, not some certainty born of fear that will open the Bible to us. We need not fear truth, however it may be known. So Luke may not have had all his geographical details straight. John (chapter 8) includes the woman caught in adultery, but not in its earliest manuscripts. Actually she, poor woman, is found at the end of Luke in some texts. Paul did not write the document from the earlier third century, 3 Corinthians. The references to slavery in the New Testament are as errant and time bound as are the references to women not speaking in church. The references to women not speaking in church are as errant and time bound as are the references to homosexuality. The references to homosexuality are as errant and time bound as are the multiple lists of the twelve disciples. The various twelve listings are as errant and time bound as the variations between John and the other Gospels.

The Marsh pulpit, and others like it, are not within traditions which affirm the Scripture as the sole source of religious authority. We do not live within a Sola Scriptura tradition. The Bible is primary, foundational, fundamental, basic, prototypical—but not exclusively authoritative. Do you hear that? It begs to be heard. Today's passage from Matthew 4 is an idealized memory of something that may or may not have happened in the way accounted, somewhere along the Tiberian shore. It looks back sixty years. What do you remember from January of 1948? Nor was it written for that kind of certainty. It is formed in the faith of the church to form the faith of the church.

If I were teaching a Sunday School class in Nebraska this winter I would buy the class copies of Throckmorton's Gospel parallels and read it with them.

We grasp for certainty, but confidence grasps us.

June 29

Credo

1. God is love.

2. Love is both mercy and justice, both compassion and holiness.

3. Compassion is more important than holiness.

4. God loves the world (not just the church).

5. The church lives in the culture. The church lives *in* the culture to transform it. (Not above it to disdain it, not below it to obey it, not behind it to mimic it, not before it hector it).

6. The church is the Body of Christ.

7. Christ is alive. Wherever there is way, truth, life. . .

8. Life is sacred.

9. Life is a sacred journey to freedom.

10. The Bible is freedom's book.

11. The Bible is a source, not the source, of truth

12. The Sabbath was made for man, not man for the Sabbath.

13. War is hell.

14. Peace is heaven. Jesus is the prince of Peace.

15. Gay people are people.

16. Women's bodies are *women's* bodies.

17. Women and men need each other. (Not like fish need bicycles, but like fishers need fish and riders need bikes).

18. There is a self correcting spirit of truth loose in the universe.

19. The founder of Methodism is John Wesley (not John Calvin).

20. The ministers of the conference are the conference. Period.

21. Ministry is preaching.

22. The fun of faith is in tithing and inviting.

23. Tithing is required. It is core, not elective.

24. Death is the last enemy. As Forrest Gump said, atop his beloved's grave, "My momma told me that 'death is a part of life.' But I wish it weren't."

25. God's love outlasts death.

June 30

July

Ben on Church

Our son is a thirty five year old lawyer in Albany, NY. He wrote a letter to the editor of the paper there, about a man in his church who had died:

"The front page article 'Religion? More reply 'none'", Oct 21, about the decline in our community, particularly in my demographic, forced me to think about why I still go to church, despite its flaws. As I continued through the paper, I found my answer in the obituaries.

"I met Dr. Wesley Bradley at Trinity UMC about five years ago. I was immediately drawn to him—to the earnestness of his handshake, to the comforting advice he offered me as a new dad, to the way he proudly strolled down Lark Street with his lovely bride as if it were their first date

"Although I did not know the extent of Dr. Bradley's professional accomplishments until I read his obituary, I knew the greatness of his grace. I witnessed the faith that had sustained him and I learned from his humble and caring example.

"The church provides a time and place for God's grace to touch and connect us. But for church I would not have known Dr. Bradley. My soul, which now grieves his passing, would have remained unaffected.

"I go to church to feed my soul. It's not the only way to do it, but I think Dr. Bradley's life of faith is worth my generation's consideration."

July 1

Christopher Morse

Recently our friend and teacher retired in New York City. Dr. Christopher Morse lectured on the history of Christian theology in September of 1976, and before and after. The lectures , built in part upon the lectures of Robert Calhoun at Yale a decade earlier, in may have been, are today still shimmering in memory, forty years later. Speech matters. On a bright May morning, some from near and some from far drove to Riverside Drive, parked behind Grant's tomb, wondered again and aloud who was buried there, peered in at the dark, historic, gothic emptiness of Riverside Church, hunted down friends at the Interchurch Center next door, sat in the venerable Union Theological Seminary courtyard, fragrant and cloistered and quiet, then in James Chapel, now filling with five decades of friends and students. The honoree asked not to preach, but only to celebrate the Eucharist, in clear Methodist fashion, as we do today. Doctoral students sang an anthem musically summarizing Morse's theological principles. Hear these words set to guitar and folk music: coherence, catholicity, conformity . . . A young student preached. Prayers were offered by another, strong, sonorous, spirited prayers by another young student, the son of a prominent NYC Methodist preacher. A simple luncheon followed, with a portrait unveiled, no eulogies or roasts or remembrances. Just 90 minutes, noon on, of grace. Then the drive home, along the coast and through New Haven, a drive most richly populated by ghosts, haunted by recollection and reckoning, riddled with gratitude. Friends, an excellent 80 minute lecture lives, feeds, and lasts a lifetime, maybe even three such. By the way, the young man who prayed so well, a cradle Methodist, a parsonage child, a brilliant future preacher, is gay. Said a proud, heart broken dad, "He will not lie. He will not stay. He will find another denomination." But the father's smile through pain was a real, though fragile, real though apocalyptic touch of grace, a holy Eucharist, love made real.

July 2

Death Certificate

Jesus died, he really died. Our earliest accounts, on all fronts, verify his death. The NT is his death certificate. The earliest account of resurrection, from 53 CE, read a moment ago, and addressed to Corinth, a nice enough city, located currently in a debt soaked nation, is that of Paul. He knows nothing of an empty tomb. For him, death is death, including that of Jesus. He is a good Greek dualist after all: flesh and blood cannot inherit the kingdom of heaven; that which is born of the flesh is flesh, and that which is born of the spirit is spirit. If you doubt the physicality of Jesus' resurrection, you have Paul on your side. Paul's atheism (his rejection of the reigning first century cultural gods) is taller and truer than yours.

But there is, he says, a bodily resurrection, only that is with a resurrection body not an earthly body, a heavenly body not a fleshly body, and what is a resurrection body, well it is definitely not an earthly body, thank goodness, given what condition my current sagging fleshly condition is in, it is heavenly, and what is that, well, it is hard to say because it is utterly different from anything here, it is sown in glory and what not, but it is definitely a resurrection body. Thanks Paul.

But empty tomb? Not so much. But the gospel is Luke not Paul, for whom there is very much an empty tomb. It is symbol to be interpreted not a doctrine to be explained. Easter manifests redemption, or restoration, a re creation in life of real life.

July 3

Dr. Wolseley

Prodigal means extremely—extremely something: wasteful, generous or abundant. The verb is (an Aorist participle): *and coming (in) to himself* (a moment in time, a process in thought). "For till then he was beside himself, as all men are, so long as they are without God in the world" (J Wesley).

But notice that the gospel, love, is hinged today on a single phrase. After his travel and squandering, and before his return and reception, the prodigal has a thought, a prodigal thought at that. All of the gospel this Lord's Lenten day turns on a thought. *When he came to himself . . . When he thought to himself . . .*

Three pulpits ago Professor Roland Wolseley endured this minister's more youthful preaching. Now deceased, Dr Wolseley was the preeminent scholar in the field of African American journalism. Through his post at Syracuse University he almost singlehandedly created the discipline, through the publication of many books, the guidance of doctoral students, and a dogged, fierce love of his field, the struggling saintly newspapers and journals of the black community. Roland went to Medill in Chicago, at Northwestern. There, in his twenties he fell under the spell of my own greatest pulpit hero, Ernest Freemont Tittle, at Evanston First UMC, then the largest UMC in the country. Tittle, a pacifist, as was Wolseley, gathered a group of graduate students for fellowship and reconciliation. Wolseley met his wife, Bernice, there, and she went on to be for many years Tittle's secretary. You can read about Tittle in Robert Moats Miller's older biography, or in Christopher Evans more recent monograph.

In those Syracuse years, Roland, a person of deep faith and quiet humor, would trace the work of Tittle in contrast and connection to what he was hearing. Occasionally, too occasionally, he would say, leaving church, 'Tittle would be proud of that one.' Another of those early 1940's graduate student couples, it happened, awaited us when we moved to Rochester, where Ruth and Vernon Lippitt then lived. These people, young in the forties, were mature the eighties and nineties, but had lost nothing of their early conviction, a combination of deep personal faith and active social involvement, found decades earlier, in the arm of a University congregation. Marsh Chapel: the seeds you plant today will flower and blossom and grow for decades, with telling affect. Faint not, fear not, flag not!

Roland also kept us alive during administrative meetings, using punctuative humor. Our trustees usually hired the same painter, a fine painter named Bogus, when the decay of the building outran their native parsimony. When they couldn't wait any longer to the paint a room, they made a motion to 'hire Mr. Bogus.' After the motion and second, with practiced timing, and with all knowing what was coming, yet unable not to laugh when it did—some things are just funny for no real reason—Dr. Wolseley would compliment the recent extravagance of the trustees in hiring Bogus, then add, speaking of Bogus, "Is this guy for real?" In eleven years I think I heard that question thirty times—"Is Bogus for real?"—and yet it always made me smile. After three hours of administrative board meeting, it doesn't take much, that is true.

Roland was a careful listener. He wanted the best for preaching and preacher, and, from Tittle, he knew the best, and he knew the rest. Once the sermon including the phrase "I thought to myself.." Afterward he asked sharply, "Why the redundancy? Just say, 'I thought.'" He was probably thinking of William Strunk, "omit needless words," a fence I have long since jumped, as you have the scars to attest. But I took his advice.

Except, today, with love and real affection for Roland who is now in heaven, we wonder . . . *When he came to himself.* There is something in that lingering middle voice construct in a language like ours that has no middle voice, only active and passive, but has lingering forms like this one. The phrase shows the mind circling on itself, *when he came to himself.* We do this in memory, come to ourselves. We do this in discovery, come to ourselves. We do this in prayer, come to ourselves. Give some Lenten minutes to memory, discovery and prayer. We do this in those moments when we realize there is more to life than meets the eye. When he have a prodigal thought. A new, wayward, slightly reckless, excessive, extravagant, prodigous thought.

July 4

Fanueil Hall

May 16 started six days of Commencement gladness, here at Boston University, across a campus and city still bruised and hurting from spring terror and death. We shall sorely and truly need together the ongoing development of a spiritual discipline against resentment (acknowledged, admitted, accepted—and then wrestled with, like love with an angel). More than 80 graduates were anointed by word and sword with a scarlet key. The dental school celebration—large, colorful, global. A certain choir learned that they would sing with the Rolling Stones, a band active when Christopher Morse was in college. Of course, with gladness, we happily recall the great, big moments of Commencement 2013. Morgan Freeman photographed with Jan Hill. Morgan Freeman cheered by students, "speech, speech . . ." And in extatraditional mode, he did. The Marsh Chapel choir, soon to sing with Mick Jagger, resplendent, redolent at Baccalaureate. The thrilled celebration of hooding like that of the theology school here in the Chapel. Music from "A Chorus Line"—perhaps generationally specific in thrill—with the Boston Pops. A magnificent Advisory Board meeting with a world class presentation on global health. Greek and Latin orations, from memory, in the original, at the BU Academy graduation, with a fine sermon given there, on "closing the opportunity gap" on the text, 'to whom much is given, from him much is required' in St. Luke. All these and others were wonderful and more than wonderful.

But come with me to an out of the way, smaller gathering, and a particularly powerful one every year. For us, the most meaningful graduation moment each year is not under the big tent but among several dozen in Faneuil Hall, where 20 or so soldiers are commissioned as second lieutenants. In crisp attire and crisp liturgy, young men and women assemble before the portraits of Sam Adams, John Hancock, and George Washington, in the cradle of the cradle of liberty. "The President of the United States has placed his trust and confidence . . ." "Do you promise to preserve, protect, and defence . . ." Then the loved ones—parents, or siblings or spouses—place the apulets upon the commissioned officers, sending them potentially into harm's way for our sakes. Freedom is not free. To see mom and dad, brother and sister, husband and wife struggling to get the shoulder boards in place, every May, is the marrow of commencement, where a courageous present enters an uncertain future. This year—by apocalypse came the gospel said Paul—one fine woman was aided by two other young women, her sister—and her partner. In Boston, Faneuil Hall. Before Adams, Hancock, and Washington. She is going to place herself in mortal danger for us. And we are going to question her practice of love? It was a very full moment, an apocalypse if you will. A touch of grace.

July 5

Frankincense

We begin. As J Edwards said, 'Resolved: to do nothing I would be afraid to do in the last hour of my life.'

I don't believe I quite heard or overheard your seasonal resolution(s).

There are no free-lance Christians. If nothing else, for sure, the child the wise visit makes space in life for real fellowship. The church is a working fellowship.

Isaiah foretold it. Here in third Isaiah, who remembers the birdsong of second Isaiah, and carries the tune back into Jerusalem, after the return from exile, after 538, when another wise Persian, Cyrus, set the people free. The birth of the Christ, by symbol of gold and frankincense, is connected to a universal liberation.

We are here to ring the bell, to sing the song, to sound the trumpet, to lift the voice. You may need, this week, to see the examples in salt and light, of faithful people. Here are some in these Marsh pews. Kind people. Kind women. Kind men. Doing unto others, as they would have done to themselves. Seeking. Seeking lasting wisdom.

With joy. Come on MLK Sunday, and hear our friend Dr Fluker, and on Monday and celebrate the King of Marsh Plaza. Come February 9 (our usual Ground Hog festival, date and place moved) and ice skate on Marsh Plaza. Come and sing hymns in the Lynn home of Alice and Yrjo—a midwinter delight! Come for brunch and the marathon on Patriots day, to our home.

Resolve this, 2013: I will be in church on Sunday. Wise men still seek Him. You find faith in fellowship, and vice versa.

St. John of the Cross: *En una noche oscura. . .*

At Marsh we minimize meetings, committees, structures, organization. We find our fellowship, across the University, as above. We take our education in the University. We partner in service with our schools and colleges of the University. We refuse to sit on a whale and fish for minnows. Come and join us! It is a great way to give, to live, to give and live, the gospel.

Here gay people are people. Here lay people are people. The eight words Methodism will need for survival: gay people are people, lay people are people. I refer you to the sermon coming January 27, 2013.

July 6

George Herbert

The poet George Herbert lived from 1593 to 1633. The English Civil War occurred soon after his death, leading to "disestablishment." Herbert was an "orator" at Cambridge, and sickly. From a young age he knew that he was called to write devotional poetry. He knew John Donne, who was a friend of his mother's. He employs both trochaic and iambic meters. He writes, among other things, of the soul's call to God, and of the claim the believer has on God. That is, in his work there is a Johannine courage. Love made me welcome, but my soul drew back. . . . You must sit down and taste my meat. . . . Herbert wrote of love. Here is a poem (you beautifully sang it a moment ago) that draws directly on John 14:17, John 6:6, and John 16:22:

The Call
Come, my Way, my Truth, my Life:
Such a Way, as gives us breath:
Such a Truth as ends all strife:
And such a life as killeth death.
Come, my Light, my Feast, my Strength:
Such a Light as shows a feast:
Such a Feast as mends in length:
Such a strength as makes his guest.
Come my Joy, my Love, my Heart:
Such a Joy as none can move:
Such a Love as none can part:
Such a Heart as joyes in love.

July 7

Gnostic Thought

Now I put it to you: how long has it been since you have had a prodigal thought? The prodigal son is prodigally reckless in departure. But he is prodigally excellent and ecstatic in return. His negative prodigality in descent is eclipsed by his positive prodigality in resurrection. How long has it been since you have *come to yourself?*

Though no one says so, and to my knowledge no one has yet so written, Luke 15 may be the most Gnostic of chapters in the New Testament. It is about gnosis, self knowledge, *coming to oneself.* As the Gnostics taught, we are trapped in a far country, a long way from our true home, like a man who has squandered his birthright, and moved from light to darkness. As the Gnostics taught, we are meant to get home, to get back home, to get back out from under this earthly, fleshly, pig slop bodily existence, and back to higher ground, to heaven, to the heaven beyond heaven, to the land of light, to the loving father, like a prodigal son returning to the home that is truly his. As the Gnostics taught, there is just one way to get back home, one key to the magic door. That way and that key is knowledge, self knowledge, the knowledge of one's own self—whence w come, wither we go. As the Gnostics taught, salvation comes from this sort of esoteric, personal, soulful knowledge. *When he came to himself . . .*

It is jarring, I give you that, to admit that this most traditional and most popular and most orthodox of parables may well have grown up outside the barn, outside the fences of mainstream Christianity. But there is nothing orthodox about the prodigal and his coming to himself. His is truly a *prodigal* thought. I need to get back home. Back to the land of light. Back to the pleroma. Back to the God beyond God. No "Christ died for our sins," here. No "lamb of God," here. No settled orthodox Christology here. No cross, no gory glory, no Gethsemane, no passion of the Christ, here. It all comes down to self awareness, to awakening, to a moment of clarity. *When he came to himself.* The parable of the Prodigal Son is the most Gnostic, most heterodox, most Johannine of them all. Stuck here in the middle of Luke, read here in the middle of Lent, interpreted here in the middle of March.

The Gospel challenges us to come out from hiding.

You cannot hide behind a distrust of organized religion today. The prodigal thought soars beyond that. You cannot hide behind a disdain for clergy, for formality, for robes and choirs and altars and candles. This prodigal thought pierces all that. You cannot behind the hideous moments in religious and Christian history—many there be—as a way to fend off the gospel, at least not this morning. The knife cuts deeper, to the deeps, to your very soul.

You cannot hide on the left behind a critique of Catholicism today. Prodigal thought soars beyond that. You may reject the celibacy of the priesthood, the sacrifice of the mass, the subordination of women, and the infallibility of the pope. But many, very many, Catholics do the same. No, the gospel undercuts your smart but narrow critique, and asks about your soul. You do have one you know.

I cannot hide on the right behind a critique of Calvinism today. Prodigal thought soars beyond that. I may reject Calvinist total depravity, unconditional election, limited atonement, irresistible grace, and perseverance of the saints. Not all saints persevere, grace is resistible, atonement limitation is not divine, election has a human dimension, and depravity, well, it certainly is present, but not total. But you know, many Calvinists, very many, would agree. No, the gospel undercuts my own smart but narrow critique, and asks about my soul. I do have one, you know.

It asks whether you are coming to know yourself? Are you? This is the parable, oddly enough, that calls the seekers' bluff. Today the Gospel attacks where you have finally no ready defense. It moves to your mind, your soul, your own most self.

July 8

A Good Meeting

When you next attend a meeting, make a rough count of the number of people who, overtly or covertly, are sending or reading email, searching the internet for birthday presents, reading online newspapers or magazines, playing solitaire, texting a person across the table with a joke about the person presently speaking, or cleaning out and through various e-files. On of the real graces, sets of talents our culture needs to thrive is the capacity, on all sides courteously and summarily to attend, or lead, a meeting. A good meeting is like an apple in the sun, beautiful and tasty and nourishing. Such a conference requires attention from all sides, much careful planning and preparation, and significant, rapid follow through. In such a meeting, the Hebrew Scripture was gradually translated into Greek, at Jamnia. In such a meeting, St. Paul condemned St. Peter to his face, and forever freed faith from religion. In such a meeting, Martin Luther refused to recant and exclaimed, *Here I stand; I can do no other; God help me.* In such a meeting, the Declaration of Independence was wrought. In such a meeting, John Wesley consecrated Coke and Asbury. In such a meeting, Elizabeth Cady Stanton and Susan B. Anthony charted the course toward suffrage. In such a meeting, Churchill and Roosevelt planned the defeat of Nazism. In such a meeting, decisions were made by Freedom Riders. In such a meeting, Universities were founded, businesses created, nations born, refugees freed, movements initiated, inventions funded, leaders anointed, and freedom protected. One such became known as the Boston Tea Party, which by the way was not a gathering of conservative politicians.

July 9

Heiss in Syracuse

Our Annual Conference in Syracuse concluded yesterday. Among many other earthly delights it included a fire alarm—no harm, no injuries—during opening worship. Imagine 1500 Methodists fleeing and stampeding out of a convention center, 'fleeing from the wrath to come.' No flames, just apocalyptic mirth and moments in the sunshine for fellowship, and for conference. It was also a truth moment. A fire alarm is ringing, right now, across Methodism. Since 2010 from Albany to Buffalo my beloved conference has lost 11% of its people. For those under 45, the disaffection is highly specific. We refuse to affirm the full humanity of gay people. Can we be surprised that people of conscience go elsewhere? What kind of future could you honestly want or expect for an excluding denomination? During the fire alarm, I took the occasion to find and meet a pastor from Binghamton, whose blog post I had read the week before. I close with Stephen Heiss's words, for they are truly my very own:

To Bishop Mark Webb, my brother in Christ!

In the spirit of the One who said the truth will set us free, and emboldened by the freedom given by grace for which Jesus lived and died, I want and need to share with you how God has led me (and many of our colleagues) in ministries to help set at liberty those who have been held captive by the tyranny against people who are gay.

In the last few years I have officiated at several weddings for brothers and sisters who are lesbian or gay. One of those weddings—the highlight of my ministry—was for my own daughter and the woman who is now her wife. They are so happy!

Further, much to my delight, I have plans to officiate in the near future at yet another wedding for two women, that their joy may also be complete.

Bishop Webb—the long bitter era of scorn and hatred against gay people is dissolving before our very eyes. Christ has broken down the walls.

Those who have lived within the law and those who have lived outside the law are sitting down together at the table of grace.

The parable of the Kingdom of God as a wedding banquet has become an event in real time for hundreds of gay couples across our state. Finally, like the guest list in Jesus' parable, those on the outside are invited to the inside of God's grace. They must come!

Nevertheless, some yet refuse the invitation.

They make excuses.

They cite Scriptures, yet offer no interpretive principle by which their claims are validated.

They prefer the "tradition of the elders" to Jesus' teachings about "not judging the other."

They screen for the gnats of sexual correctness while the elephants of consumer materialism, environmental degradation, and global starvation pass right by, completely unnoticed.

We cannot judge them, of course, for they too are given grace.

Who among us can say we have always accepted every invitation toward grace and away from judgment?

And so, grace abounds!

Further, the harvest of that grace is found everywhere—even in the church!

With regard to homosexuality, we who count ourselves as United Methodists have been wandering in the wilderness of uncertainty about all things gay for 40 long years. Now the Promised Land is coming into view.

During those 40 years we have attempted to trap gay folks in nets of shame.

We stalked them with bible verses.

We legislated against them—whereas this, and whereas that.

We sent them to trials.

In righteous rage we lifted stones against them.

Now, in our own time, we are dropping those stones, one by one —at first—mothers, dads, sisters, brothers, school mates, talk show hosts, the neighbor next door.

We were learning.

Then—psychologists, pediatricians, sociologists, school teachers, neuro-scientists, biologists, counselors.

We were learning.

Then—Anglicans, Episcopalians, Lutherans, United Churches of Christ, Presbyterians, Reformed Jews.

We were learning.

And now—baseball players, bible scholars, theologians, professional ethicists, Sunday school teachers, pastors . . . and bishops. We are learning. We are finally learning that being gay harms no one.

July 10

M. Robinson

As our Calvinist Lenten preaching partner this Lent, M Robinson, writes in *The Death of Adam*, and in *Absence of Mind*, prodigal thought is soul thought, and meant to change your life.[1] She is a powerful voice today honoring the mind. A prodigal thought is a tussle between the mind and the world, the mind and the soul, the mind and itself. Give her voice some space in your mind:

"It all comes down to the mystery of the relationship between the mind and the cosmos" (3).

"Consider . . . The deeply pensive solitudes that bring individuals into congregations and communities to be nurtured by the thought and culture they find there. . . . The mind as felt experience" (9).

"We suffer today the exclusion of the felt life of the mind" (35). . . . "A central tenet of the modern world view is that we do not know our own minds, motives or desires" (59).

"The mind is an illusion according to modern theory. . . . The renunciation of religion in the name of reason and progress has been strongly associated with a curtailment of the assumed capacities of the mind" (75).

"Yet we have . . . A singular capacity for wonder as well as for comprehension (72).

"For the religious, the sense of the soul may have as a final redoubt, not as argument but as experience, that haunting I who wakes us in the night wondering where time has gone, the I we waken to, sharply aware that we have been unfaithful to ourselves, that a life lived otherwise would have acknowledged a yearning more our own than any of the daylit motives whose behests we answer to so diligently" (110).

"Soul is . . . a name for an aspect of deep experience" (116) . . . "The self that stands apart from itself, that questions, reconsiders, appraises" (119).

How does your soul fare? Are you open to the challenge of a prodigal thought—in memory, in discovery, in prayer?

July 11

---

1. Marilynne Robinson, *Absence of Mind* (New Haven: Yale University Press, 2010).

Matriculation 2013

Dear Lord:

As we step forward into this new season, may we walk together, aware of those who have come before us, back *to* 1839, and those too who lived a dream before us, back *in* 1963.

As we set foot in this new semester, a small step for each individual, but a giant one for a class of 3800, help us to carry with us a humble gratitude for those parents and others who helped launch us, who have guided our trajectory thus far, and who have funded our freedom here.

As we walk together soon under the leaves of autumn, and another year, let us say a quiet word in prayer for those in Boston who knew real loss this past April, who knew pain then and fear then, damage then and death then, here in Boston, just a few months ago, under the bright buds of springtime.

As we lean in, lean forward, into this open, new range of experience, a year of learning—the promise, the privilege, the gift, the joy of another year of learning—let us do so with measured steps, steps that keep the rhythm of health, follow the trail of goodness, and balance the left foot of adventure with the right foot of prudence.

As we sally forth, Dear Lord, may we walk *together*, neither racing ahead nor lagging behind, but running *together* the race that is set before us, watching for kindness to receive and kindness to share and kindness for others, during the quest for learning, virtue and piety.

(Pause)

Bless us we pray with this spirit of remembrance, of gratitude, of compassion, of prudence, of kindness in this one year, walking together, 2013.

July 12

Myrrh

We begin. As J Edwards said, "Resolved: to do nothing I would be afraid to do in the last hour of my life."

I don't believe I quite heard or overheard your seasonal resolution(s).

Resolve, 2013: to leave behind debt and regret.

On January 1, 1863, here in Boston, at the Boston Music Hall, F Douglass and many others sang. The Handel and Haydn society sang. One of their members, Harriet Beecher Stowe, sang. Why their birdsong, good news of great joy? In the cradle of liberty? Emancipation. Real change is real hard, but change does come. Lincoln said (12/62): "The dogmas of the quiet past are inadequate to the stormy present."

Stowe wrote: he is coming like the glory of the morning on the wave . . .

Regret is the shortest definition I know of hell. Let your regrets be few. Prize your time, your body, your heart. "To thine own self be true" (that's Shakespeare by the way, not the Bible). Let us leave behind the regret of gun violence, the regret of dehumanization of gays, the regret of environmental predation, the regret of children in poverty, the regret of unruly rouge nations, the regret of selfish living. Let your freedom be not only the freedom of the will, but the freeing of the will, to love.

Debt is the surest measure I know of hell. Debt is an actuarial prison. "Neither a borrower nor a lender be" (again, Uncle Will, not the Holy Book). An undergraduate degree is a wonderful thing, but not worth a mountain of lasting debt. Travel light, cloak and staff. Go where they will pay you to study, if you can.

Yes, I am concerned about national debt. I am. A $4T budge with $3T income—this does not compute. Even churches balance their budgets (I have 35 Decembers of fist fights, I mean finance meetings, to show). Debt is a bad gift to grandchildren. But I am even more concerned about your personal debt. Lord forgive us our debts!

Get rid of your debt. Get rid of your regret. This year.

Find the freedom to live in love.

You are hiding out there. I know you are. I am hunting for you. You are out there. In a Beacon St. apartment. Up on the north shore. Munching bagels on the Cape. Out in Newton, enjoying the Marsh Choir. I have been searching for you, for six years. Against the fierce New England wind of post Christian secularism, righteous anti religious fervor, mixtures of bad Calvinism or Catholicism, Sunday hockey, and a kind of intellectual life that is always just a bit short—of wonder, mystery, and magi wisdom. I am hunting for you. But I don't find you yet. I search, but you are too well hidden.

Can you give me a little *tweet tweet*?

Congregation? Clergy? Choir? Radio?

July 13

Psalm 91: Charles Wesley

When we have nothing else to go on, there is something irreducibly solid, something strong and good—the divine voice in the faith of Christ—-to which we may cleave and cling. Finally, this is what brings you to the pew and me to the pulpit and us to the church, the hope that something may be said and heard that is divine, saving, satisfying and true. In the silence that follows all our speaking, like the priestly verses that follow the human voice in this psalm, we may hear something that changes everything. So Charles Wesley, as ever, in perfect pitch:

Let us plead for faith alone
Faith which by our works is shown
God it is who justifies
Only faith the grace supplies
Active faith that lives within
Conquers hell and death and sin
Hallows whom it first made whole
Forms the Savior in the soul

July 14

Psalm 91: Destruction and Evil

Deliverance from noonday destruction

It is in the heart of the Psalm that one senses the singer's desperation. There is an irrational side to his message. "Thousands will fall but you will be spared." It will not help us to ask about the ethics of this promise. Nor will it help us to question the sense of destiny involved here. I hear this psalm in another way. I hear it as a father's prayer, or a mother's dearest hope. I cannot help but think that this psalm perfectly captures the hope, the visceral hope, which this decade has been on the minds of our own parents of soldiers and sailors. Noonday destruction will not come near you. I pray that noonday destruction will not come near you.

I remember a Day Care center where I used to see notes pinned to the coats and sweaters of daycare toddlers. This psalm is a note pinned to the shirt of a loved one heading into danger. When there is nothing else we can give our daughters and sons we want them to have faith. Faith to go forward, bravely, without being sure of what they will find at noonday. And we are passionately desperate for one hope: that they will come home. And we sing the song without any chords of doubt, because we want to admit none. We make no uncertain sound because we want our beloved to carry no worry, but to be armed with the confidence of the Lord. This is a battle hymn. It is the kind of song you sing to yourself when all about you there is mayhem. If I were a chaplain it is the kind of psalm I might give to a soldier to memorize by day and recite by night in the face of mayhem. "You will not fear the destruction that wastes at noonday."

July 15

Psalm 91: Illness and Tares

Deliverance from Illness

Our writer is not a philosopher. He is a musician, perhaps, but not a systematic thinker. He has one interest: getting by, getting through, getting out, and getting home. So he does not worry about the small stuff. In fact, I have a sense that the psalmist is desperate. His song is one for that point on the road when you just have to go ahead and risk and jump. You have made your assessment, you have made your plan, you have made your study, then you have prayed. Yet you see all the pestilence about you in homes and institutions and nations, so you wonder, is it worth the risk? You are not sure.

This hymn of the heart is one you sing when you are not sure, but you are confident. Not certain, but confident. You can be confident without being certain. In fact, a genuine honest confidence includes the confidence to admit you are not sure. Faith means risk. Isn't that part of what we mean by faith? Our writer is at that point, the point of decision. Once you are there, you have to choose between walking forward and slinking away. It becomes very simple. Either God lives or not. Either God is in Christ or not. Either God in Christ touches us by Spirit or not. Either we move forward in faith, or not. Choose. And the Psalmist wants his student or grandson or parishioner to choose in faith. So he urges: abide in the shadow of the Almighty. . . . "He will deliver you from the deadly pestilence."

July 16

Psalm 91: Snares

Deliverance from Snares

Our singer is a person of simple faith. He has one, and only one, word for us: You are covered. Abide in the shadow.

We could make many complaints about this hymn and its singer. He has a dangerously simple view of evil, especially for the complexity of a post-modern world. He has a way of implying that trust, or belief, are rewarded with safety, a notion that Jesus in Luke 13 scornfully dismisses, and we know to be untrue. He has an appalling lack of interest in the scores of others, other than you, who fall by the wayside. He seems to celebrate a foreordained, foreknown providence that ill fits our sense of the openness of God to the future, and the open freedom God has given us for the future. He makes dramatic and outlandish promises not about what might happen, but about what will be. As a thinking theologian, this psalmist of psalm 91 fails. He fails us in our need to rely on something sounder and truer than blind faith. He seems to us to be whistling past the graveyard.

And yet . . . for those who have walked past a February graveyard or two, for those who have walked the valley of the shadow of death, for a country at war for a decade now, for a world searching to match its ideals of peace with its realities of hatred, for you today if you are in trouble, and who are worried today about others and other graves and other yards, and who have seen the hidden traps, unforeseeable dangers, and steel jawed snares of life, there is something encouraging about this simple song: "he will deliver you from the snare of the fowler."

July 17

Psalm 91: Winter

There come wintery episodes in the course of a snow battered lifetime that place us deep in the shadows. If the shadow is dark enough, we may not feel able to move forward, for our foresight and insight and eyesight are so limited. We may become frozen, snowed in.

You may have known this condition—of confusion or disorientation or ennui or acedia. You may know it still. The death of a loved one can bring such a feeling. The loss of a position or job can bring such a feeling. The recognition of a major life mistake can bring such a feeling. The recollection of a past loss can bring such a feeling. The disappearance of a once radiant affection, or love, for a person or a cause or an institution can bring such a feeling. The senselessness of violence inflicted on the innocent can bring such a feeling.

(Over the years I have grown frustrated by my own mother tongue in various ways. English places such a fence between thought and feeling, when real thought is almost always deeply felt, and real feeling is almost always keenly thought. We need another word like *thoughtfeeling* or *feltthought*. When C Wesley sang 'unite the pair so long disjoined, knowledge and vital piety, learning and holiness combined, and truth and love let us all see' he described something so bone marrow close to my own life, happiness, hope, ministry, faith. And he also I think was wrestling with the limits of our beautiful language. Anyway, you by nature and discipline live the *thoughtfeeling* gospel, and for that I am lastingly thankful.)

Be it then thought or feeling or *thoughtfeeling*, there do come episodes, all in a lifetime, that place us, if not in the dark, at least well into the shadows. You may have known all about this at one time. You may know it still.

Come Sunday, some snippet of song, or verse, or preachment, or prayer, it may be, will touch you as you meander about in the dim shadow twilight. Hold onto that snippet. Follow its contours along the cave of darkness in which you now move. Let the snippet—song, verse, sermon, prayer—let it guide you along. So you may be able to murmur: "I can do this. . . . I can make my way. . . . I can find a handhold or foothold. . .I can abide in this shadow. . . . For now I can abide here. . . . I can make it for now, at least for now, for the time being.'

This Lent we shall await a word about war and peace, about drones and defense, about our beloved country in this year of our Lord. We will rightly desire a word of interpretation about a passage in Scripture—Old Testament, Gen. 22, or Epistle, Rom 10. or Gospel, Luke 4. This Lent we will rightly desire a communication about how to live, in discipline and obedience and faith, during a time of penitence and preparation and we will want a word from our Lenten conversation partner Marilynne Robinson. All in due time. Today , first, though, the word, near to us, on our lips and in our heart, is a word of faith, the given courage *to abide in the shadow*. Health is such a word, and very salvation, for those who are stumbling a bit and stumbling about in the dark today. On this plea for faith all our other attentions depend. So says the 91 Psalm.

Today the psalmist lifts a hymn of faith, a song of courage in the face of adversity. He speaks from his experience. He teaches, like a grandfather teaching a grandson. Spinning a fishing fly. Boiling the sap down in the sugar house. Watching a basketball game. Watching the sunset.

July 18

Restoration

The rites of spring include the annual, the ritual replacement of the dock down by the water's edge. It is one thing to build a dock, another to rebuild one.

How fondly I remember our first year on the lake, the joy of building a dock. To the work of carpentry I bring (others will bear eloquent witness) a rare combination of two personal traits, a combustible combination in any field. To carpentry I bring a frightening combination of rabid zeal and expansive ignorance. Zeal and ignorance are the hallmarks of my carpentry. Hence, on that first spring day, imagine my excited joy as plank after sweating plank cascaded from the flatbed truck. Hovering over the victim wood, with sun now high in the sky, and the lake at deep blue, I reached, tenderly, for hammer and saw. In a flurry, in a flash, it was all over. The dye was cast. 30 planks had become two rectangles. A jumble of a wood pile came gradually to resemble what, with some kindness, we might call a dock. A very rudimentary creation. A little sweat, the joy of building, nails flying, and occasionally addressed with accuracy, a hammer swinging away with lightening speed and like lightening seldom hitting the same place twice. What joy to create! And what relative ease. The wood is fresh, the nails are new, the body is young, the air is warm, the fresh prospect of a job completed looms in the air. To build, to build, perchance to dream. Ah.

But now the winters have taken their toll. And now the ice and snow, hard to control, have shoved and crushed. And now the boards are broken. Some are missing. The nails angle outward like gnashing teeth. A whole section of a section has gone to sleep with the fishes, as we say. Neptune has demolished what Zeus intended. Old Man Winter and Father Time and Mother Nature have taken apart one's artful handiwork, one's thing of beauty, a joy forever. In short, we have an opportunity to succeed.

And who wants this kind of success opportunity? Not us. No way Jose.

Give us morning in America, not twilight! Give us ruddy youth and not, well, maturity! Give us the left coast not the right! A home where the buffalo roam, where the deer and antelope play, where seldom is heard a discouraging word! Give us an open frontier to conquer, not old cities to rebuild! Give us new nails, new boards, new projects! History (said Henry Ford) is bunk! Give us suburbs not cities! Give us sprawl and mall not city hall! Give us something new in religion, not the complex twistedness of experience! Give us easy health, not healing work! Give us brand new companies, not these hundred year old corporations with history and commitments and values and traditions! Give us babies not teenagers! Diapers not drivers licenses! Tom-toms not pom poms or senior proms! Creation. Building. The first frontier. Go west! Not your father's Oldsmobile. Give us the natural simplicity of Christmas, not the historical complexity of Holy Week. Give us new denominations, not these older worn out, bruised, superannuated, flea bitten, elderly churches. Give us a brand new cathedral, not one that needs upkeep. Give us the flat and easy, not the deep and dark and wide.

And for God's sake get rid of that cross.

It is one thing to build a dock. There is joy in Mudville over any building.

But it is another thing, quite another, for us anyway, to rebuild. Creation—ok. New Creation—no way.

July 19

Church in 2013

So what are we in my beloved church to do in 2013?

After Tampa, in May, I determined to spend six months in prayer, and visitation. By phone or in person I spoke with 31 trusted friends. I meditated on their counsel, and came to only four fairly meager conclusions. 1. We need steady ongoing conversation, conference among elders, in season and out. 2. We need to follow the money. 3. We need to focus on pastoral care for gay people. 4. We need to focus on pastoral embrace for lay people. Many young elders are leaving the church. Many middle age elders want to split the church. Many older elders are using covert, hidden means to address the situation. I will not leave, split or dissemble. So that means finding another path. I will have to go deeper. A couple thoughts.

One: There is something in this journey that will call me out and down further into faith. The language of the psalms fills my heart. I prayed and heard this: You will have to go down deeper.

Two: One part of the path is in regard to our ministry, the other part, regards money. In a way, the first part is easier. That is, most churches over time can come close to doing what we do regularly here at Marsh Chapel: marry gay people, hire gay clergy, minister directly to the gay community, and speak frankly, as today, about the full humanity of gay sisters and brothers. The second part is harder, about money. We will need means to keep from sending money, by apportionment, to fund the dehumanization of gay people, whether in America or in Africa. Fortunately, our general funds are several, not single, and local church treasurers, at the direction of the lay vote in the charge conference, can send to some and not to others. This will take some careful planning. My own investment will be to continue to lift my voice, to continue in eight words that form the future for my church: *Gay people are people. Lay people are people.*

July 20

Henry Vaughn

    The poet Henry Vaughn lived from 1622 to 1695. He fought on the Royalist side during the great war. Vaughn is known as one of the best followers and imitators of Herbert. In 1649, Charles I executed Oliver Cromwell. The Church of England was disestablished and the Book of Common Prayer was outlawed. The King was understood to be anointed by God. Incidentally, his brother was an alchemist. Vaughn lived during a dark time, and his poetry evokes his time. He recalls the great Pseudo-Dionysus and the Cloud of Unknowing. He celebrates night and the darkness of God. It is no accident that he bases this poem on Nicodemus at night, John 3:2ff. Here some verses from this wondrous work:

The Night
Through that pure Virgin Shrine
That sacred veil drawn o'er thy glorious noon
That men might look and live as glow-worms shine
And face the moon:
Wise Nicodemus saw such light
As made him know his God by night.
Most blest believer he!
Who in that land of darkness and blind eyes
Thy long expected healing wings could see,
When thou didst rise,
And what can nevermore be done,
Did at mid-night speak with the Sun!
O who will tell me, where
He found thee at that dead and silent hour!
What hallowed solitary ground did bear
So rare a flower,
Within whose sacred leaves did like
The fullness of the Deity. . .
Dear night! This world's defeat;
The stop to busy fools; care's check and curb;
The day of Spirits; my soul's calm retreat
Which none disturb!
Christ's progress and his prayer time;
The hours to which high Heaven doth chime. . .
Were all my loud evil days
Calm and unhaunted as is thy dark Tent,
Whose peace but by some Angel's wing or voice
Is seldom rent;
Then I in Heaven all the long year
Would keep, and never wander here.

But living where the sun
Doth all things wake, and where all mix and tire
Themselves and others, I consent and run
To every mire,
And by this world's guiding light,
Err more than I can do by night.
There is in God (some say)
A deep but dazzling darkness; as men here
Say it is late and dusky, because they
See not all clear;
O for that night! Where I in him
Might live invisible and dim.

July 21

Eliot

The poet T.S. Eliot was born in America, yet lived most of his life in England until his death in 1965. He was the greatest poet of his age, and one of the greatest of any age. While our generation does not cling to him as did an earlier one, and this itself is a pity, nonetheless he touches us too. To him we owe the rediscovery of the metaphysical poets. Eliot found God's presence in God's absence. Like Herbert's mature claim upon God, like Vaughn's love of night, Eliot's presence in absence seems strikingly close to the spirit of our own age. I dedicate this reading to my dear dad who died three years ago, an authentic lover of the word.

July 22

Tweet, Tweet

The gospel is the beauty of a bird in song.

We begin. As J Edwards said, "Resolved: to do nothing I would be afraid to do in the last hour of my life."

I don't believe I quite heard or overheard your seasonal resolution(s).

You still may be hunting, searching.

The gospel is the gift of the Christ child to us, God's gift of faith, of fellowship, of freedom—beyond thought and beyond intuition and beyond demolition. If God is for you, who is against? The gospel also is our gift to the Christ child. Odd, no? The gospel heard and spoken and lived is our gift to Christ, like the story which Matthew narrates, Mt 2, is his gift to wordflesh.

Search and hunt they did, these wise men. The very presence of the wise at the outset of the gospel is the rejection of fundamentalism near and far. Swinging like an angel sword before the garden of Eden, here come the magi, making sure that any gospel worthy of the name fears nothing human, fears nothing known or knowable, fears nothing true. Biblicism be gone, say the kings. Their presence is the celebration of the liberal gospel, the gospel of liberality, your birthright, Marsh Chapel. The gospel (not that there is any other) that honors what we know, while admitting what we do not. The gospel that remembers our history, including its horrors. The gospel that eschews easy measures of the divine, which by definition is un-measurable. The gospel that has arms big enough to embrace the big bang, and evolution, and real random chance, and the unknowable God in whose love, alone, we are at all known. To be good news, the gospel must be true, all truth, the whole truth and nothing but the truth. Otherwise it is not good, and not news. Searching can exhaust the searcher, star at night, out to the east, following forever. Truth. Science. History. Psychology.

Our five grandchildren and their overseers visited us at Christmas. The oldest is five, leader of the pack. I heard them playing hide and seek. She taught them a song, a birdsong. When they ran out of hunting energy, and were stumped, humans at the edge of knowledge, ministers at the edge of energy, she would call out, in song, "can you give a little *tweet-tweet*'" And repeat, and repeat. Then, from under the bed, would come the birdsong response, "*tweet, tweet.*" The gospel is not only the Christ gift. The gospel is our gift to the Christ.

July 23

Young Death

We stood with 500 eighteen year olds gathered Thursday evening past, in the wake of the death of our 18 year old student. For many, in their teens, a first harsh encounter with death. In a secular gathering they offered a secular prayer. Some came to themselves that evening, thinking:

We mean to be thoughtful, and to be together in our thoughtfulness.

We are not alone in our thoughts. We have each other to lean on.

We will lean on our friends, those with whom we can share a hug.

We will lean on our groups, classes, dorm and hallway neighbors, those who know our names and call us by name.

We will lean on our own traditions of memory and hope, so significant, now, those words and events and stories that place all experience in ultimate perspective.

We will lean on our religious traditions, wherein we sing and kneel.

We will lean on our faith, that dimension of life that is deepest and truest to our own most self, our soul, the dimension of deep experience.

We will lean on some snippets and memories of words and phrases—goodness and mercy will follow me, let us love one another, love is God, let us watch over one another in love.

We may be moved to wonder again, at life, the meaning of life, the boundaries of life, and our own choices and actions and words therein.

We will be thoughtful and we are not alone in our thoughts.

July 24

Beginnings

Keep a list this week of beginnings, new year celebrations of different kinds. A first paper submitted. A first date enjoyed. A first real conversation in friendship. A first blistering failure. A first day on the job. A first ache in the bones to hint at the advent of autumn in life. A first handshake. A first argument. A first genuine disappointment. Whatever 'years' begin in the next week, take a moment to savor them or at least to consider them. You can do so with confidence, as we hear in a moment: *His good Spirit, which shows me the path to Life, guides and leads me upon a level road, therefore I begin this year in Jesus' name.*

July 25

Experience

We are entering a new year, whether with the academics at matriculation, or with those following this season's autumnal sports, or with the hikers and campers as fall arrives. Our Holy Scripture and our Cantata this morning both offer us insight for a new day.

In particular, those of you who may find yourself outside of the religious traditions around you, or the tradition, if any, in which you were raised, may be heartened to hear the music and word this morning.

Our community of faith at Marsh Chapel, Boston University, shares with other such communities, far and near, an alertness to the meaning in beginnings. *Jesus shall be my everything. Jesus shall remain my beginning. Jesus is my light of joy.* So the duet affirms in just a few moments. Beginnings remain. The start of something new stays with us long after the newness has been spent. We recognize the power of new beginnings.

Look at the few days of this week and weekend.

Thursday, hundreds of students and other gathered within the Jewish community to celebrate Rosh Hashana, the start of the Jewish new year. Songs, prayers, readings, teachings were deployed to plumb the depth of meaning in the return of the year's opening.

Saturday, many hundreds of students and others gathered for feasting and dancing at the celebration of Raas Lela, the seasonal and communal recognition of what is new this autumn. Songs, prayers, readings, teachings were deployed to plumb the depth of meaning in the return of the year's opening.

Boston University is proud to host the largest Hindu student association in the country. Their yearly Saturday evening festival provides a colorful, fervent, rhythmic opening to the rest of the year. The dance and the meal seem to pray, as does our cantata: *bless all faithful teachers, bless hearers of the word, may peace and loyalty kiss each other, thus we would live this entire year in blessing.*

This evening, this Sunday evening, yet another several hundred students and others will gather to share a common meal, a common table, a common reading, a common address, a community of fellowship. The event is the feast of Eid, in which our Muslim community completes Ramadan and enters the year following those days of discipline. Songs, prayers, readings, teachings will be deployed to plumb the depth of meaning in a sort of return to the year's opening. *Let us complete the year to the praise of the divine name.* So the meal suggests, as the cantata affirms.

All of these events this year will have been located in the same space, in the same week, in the same University, on the same street. They happened and will have happened in the very same room. In engaging difference, in embracing alterity, we do well not to minimize the variations present. We also do well to recognize the common hope present. Community emerges from diversity when diversity is longing for unity. Without that common hope there will be no common faith and then over time no common ground.

In addition, the Christian community will be gathered for worship, here in the nave of Marsh Chapel and across the airwaves, and later in through the afternoon and week for other Christian services—three Catholic masses, an Evening Ecumenical Sunday Eucharist, prayer and devotion preceding the Inner Strength Gospel Choir practice, a Monday evening Orthodox communion, a Wednesday evening ecumenical and Episcopal Evening Prayer, a school of theology service, a moment of Thursday silent prayer, a Common Ground Thursday communion service, and other services, all located here in the Chapel. Next Sunday afternoon we will celebrate at 2pm the baptism of Nathan Hutchison-Jones, one of several infants baptized this year. It is an hour of new beginnings as well. Beginnings remain. Beginnings reverberate. Beginnings resound through time and space. And every dawn, every morning awakening, is one such new beginning. How seriously, studiously, and curiously, famously wondered Howard Thurman, have taken our moment of waking from slumber, morning by morning?

July 26

Faith

This is a day of new beginnings. As by potential at least is every day, and every Lord's Day. Now is the acceptable time. Today is the day of salvation.

Our love of Holy Scripture impels us to listen, again, just a bit more closely, to the new beginning announced in Matthew 21.

One portion of our passage explores the perennial religious issue of authority. The pages of the New Testament themselves were composed and collected in no small measure as a way of exploring authority. 'By what authority?' is the question Jesus parries with another question which puts his interrogators on the horns of a dilemma. When something new is on the horizon, this question invariably arises. In a new year setting, a day of new beginnings, when something big and new is in the offing, it may be worth asking: On whose authority shall weighty and consequential decisions be taken? It is at least worth thinking about: by what authority?

Another portion of our passage tells of two sons and the opportunity to work the vineyard. It is easy for us to hear the acclaim reserved for the first, who goes ahead and does the work, and to hear the criticism of the one who pays lip service to the stewardship of the vineyard, but goes another way. For Matthew, at least, here, at least, the surprising gospel is that those not attired in the formal clothing of faith, those even who are engaged in the most secular and ancient of professions, seize the day, and take up the labor and tend the vineyard. Not the membership list, but the prospect list. Not the clergy, but the laity. Not those at the center, but those on the periphery. Not the nominally present, but the actually absent. Not those who have cleaned the outside of the cup, but those who have had the inside washed and laundered and pressed and put to service. Not those who say a comfortable yes, but those who say an honest no, yet whose lives say yes, when others' lives say no. Here, at least, to the extent one understands the phrase, one hears an initial encouraging word for those who may be "spiritual but not religious." The vineyard awaits those who will tend it. This perhaps is what John Wesley meant to say as he preached, "if thine heart be as mine, then give me thine hand."

Paul says it clearly: *Do nothing from selfish ambition or conceit, but in humility regard others as better than yourselves. Let each of you look not to your own interests, but to the interests of others. Work out your own salvation with fear and trembling.*

It may be that on reflection, the first son had a vision of what such a vineyard could look like over time, what such an unusual kind of labor could feel like over time, what such a new start to a new year in a new way could become over time. It may be that on reflection you will have a vision of what such a vineyard, God's garden, could look like over time, with a little effort, what such an unusual kind of labor, faith working through love, could feel like over time, and what such a new start to a sober and loving life this autumn Sunday could become over time. If so, you may silently whisper, walking or driving home, *Lord God we praise you, since you with this new year send us new fortune and new blessing and still think upon us in grace.*

July 27

Marsh Spirit

Ecclesia. Symphonison. Pragmata. Church. Agreement. Issues . . .

Welcome to the ministry of Marsh Chapel! Here you will find a heart in the heart of the global city, and a worship service in the service of the global city. Here you will find passionate interest in matters related to gospel voice, personal vocation, and congregational volume. I look forward to knowing your name!

Please take advantage of the opportunities here for ministry, for music, for hospitality and for international engagement. Find your way to your own true interests in our midst. Get to know Br. Larry, Dr. Jarrett, Mr. Bouchard, and Rev. Longsdorf. I look forward to their knowing your name!

For Marsh Chapel to be a if not the leading liberal pulpit in the country, an if not the exemplary collegium for vocational discernment in our time, and a if not the largest University congregation in the country, we need you. We need your Sunday presence, your tithing generosity, your acceptance of service roles, your prayer before worship and night and day, and mainly your own best self.

Our preaching this year, September 2014 to May 2015, will cycle around and through an engagement with Spirit. We will of course follow the common lectionary, and offer ordered 11am Sunday worship in the Marsh tradition. The sermons will test the spirits (1 Thess. 5) to see if any be of God (1 John 4). The sermons will speak with those who are "spiritual but not religious."

In particular, the first Sunday sermons, normally delivered from the chancel, will explore "The Marsh Spirit." What is the particular, soulful spirit of our community here, over 60 years? What makes Marsh Chapel, Marsh Chapel? Then, also, once each month a theme sermon, will explore what the Spirit is saying to the Church on issues of moment (the moral equivalents of war, religion on campus, safety and student life, drones, law and love in the United Methodist Church, and other). Advent and Lent will give us seasons of Spirit cycles. In Lent, we will debate Jonathan Edwards, but on the matter of Spirit.

So find your way to the Paraclete. Open your door to the Spirit of Truth. Study a little about the Holy Spirit. Channel your inner Third Person persona. And get ready. The word this year: Spirit.

We began in a more general way a bit last week.

The Spirit offers grace in invitation, compassion, vocation, and aspiration.

We are a people alive in welcome to others, because we have been welcomed. Frost: You come too . . .

We are a community attuned to hurt, for we have known that pain. Frost: Treason, to go with the drift of things . . .

We are a congregation that has developed a culture in which a sense of calling is celebrated. Frost: Yield who will . . .

We are a gathering of women and men who look out, and look down, but who regularly look up, to aspire to height and heaven and wholeness. Frost: It asks of us a certain height . . .

July 28

Marsh Spirt: Inquiry

Our spirit at Marsh Chapel is one of inquiry. We are learning together: from each others' voices, through each others' thoughts, out of each others' conflicts, with each others' histories and mysteries.

The Marsh Spirit includes the experimental creativity honored by Daniel Marsh, by Howard Thurman, by Huston Smith, by Floyd Flake, by Robert Neville, and by our learning together in these years.

The Marsh Spirit, which we explicitly explore, this year, on our Eucharist Sundays, is an unabashedly liberal one. Compassionate, not permissive. Curious, not fearful. Coherent, not chaotic. Traditional and Scriptural, but not unreasonable or impersonal. "Test the spirits, to see whether any be of God." Scriptures of every religious tradition direly need to be fettered by our experience and our reason, alongside our traditions of understanding.

Liberal in the Christian, Protestant, Methodist, Bostonian, Personalist manner.

Theologically liberal, that is, not necessarily politically so, all the way. For instance, often you have heard our voice inquiring about the health of gambling. Citizens of the Commonwealth of Massachusetts might want to inquire about virtue and vice in publicly embraced gaming. Have you lived near Atlantic City or in Oneida NY? You might want to inquire of those who have, what the consequences have been. We have lived near a major casino: blighted neighborhoods, children left for hours in back seats, people with cash to use for slots but not for heath care, a few solid jobs and many, many poor people made poorer and poor children made poorer.

Our College of Arts and Sciences has a hospitality table in the main hall for the first week of classes. Here is a place where information of moment and meaning may be given over to those in need. Call it a sermon table.

Three students were discussing the heat and humidity, the first week and first weekend, causes curricular and extra curricular. Said one, pointing down the hall: *I had a class in that room. It was terrible.* A passerby asked: *Which was terrible—the room or the class?* Well, in this case, it was the room.

But there along Commonwealth Avenue, inside a great Cram and Ferguson building, there arose a momentary insight into the troubles of interpretation. Which—room or class? In order to know, to hear properly, you have to dig a little deeper, ask a question or two, probe and inquire.

Our spirit at Marsh Chapel is one of *inquiry*. We are learning together: from each others' voices, through each others' thoughts, out of each others' conflicts, with each others' histories and mysteries.

We inquire after truth. That which has been believed always and everywhere by everyone, as John Wesley put it. Nothing human is foreign to us—*nihil humanum*, as Terence put it.

How shall we do so?

July 29

Marsh Spirit: Talk

In chapter 8, verse 15, Matthew begins to give advice about how to life in community. Community involves difference, but also can involve hurt. Communication makes community. Matthew's Jesus teaches us to speak to each other in our presence and not of each other in our absence—to each other in our presence not of each other in our absence.

This week I received a triangulating e-mail. It came from the leader of an organization I dislike, seeking support for a person I do like. I loathe one and love the other. The triangulation in the communication forces me either to support an organization I do not like or to disappoint a person I do like. What do you do in such a situation? The kinder approach from the organization would have been a visit, or a phone call, in which sensibilities could be explored. But now we have the e-document: eternal, irretrievable, international, indelible. And the tangled triangle. It will take 3 hours or more to unbind and loosen this knot. You know, there was a time when people had to come and see you before they so complicated your life.

I think on inquiry, that Matthew 18: 15 teaches me how to respond. I shall not send a steaming reply, tempting as that would be. I shall not reply from a distance at all. I must go and see my interlocutor. I must make a visit to the author of the e-mail and find a way through the horns of the dilemma, the Scylla of support for an organization I dislike and the Caribdis of hurt to a person I do like.

In verse 17, Matthew provides a further suggestion, to use if the earlier ones fail. Tell the whole church, his Jesus says. We are clearly hearing overtones of what was needed in Matthew's community, toward the end of the first century. Jesus may well have taught in such fashion, though the use of a Greek word like 'ecclesia'—twice here—probably indicates this is later material placed on Jesus' lips. But the import remains—gather the community for deliberation. Get things moving in the community—get people walking together!

July 30

Marsh Spirit: Remember

In chapter 8, verse 16, Matthew quotes from Deuteronomy 19. That is, he goes back to the basics, back to the starting point, the Old Testament, back to kindergarten, if you will, as many have gone this week.

New York City has more than doubled, from 20K to 55K, the number of 4 year old children in free universal pre-kindergarten. Who says things cannot change for the better, and quickly? In Albany our four year old granddaughter entered a similar program and her Dad wrote:

"According to Anne, Sally's drop off went very smoothly. True to form, Sally walked into the school confidently and eagerly and, unlike many of the other kids, refused to hold her mother's hand. She knew right where her classroom was and where to go, found her cubby right away, put her things in it, greeted and hugged her new teacher, and then found a book, sat down on the carpet in the spot marked for her, and started to read quietly while the other kids filtered in. I'm so proud of her!!!"

Robert Fulghum had it right a generation ago: Everything I have ever needed to know I learned in kindergarten:

1. Share everything.

2. Play fair.

3. Don't hit people.

4. Put things back where you found them.

5. Clean up your own mess.

6. Don't take things that aren't yours.

7. Say you're *sorry* when you *hurt* somebody.

8. Wash your hands before you eat.

9. Flush.

10. Warm cookies and cold milk are good for you.

11. Live a balanced life—learn some and drink some and draw some and paint some and sing and dance and play and work everyday some.

12. Take a nap every afternoon.

13. When you go out into the world, watch out for traffic, hold hands, and stick together.

14. Be aware of wonder. Remember the little seed in the Styrofoam cup: The roots go down and the plant goes up and nobody really knows how or why, but we are all like that.

15. Goldfish and hamsters and white mice and even the little seed in the Styrofoam cup—they all die. So do we.

16. And then remember the Dick-and-Jane books and the first word you learned—the biggest word of all—look."[1]

July 31

1. Robert Fulghum, *All I Really Need to Know I Learned in Kindergarten* (New York: Ballantine Book, 1986).

August

A. A. Childs: A Story from a Mentor

The good news of liberty in Jesus Christ goes beyond death. Death is a serious enemy, even the final enemy. But the gospel transcends death, though its victory is hidden from us. God overcomes, Father Son and Holy Spirit.

Some time ago, in a small upstate village, there lived a man and a woman. They were of middle age and middle class. In fact, they ran their own business, a "mom and pop" store. Through the village, the man was known for the attention which he showed his partner. He doted on her. He opened doors and bought flowers and made compliments. For her part, she also was devoted to her man. She stood by her man. She baked and sewed and entertained. In church, they sat in the front pew, holding hands for the Sunday observance.

The pastor in the town for years admired them, and during wedding services would quietly pray, Lord make these young people like them, devoted to each other. One night the pastor was invited to visit the home of these two lovebirds. After the usual chitchat, it became clear that something was afoot. Wringing his hands and sweating, the man awkwardly asked, at last, whether the pastor would have any qualms about performing a wedding ceremony. "Not at all," the parson replied. "For whom?" Silence followed, the man coughed, and the woman blushed. Dimly, the pastor realized that the wedding was to be theirs. Yes, they had come to the village many years ago, had fallen in love and worked together, and then lived to together, first in aid of their business, and then as the townsfolk began to refer to them as MR and MRS, they began to relax and enjoy one another. They were very happy.

The wedding ensued, quietly performed in the parsonage living room.

Exactly one month to the day after the wedding, late at night, the parsonage phone rang. The man, panic stricken began in a rush, "It's all over." Our marriage doesn't work. Please come and help us." The pastor took the two aside to hear their confessions. "For years, you were so happy, and now, married, you are not? What has happened?" The man began, "Well, it used to be, you know, I just never knew whether she would stay. We weren't really married. She was free to go. So every day was special. I watched what I said, and I watched what I did, and I watched her. I wanted to please her. But somehow, after that ceremony, I let down. I guess I figured she was there to stay now, so it didn't matter. I think I took her for granted." And he cried. The woman also reported, "It used to be that every day was an adventure. I knew he could leave at any time. Every meal might be our last. Then we actually got married and I let down. I guess I figured it didn't matter as much now. I think I took him for granted. Pastor, what are we going to do?" After more hours of tears and talking, the pastor finally prepared to leave the home. As he left he commanded the couple to promise each other that from that moment forward, they would live as if they were not married. He said to the husband, "You are to live as if you have no wife."

With these and other stories, A. Allison Childs preached The Holy Spirit, the gospel of love that transcends death, and interpreted the scripture, I Cor. 7:25.

Many years ago, a young seminarian was assigned to preach in a mission chapel in the inner city of Rochester. As he arrived, he noticed that the mission captain had placed a sermon title in the window, "Jesus Saves." Although the young preacher had actually pre-pared another theme, he good-naturedly ascended the pulpit and preached the saving love of Jesus. The next Wednesday, night the seminarian returned, and found that again the ser-mon title had been placed in the mission window, "Jesus Saves." This time, toting a goodly message on some other weightier theme, the preacher asserted himself and inquired about this practice of a single title. " I have prepared another message this week," he reported. The mission captain smiled and quietly replied, "No. Not here. Here we preach one message, one only, "Jesus saves." For the next twelve weeks, the young preacher addressed this same theme. To his surprise, he found that there was indeed much variety within it, and that, gradually his little flock of hearers grew and was strengthened, and that he himself grew in faith. He resolved, from that point forward, whenever he preached, and whatever the theme, to try to find a good word to say about Jesus.

With these and other stories, A. Allison Childs preached the Son of God, the gospel of love that transcends death, and so interpreted for us John 20:19.

Several decades ago, a poor boy was growing up in a small town along the Finger Lakes. His family worked hard, but had little extra, and so he would work himself on a neighboring farm. There he became friends with the farmer's son, a boy about his own age. They became fast friends, cleaning the barn, and milking, chasing the cattle in the summer, filling the hay mow. At Christmas the farmer gave both boys trumpets. They sat down together and carved their names into the handles. Then they fell to practicing, and found the joy of music. Every night, after chores, the poor boy would cross the valley and ascend the hillside where his home lay. Then, as night fell, he would turn and face across the valley toward his friend, and slowly play a melody. Then, with the other trumpet, the friend would reply. "Day is dying in the west. . ." For some years this was their habit, and the farm folk and villagers in this Finger Lake region came to rely on the trumpet duet as a call to evening prayer.

Then, the farmer's son was drafted and, in short order word came that he had died in the great world war. The poor boy was devastated. He had known little of the comfort of life, and little of friendship, and now, what he had known, was taken away. He became bitter, and his life drifted on, building itself around the heartache at the center of his soul. He grew old. One day the pastor came to call. The pastor dreaded the visit in this home, because there was so much hurt, and so little comfort. On this day he happened to ask if there was any good memory, any happy memory that the man could share. After some silence, the man replied, and told the story of the two trumpets. He told of his friendship, his love of music, his acceptance in the farmer's home, his bitterness at the tragic loss. The pastor asked to see the trumpets, and then asked if he might borrow them.

Some weeks later, the old and bitter man was seated rocking on the porch, in the summer heat. Suddenly, a familiar tune came his way. From his left afar off he heard, "Day is dying in the west. . ." and then from the right "Holy Holy Holy. . ." It came closer. . . and closer. . . and with every verse, somehow, a bit of the faded memory came clearer. Two boys, high school age, came playing the trumpets, grateful for their use, prompted by the pastor to offer this tribute. What a precious gift a friendship is, the old one thought. How lucky I am to have known even briefly, its power.

With these and other such stories A. Allison Childs preached the kingdom of God the Father, the gospel of love that transcends death, and interpreted for us the meaning of the psalmist, Psalm 100.

August 1

Absence and Evidence

On the Sacred, Marilynn Robinson: "So I have spent my life watching, not to see beyond the world, merely to see, great mystery, what is plainly before my eyes. I think the concept of transcendence is based on a misreading of creation. With all respect to heaven, the scene of miracle is here, among us. The eternal as an idea is much less preposterous than time, and this very fact should seize our attention. In certain contexts the improbable is called the miraculous.

What is eternal must always be complete, if my understanding is correct. So it is possible that time was created in order that there might be narrative—event, sequence and causation, ignorance and error, retribution, atonement. A word, a phrase, a story falls on rich or stony ground and flourishes as it can, possibility in a sleeve of limitation. Certainly time is the occasion for our strangely mixed nature, in every moment differently compounded, so that often we surprise ourselves, and always scarcely know ourselves, and exist in relation to experience, if we attend to it and if its plainness does not disguised it from us, as if we were visited by revelation."

Absence of evidence is not evidence of absence.

Not everything measurable is meaningful, and not everything meaningful is measurable.

The greater the sea of knowledge, the longer the shoreline of mystery surrounding it.

The world does not lack for wonders, but only for a sense of wonder.

August 2

Allegiance

You will pledge allegiance to someone, and maybe, already, you have.

Beware the dark danger of allowing lesser loyalties to eclipse the one great loyalty.

You are pilgrim not a tourist, a pilgrim not a tourist.

You are here on a journey not a lark.

We are a pilgrim people, stumbling our way forward, as Robert F Kennedy tried to remind us 45 years ago, weeping with those who wept in Indianapolis, the night King was murdered. Kennedy preached:

"We can move in that direction as a country, in greater polarization –black people amongst blacks, and white amongst whites, filled with hatred toward one another. Or we can make an effort, as Martin Luther King did, to understand and to comprehend, and replace that violence, that stain of bloodshed that has spread across our land, with an effort to understand, compassion and love.

For those of you who are black and are tempted to be filled with hatred and mistrust of the injustice of such an act, against all white people, I would only say that I can also feel in my own heart the same kind of feeling. I had a member of my family killed, but he was killed by a white man.

But we have to make an effort in the United States, we have to make an effort to understand, to get beyond these rather difficult times.

My favorite poet was Aeschylus. He once wrote: "Even in our sleep, pain which cannot forget falls drop by drop upon the heart, until, in our own despair, against our will, comes wisdom through the awful grace of God."

What we need in the United States is not division; what we need in the United States is not hatred; what we need in the United States is not violence and lawlessness, but is love and wisdom, and compassion toward one another, and a feeling of justice toward those who still suffer within our country, whether they be white or whether they be black.

Let us dedicate ourselves to what the Greeks wrote so many years ago: to tame the savageness of man and make gentle the life of this world."

Something, or someone, will claim your allegiance. Beware giving the sacred dimension of your heart to something less than worthy of your heart.

Ask: Who are you? What do you believe? How do you love? To what are you called? Whom shall you forgive?

To what do you give your highest allegiance. The old Boston personalists counted cooperation as the highest good. Bodily cooperation—health. Social cooperation—civilization. Climactic cooperation—nature. Personal cooperation—the beloved community.

Love is the norm, not a mere virtue. Love is the power that makes virtue possible. Love is who we are meant and made to be.

Have you truly selected one just need, one issue in justice, and applied and invested yourself with allegiance?

August 3

Amnesia and Soul

Sometimes the trouble is amnesia. I am getting to the point that I need a solution or two to daily amnesia. Where are my glasses? Keys? Sermon notes? I should say, when I lay them down, 'I am putting my glasses on the bureau.' But we know a bigger, that is to say, a real sort of amnesia, too, that sometimes sits right with us in the pew, right beside us in the arm chair. What am I doing here? What is the point of all this struggle? I seem to have lost my way. I find it greatly comforting, on a daily and weekly basis, to see that in the very marrow of the Scripture, my wandering forgetfulness is known, shared, experienced, addressed. The recognition of a lost path, a way forgotten, an amnesia about something that really matters—this too is a summer grace. The student of Paul who honored Paul by writing pseudonymously a letter to the Colossians in his name had us in mind here, or had this in mind at least, our amnesia. Remember: you have been raised. Remember: seek the good big high great things. Remember: your life is hid with Christ in God. Remember: you are wearing a new nature, a renewed nature, which connects you in love to every other. "Christ is all, and in all."

Then sometimes, too, the unexpected arrives, supplanting security with radical change, unplanned and unforeseen. A good morning to listen to the radio service, or, better, to find your way to church can be this very moment of cataclysm. It is only sparing help to recall that many others in the history of the race have woken up, suddenly, to discover that all the barns full of grain carefully and responsibly stewarded cannot get us past a great loss, a loss of life, a loss of self, a loss of soul. Faith is only faith when it is all you have left to go on. (repeat) Then it is faith, for that is what we mean by faith, walking ahead into the dark. Sometime go through the pages of the Scripture and just watch for the number of occasions when the people in the Bible are suddenly and unexpectedly accosted with trouble, through no fault of their own. In St Luke today, the man is a prosperous farmer. But in other spots he is a favorite son thrown in a pit, a patriarch wrestling with a demon, a leader dying in a cave, a scout frightened by grasshoppers, a prophet unheeded until too late, an Apostle who knows about a thief in the night, a disciple who thought his betrayal would go unnoticed, a king who expects wrongly that his son will be honored, a father whose son leaves home, an honest worker who loses his job, a woman who has to plead until blue in the face before a judge who could not care less. And then: a Savior, a man of compassion, an embodiment of love, a healing teacher, a Lord, a Messiah—crucified. In the summer, for us, sometimes, it can be restorative to see that we have company on the days when night falls early. "One's life does not consist in an abundance of possessions." Or positions.

Right now our land and landscape are covered with a vast carelessness. A vast carelessness regarding the poor. A vast carelessness regarding the children of the poor. A vast carelessness regarding the other—otherwise oriented, otherwise abled, otherwise viewed. We have made some headway, by the Dow measurement anyway, in the building of better barns. (Nor should we, nor do I diminish the importance of bodily, physical, fiscal health.)

But the parable today though brutally admonishes us that love is for the wise. The body is not the soul. Fool! Today your *soul* is required.

August 4

Anderson Deliverance

Here is restoration from my neighborhood: Several years ago, a young man from my neighborhood, upstate New York, one Batavia boy, set out for the Marines. He did a couple of tours. Then a job opened up in journalism. He was young! First he went to South Africa. And then to Israel. Later, he chose to transfer to Lebanon. Free, healthy, successful, gaining influence—what a life. Then one Saturday he went early to play tennis in Beirut. Along the way, a black sedan pulled him to the curb. He was blindfolded, stuffed in the truck and whisked away, carted from basement to tenement to apartment. He spent all day and all night hooded and chained. For six years.

It's one thing to build a life—free, healthy, successful, influential. Another to redeem a life.

I remembered Terry Anderson's story again this week. In the darkness, in the bondage, through the terror, out of the misery he found . . . a new life, a new creation. He found faith. Or faith found him. He read the Bible, cover to cover, more than 50 times. It was his only story. As it is ours.

50 times, he watched Moses slay the Egyptian.

50 times, he saw Israel run from Pharaoh.

50 times, he heard the chariots chasing God's folk.

50 times, he wondered at the Red Sea parting.

50 times, he gasped as the returning water drowned Pharaoh.

50 times, he fidgeted as Israel just wandered and wandered in wilderness.

50 times, he heard the promise of milk and honey.

50 times, he sat with Moses on Mt. Nebo.

Then, as Moses lay dying for the 50th time, a knock came at Anderson's door. And again he was whisked away, but this time, by grace, to freedom. Do you remember his landing in New York? Do you recall his walk across the tarmak? Do you recollect his drive—they closed the highway to all traffic—to Midtown? Do you remember his words? "I have faith in God."

It's one thing to grow up in Batavia and build a life.

It's another thing, hooded and chained and trapped in later life to see life redeemed. And some bondage comes to us all. That's power. That's restoration. That's power.

August 5

Arrival

Sometimes we arrive in worship with a personal, compelling need. We find our familiar pew. We turn at the appointed hour to the radio frequency. We enter a spirit of prayer. Sometimes we bring, or are brought by, a compellingly particular concern.

You may come with a fractured relationship.

Draw near in faith, and take this holy sacrament, this summer grace, to your comfort.

You came as a still wounded city, not so much strong as getting stronger.

Draw near in faith, and take this holy sacrament, this summer grace, to your comfort.

You may come with amnesia about your salvation already wrought in Christy.

Draw near in faith, and take this holy sacrament, this summer grace, to your comfort.

You may come in the throes of a mortal struggle between body and soul, bigger barns and a farther shore, carelessness and care.

Draw near in faith, and take this holy sacrament, this summer grace, to your comfort.

August 6

Authority

Religions wrestle with authority, all the time, everywhere. The current change in Rome, and the ascendancy of Francis, our brother, whom we honor, encourage, and celebrate, recalls for us centuries of struggle over authority. To the Calvinist right, all authority is vested in Scripture. The Bible is the only full authority, 'sola scriptura,' an historic, in some ways tragic manner of interpretation of life and love. To the Catholic left, final authority is vested in the Bishop of Rome. Before we, or more specifically I, become too critical of these vested stations, we, or I, must also recognize that at some point, some one has to break the tie, make the decision, guide the church, be 'primus inter pares,' whether in the form of a breathing holy person or in the form of a spirited, breathing holy text. My own tradition attempts to have it all or both ways, not always with shining success. Methodism combines catholic tradition, reformation message, puritan discipline, Anglican liturgy, and pietist feeling. Methodism interprets Scripture through Tradition, and Tradition through Experience, and Experience through Reason. Such a separation of powers, by the way, has great advantages in a university setting, like this one.

August 7

Clucking of the Hens

Our mentor and friend Rev. Russell Clark, a Colgate and Boston University graduate, served a small church in Oriskany Falls , NY for many years. He dodged and weaved as appointments elsewhere were offered, to bigger churches and salaries. He stayed. He fell in love with a quieter life, natural beauty, the intrigue of pastoral ministry, the mystery of the cotidian. The Clark home sported a large twirling book shelf in the living room, filled with novels and histories and poetry.

His lay leader died after some years, to the regret and lasting hurt of the community. People are not replaceable. The widow, usually of regular perfect attendance in worship, stayed home, for some time. At last in Lent she appeared. Russell asked her how she found her way through the morass, the mess, the maze of grief, and got back home to church. "Well, it was not the scripture, though I love all the scripture. It was not the hymns, though I sing them to myself day by day. It was not your visits, though they were most gracious. It was not the family care and feeding or that of the neighbors. It was not my personal faith in the resurrection, though I do have faith. It was not even prayer, though I practice formal prayer, evening and morning, at meals and at bedtime.

"It was just this: the chickens had to be fed every morning. So I had to get up every morning. Once I was up, the rest of the day—and at last, over longer time, the week and month, including Sunday morning—seemed to fall in line. It was the chickens. The clucking of those hens. The clucking of those hens meant more to me, in healing, than all the hymns of Easter. The regularity of feeding them, early in the morning, restored me, over time. The clucking of those chickens meant more to me than al the hymns of Easter."

August 8

Driver

Speaking of speech, my former teacher Tom Driver recently remembered:

"I was twenty-five years old in 1950, a bachelor newly arrived in New York City to attend graduate school. I bought a single ticket and went alone to see director Harold Clurman's production of *The Member of the Wedding*, by the southern author Carson McCullers. With the rest of the audience, I was put under a spell by Ethel Waters singing "His Eye is on the Sparrow." There came another spell at the final curtain. The play's central focus has been the longing of a pre-adolescent girl to escape from her loneliness. Young Frankie Addams (played by Julie Harris) wants to be part of the forthcoming wedding of her older sister. This privilege is not readily granted, but In the last scene, the way becomes clear, and she exclaims with joy: "The wedding will be the we of me." Curtain.

"I will never forget what happened next. There was long applause and several curtain calls. And then we just sat there. No one wanted to leave. The strangers sitting next to me were just as slow to move as I was. After a few moments we hitherto strangers began to talk to each other. The theater had become the "we" of us. The performances on stage (and everything that Harold Clurman and the crew did to enable them) had performed something over and above the *dramatis personae* roles. They had created for that brief moment in time — less brief than most such occasions — a community of people whose lives otherwise did not cross. It is called theater magic, which means no one quite understands it and can never predict just when it will occur. But when it does, our joy is immense. It is similar to an experience of religious transcendence.

"In an age in which the term "public" has been denigrated in favor of "privatization," when housing is increasingly "gated "if it is affordable at all, when public education and health care and transportation and all manner of intrinsically social services are either neglected or attacked as impingements upon "liberty," when guns are thought to be necessary almost everywhere in the name of freedom and self defense — in such a time, the liminality engendered by ritual, theater, and religion, carries an important potential."

Our gospel then raises for us the question of authority.

August 9

Exemplum Docet

You can hear restorative words every week:

"Hello, my name is John, I am an alcoholic." Restoration.

"I enrolled to start my education again." Restoration.

"I just called, Dad, it's Easter. I know we haven't gotten along very well. But I wanted to be in touch." Restoration.

"She joined the Y last month. She had to start again toward health." Restoration.

"This meeting is about changing our company to save it." Restoration.

"We are here to try to prepare our church for the next century."

"I took communion because I wanted my life to change." Restoration.

"In the time I have I will share my heart with those I love."

"Hi Mom. I went to church today. It felt good to be there.: Restoration.

"I'm 45 years old, and I've never been able to commit to anything or anyone. With you, I am going to try." Restoration.

"For 30 years there has been a woman inside me waiting to come alive, to be. I have crying other people's tears. No more." Restoration.

"I made a mistake when I was 19. I have been beating myself up for it ever since. I guess I'll move on." Restoration.

"Today you made me happy. I haven't laughed like that since school. Where have I been all these years?" Restoration.

August 10

Fragrance

But what of our gospel? What form of authority does the Gospel of John prefer, select, elect, prize? Ah, glad you asked. No church in John, just a communal experience of Christ. No leadership in John, just the deeds and words of the risen, I mean crucified, I mean incarnate, I mean spirited One. No worries about ethics in John, no catalogue of virtues or vices, just a single command, to love. No hierarchy, patriarchy, oligarchy, ecclesiology in John. Just this: Spirit. Another Counselor. With you forever. A guide into all further truth. How is that going to work? Exactly. That is why we have the letters of John, uno dos y tres, because, clearly, it did not. The letters add in: leadership, orthodoxy, ethics, teaching, form, all. They wake from the Johannine dream. But what a dream! A spirited dream of spirit befitting any high Calvinist view of Scripture and any high Catholic view of clergy. A dream of Spirit, leading to truth, over time. A fullness of fragrance, spirit in life. As in Proust, "What matters is to transform common occurrence into art (NYRB, 3/13)."

You will recognize the story of the anointing at Bethany. Sort of . . .

It is like the familiar parable (sic): A man was going down from Jerusalem to Jericho and saw a man who had fallen among thieves, so he went and he asked his father for his inheritance. The father gave him seeds to plant, but most fell on rocky ground. He appealed to a judge, who would not listen, and then to a dishonest steward, who would listen, but who stole the rest of the seeds, and then planted them and they multiplied thirty, sixty and a hundredfold. But he left 99 of the fold and went after a lost sheep. On the way, he stumbled on a lost coin, and put it in his tunic. This will be like a mustard seed, he thought, which is small but grows a big plant. He went back to his father and said, I am not worthy to be a son, but make me a worker in a vineyard, and pay me as much as you pay those who started at dawn. Which of these do you think proved neighbor to the man who fell among thieves?

I know you remember that one.

That is, John has somehow combined a story which was also known to Mark, and used by Matthew, with a story from Luke, unused by Mark or Matthew, and has added his own special ingredients, Johannine special sauce if you will. Or maybe a redactor re-edited portions of this passage. For the record: John has added Judas as the stingy knee jerk liberal; John has added Judas' motive, not so liberal, of greed; John has not kept Mark's ethical admonition, "For you always have the poor with you, and whenever you want you can do good to them." (But Matthew also apparently erased that sentence, for who knows what reason.) John also has misplaced or erased the fine conclusion, which Mark writes and Matthew copies, *wherever the gospel is preached in the whole world, what she has done will be told in memory of her.* John also neglects to repeat that Jesus said of Mary's act that *she has done a beautiful thing for me.* In other words, what has been told in John was not so much in memory of her, though perhaps in the rest of the whole world it was so. Most delicately, Mark and John both use a rare adjective, rendered her by the English word 'pure,' which comes in the original from the same root as the word 'faith.' The gospels repeated an admonition from Deuteronomy 15, "the poor are ever present," not at all to discountenance care of the poor (so important to us, and rightly so), but to lift the fragrance, the wonder at the heart of the gospel, to the highest level. (Bultmann, perhaps rightly, hears here a reference to the full fragrance of *gnosis* spreading throughout the world.)

John, alone, fills the room with fragrance. That is his point, here. Incense, the sense of the holy, the mysterium tremendum, the idea of the holy, the presence. Resurrection precedes crucifixion in this reading. Crucifixion is merely a coming occasion for incarnation in this reading. Incarnation is a lasting fragrance in this reading, the fullness of fragrance.

August 11

Friends

My friend Rev. John Holt says of his work in ministry: "we are trying to help people discover their spiritual side so that they can make a difference for good in the world." That is what I am trying to do in and from this pulpit, trying to help people discover their spiritual side so that they can make a difference for good in the world.

Our poetic friend George Herbert wrote:

Love bade me welcome: yet my sould drew back, Guiltie of dust and sinne.

But quick-ey'd Love, observing me grow slack From my first entrance in,

Drew nearer to me, sweetly questioning, If I lack'd any thing.

A guest, I answer'd, worthy to be here : Love said, You shall be he.

I the unkinde, ungratefull? Ah my deare, I cannot look on thee.

Love took my hand, and smiling did reply, Who made the eyes but I?

Truth Lord, but I have marr'd them : let my shame Go where it doth deserve.

And know you not, sayes Love, who bore the blame? My deare, then I will serve.

You must sit down, sayes Love, and taste my meat. So I did sit and eat.

A friend, of some more years than I, brought her children to worship on Christmas eve. Afterward, she asked each one—6,8, and11 years old—what they most liked. Said 6,

"I especially liked the candle, except the wax dripped on my finger and that hurt." Said 8, "I liked communion and the way the choir music drew us forward, together, into it." Said 11, "I like the way you feel after you have been to church." 6,8,11—they came to themselves. And grandma did too.

Our neighbor Ron Dworkin wrote before his death: "I shall take these two—life's instrinsic meaning and nature's intrinsic beauty—as paradigms of a fully religious attitude to life. . .These are not convictions that one can isolate from the rest of one's life. They engage a whole personality. They permeate experience: they generate pride, remorse and thrill. Mystery is an important part of that thrill." *(NYTRB, 68, 3/13)*.

My friend Frank Halse has written of the presence, recently, a letter and seven poems. Frank is a double Terrier, CLA\STH, now in his late eighties, a widower, living alone in the great snows of the Tug Hill Plateau. He was the Protestant Chaplain at Syracuse University from 1965 to 1975. He drew a short straw and did marvelous ministry. He is a poet, and now his poetry is all about presence:

Dear Bob,

Joyce's death left me empty. Stunned even. That emptiness stayed for the 1st year. Then, two years ago, I began to be bumping into something that I finally put a name down. 'The Presence." My first experience with the mystic corners of our world.

I felt unprepared and awkward, but in time, I began to experience what can only be described as whisperings quietly in my ears.

August 12

Gospel

My Lord and My God
Resurrection Grace offers us gracious allegiance and resurrection reverence
Jesus Christ our Lord who commands allegiance
Jesus Christ our Lord who inspires reverence
A way to live and a way to love, doing and being
David sings so in the Psalms: my Strength and my Might
Peter preaches so in Acts: He is exalted as Leader and Savior
John teaches so in the Apocalypse: Alpha and Omega
Strength and Might!
Leader and Savior!
Alpha and Omega!
Lord and God!
Have we received Him this Easter with song, and word, and lesson, and love?
Lord and God.

The Gospel of John is so different: four resurrection stories, the figure of Thomas, Thomas doubting faith, his seeing that is believing and believing that is seeing, his friendship with the estranged, he (alone) gets the meaning of the story right.

To live in resurrection grace is to find, to be found, by the true Lord and the real God, to accept allegiance and reverence.

August 13

I Expect Great Things

45 years ago, Martin King was killed. But he transformed our land. His words transformed our rhetoric. His marches changed our culture. His leadership fashioned a new middle class. His hope kindled our hope. His courage inspired our own. 45 years ago. I love a story he told many times about power, redeeming power. So hidden we miss it, in borrowed upper room, in a tragic crucifixion, in a temporary tomb, in a woman's report of resurrection, in little hands, scrubbing, scrubbing, scrubbing to finish the new creation . . .

The gnarled hands—the cross, Good Friday. The expectation—the resurrection, Easter. (No matter who you are today, somebody helped you to get there. It may have been an ordinary person, doing an ordinary job in an extraordinary way.) Here is restoration from your neighborhood:

> There is a magnificent lady, with all the beauty of blackness and black culture, by the name of Marion Anderson that you've heard about and read about and some of you have seen. She started out as a little girl singing in the choir of the Union Baptist Church in Philadelphia, Pennsylvania. And then came that glad day when she made it. And she stood in Carnegie Hall with the Philharmonic Orchestra in the background in New York, singing with the beauty that is matchless. Then she came to the end of the concert, singing Ave Maria as nobody else can sing it. And they called her back and back and back, and she finally ended by singing, "Nobody Knows the Trouble I've Seen." And her mother was sitting out in the audience, and she started crying; tears were flowing down her cheeks. And the person next to her said, "Mrs Anderson, Why are you crying? Your daughter is scoring tonight. The critics tomorrow will be lavishing their praise on her. Why are you crying?"
>
> And Mrs. Anderson looked over with tears still flowing and said, "I'm not crying because I'm sad, I'm crying for joy." She went on to say, "You may not remember, you wouldn't know. But I remember when Marian was growing up, and I was working in a kitchen till my hands were all but parched, my eyebrows all but scalded. I was working there to make it possible for my daughter to get an education. And I remember Marian came to see me and said, 'Mother, I don't want to see you having to work like this.' And I looked down and said, 'Honey, I don't mind it. I'm doing it for you and I expect great things of you.'"
>
> And finally one day somebody asked Marian Anderson in later years, "Miss Anderson, what has the been the happiest moment of your life? Was it that moment in Carnegie Hall in New York?" She said, "No, that wasn't it." "Was it that moment you stood before the Kings and Queens of Europe?" "No, that wasn't it." " Well, Miss Anderson, was it the moment Sibelius of Finland declared that his roof was too low for such a voice?" "No, that wasn't it." "Miss Anderson, was it the moment that Toscanini said that a voice like your comes only once in a century?" "No, that wasn't it." "What was it then, Miss Anderson." And she

looked up and said quietly, "The happiest moment in my life was the moment I could say, 'Mother, you can stop working now.'"[1]

Marian Anderson realized that she was where she was because somebody helped her to get there. That's restoration. In the mother's gnarled hands—the cross. In the mother's voiced and great expectations—the resurrection.

August 14

1. Martin Luther King, "A Knock at Midnight."

John

One man asked another, "Tell me, in just one word, how is your life?"

His friend replied, slowly, "In one word? In one word, my life is, well . . . good."

Sensing something, the man asked again, "Then tell me, in just two words, how is your life?"

His friend replied, slowly, "My life, in two words? In two words, my life is, well . . . not good."

Both the brevity of life and the strange estrangements of our experience in life, place us, if we are honest, come Sunday, somewhere between the first and second replies, between good and not good.

We know the thrill of victory and the agony of betrayal. We know the joy of birth and the pain of death. We know the exuberance of growth and the hurt of departure.

The Gospel of John ended last week, with its concluding sentence, 'These things are written that you may believe that Jesus in the Christ, the Son of God, and that believing you may have life in his name. Jesus: Lord and God, doorway both to allegiance and to reverence. Jesus: word incarnate, good shepherd, feeder of thousands, alchemist of water and wine, healer of the blind, raiser of the dead, doorway to grace, freedom, love, spirit, community, and friendship. Only believe, only believe. Live in tune with the universe.

Startling then, today's lesson, added twenty years after the Gospel conclusion. A simple meal, of 153 fish, breakfast with Jesus. Different language and imagery here. A different, now heroic role, for the robbing and disrobing Peter, here. A different voice for the beloved disciple here. A different reflection on death and life here. A different prediction of Peter's martyrdom here. What is the meaning of this strange breakfast?

Just this: for all the grace, freedom and love, all the spirit, community and friendship rightly trumpeted in the Fourth Gospel, people are still people. This chapter is about fishing and farming, about catching and tending, about boats and fields, fishermen and shepherds. In church language, that is, 21 is about evangelism and pastoral care.

You are leading a Christian life, you are committed to the way of discipleship, the path of love. Then, and so, you will need to receive and give invitation and comfort.

The deep resonance of Handel's Messiah, its third part sung gloriously today, undergirds our good and not so good life with triumph, with the triumphant song, with the triumphant promise, with the triumphant promise of redemption, heaven, hope, healing, wholeness, God. In a word, today, triumph.

August 15

Level

Our Scripture, today in particular and every day in general, promises the presence of the spirit of truth, loose in the universe. The potential for harm is, like death itself, ever present. The potential for living grace, like life itself, is ever present. The psalmist sings of a living grace. Lydia embraced such a living grace. John, ever unique, names this grace with a new name, the *paraclete,* the counselor, the advocate, the holy spirit, who abides in the experience of peace.

For all the familiarity of these lines from John 14, the actual meaning, in history and theology, is darkly or obscurely understood. In particular the novel figure of the paraclete, related in some manner to the holy spirit, to this day is a source of wonder and perplexity for those who study these passages. We are standing on a high precipice, ice beneath our feet, wind swirling about our temples, as we receive the promise of the counselor. The living grace of the living God we know in living. Our scripture assumes that we shall be in need of some counseling, some advocacy, some aid. We are.

Today such sustenance is given in a living grace, a lively grace that teaches and reminds. Let me show you. Let me remind you. We need to learn and remember, though, the clear statement here. You will be taught, reminded. This is you plural, friends. You all. The gift of the living grace is made to the gathering, the community, the whole. Not to you but to YOU. These things I have spoken to you (plural). While I am still with you (plural). The spirit sent will teach you (plural). Reminding of all that I have said to you (plural). Peace I leave with you (plural). My peace I give to YOU (plural). Not as the world gives do I give to you (plural).

Living grace makes of us a community by making of us an addressable community, speaking to us together: *speaking us together.* We may deconstruct the Scripture, but Scripture reconstructs US. The gospel, spoken and heard, reshapes us into a living grace. Reclothes us in our rightful minds. . . . That is, in our situation, our *shared* situation, we are promised something, but the promise is to the plural you. You, You All, All You All. Our way forward, that is, on the strength of this Gospel, lies in forms of partnership—meaning is found in community, belonging is found in fellowship, empowerment is found in friendship. Each one's death diminishes me for I am a part of humankind. The dark mystery of the Counselor remains, but there is nothing unclear about the spirit's attention—focused on the common, the commonwealth, the common good.

The far too familiar lines of this strange moonscape of a passage come to a crashing conclusion. "Let not your hearts be troubled." Heart-S. We are, at heart, gifts of one another to one another, hearts whose heartbeats are felt by one another, souls whose soul is born in soulful connection to one another, meant to live for one another.

On television sometimes I hear some commentator say, 'Let not your heart by troubled.' I want to write in the S at the end. It changes everything. Heart-S.

Living grace is the grace to live together, which takes wisdom, power and goodness. This is why, may I gently say, connecting with a community of faith is so primary, so irreplaceably important. We worship *together* come Sunday. Together we search for wisdom, power, goodness.

Wisdom forms design, power allows action, goodness does good. Research, policy, practice. Teaching, deaning, pastoring. Preaching is over all. Eucharist is over all. Grace is over all.

Let us receive some wisdom about anger. Our anger is real, and needs to be felt, seen, heard, understood and processed as real. I refer you to the sermon of April 21. You will not get away from the marathon bombing without facing your anger, your hatred, even, for those who did this. Be angry, the Bible says, but let not the sun go down on your anger. Hate what is evil, the Bible says, but overcome evil with good. We need to acknowledge that anger, even confess it, even speak it, so that we do not repress it. Beware, my friend, beware the return of the repressed. You have reason to be angry. Oklahoma, Nineleven, Columbine, Sandy Hook, Virginia Tech, Boston. But you also have resources with which to deal with it.

Let us receive some power regarding hatred. Romans 12: 9 I get. . .It is the later verse, 20, 'feed your enemy . . . and so pour burning coals on him' that is harder to interpret. We may in part finally understand, at a gut level, Paul's admonition. Is there any other way to channel the anger and honest hatred of evil that we feel? What a wise leverage, a Syracusan, a Archemedian leverage of anger for good, of hatred for love. Let us together try it. We have the possibility of regeneration right here, a living grace. Shmuel Eisenstadt distinguishes irreversible collapse from "collapse with a possibility of regeneration or renewal" (eg UMC) . . . "ability to reflect on themselves . . . reference to shared, lofty visions . . . allows reshaping . . . allows continuity . . . e.g. Roman Empire and Han Dynasty." This is why, may I gently say, connecting with a community of faith is so primary, so irreplaceably important. We worship *together* come Sunday.

Let us receive some goodness for the journey.

One wrote: "We just wanted to thank you all for your kindness and hospitality. On Marathon Monday, when our race came to an end at Mile 25, we were so disoriented about what was going on. Without any cell phones or money, we wandered the streets a while confused about what to do and worried about our loved ones at the finish line. We met wonderful people that day,. Some gave us money to get a taxi, but there were none to be found, others told us to go to the chapel and walked us to your doorsteps. Everyone at the Chapel was so nice and helpful, bringing us food, hot tea, and letting us use your phones. We felt safe! You helped us to reunite with our families. Thank God that they were OK and thank God for all the wonderful and kind people who we met that day at Marsh Chapel. With love . . ."

Another wrote: "I want to express my gratitude and that of my entire family for the comfort and care provided to us on 4/15. We sought refuge and we received that and more. . .Your staff was wonderful and their comfort was most appreciated. It is hard to understand how someone can cause so much pain. The benefit of being reminded in tangible ways of the goodness and kindness of others helps to create a sense of balance—thank you for that. Sincerely . . ."

It will take the wisdom, power and goodness of another generation to design, build and desire a better world. Here is our prayer for them, the class of '13, but it is truly a prayer for us all.

August 16

Life

In a word, triumph. In two words, evangelism and pastoral care, work and structure, laity and clergy, world and church.

Breakfast is a simple meal. The worst hour of the day, the worst food of the day, the worst attitude of the day, everything and everyone more human than not. Carried by triumph, we re-enter the world of invitation and compassion, the world of the preacher and the pastor. Every week, you are encouraged to make one invitation to another about what you find lastingly good. *Come to worship with me.* Every week, you are encouraged to offer one compassionate word to another from the source of lasting compassion. *I will pray for you.*

Public worship places us in the necessary presence of others who are not our own kith, kin and kindred. With the child behind us, the student beside us, the professor ahead of us, the widow across from us, we worship God. We perceive again the utter variety and actual need of others. It is a cautionary move against the prevailing winds about us, including tornadoes, including dehumanizing techno-communication and distance drone aerial bombardment. A woman will receive that email. I might have seen her, or her kith, kin and kindred, in church. A child will be harmed by that bomb. I might have seen his kith, kin and kindred, in church. Public worship places us in the necessary presence of others who are not our own kith, kin and kindred. So crucial, saving, significant, then the simple invitation: join me for worship.

Compassionate pastoral care, personal kindness, a willingness to listen—feed, tend, sheep to sheep—connects us to the deeper dimensions, those for which life is given. Fifty years ago M L King sat writing in a prison cell in Birmingham Alabama. He wrote the famous Letter, which bears your re-reading this afternoon, addressed to pastors, fellow clergy, who could not or did not or would not hear: "when you suddenly find your tongue twisted and your speech stammering as you seek to explain to your six year old daughter why she can't go to the public amusement park that has just been advertised on television, and see tears welling up in her eyes when she is told that Funtown is closed to colored children, and see ominous clouds of inferiority beginning to form in her little mental sky, and see her beginning to distort her personality by developing an unconscious bitterness." While most of us will not regularly write such a momentous letter, in our pastoral that is personal correspondence, we will write. You know of another's inattention, another's pain. You can sit down, put pen to paper, and select some caring words—sorry, condolence, hope, help, prayer. You can imagine another opening the mailbox, holding the letter, seeing the penmanship, removing the page, reading the card. Feed my lambs. Tend my sheep. Feed my sheep.

It is not I believe that the Fourth Gospel diminishes or discounts invitation and compassion, evangelism and pastoral care, laity and clergy. It is just that the writer(s) had bigger fish to fry and sheep to tend of another fold. So along came—someone—who wrote 21 for us, to remind us. In a word—good. In two words—not good. Your life in Christ requires invitation and compassion, beginning again every day at breakfast.

Triumph, triumphant joy, triumphant promise comes your way. Put them to work this week.

I know that my Redeemer lives.

(S) Behold I tell you a mystery.

The trumpet shall sound and the dead shall be raised.

(S) Death is swallowed up in victory.

But thanks be to God who gives us the victory.

(S) If God is for us who is against us? *If God is for us, who is against us?*

Blessing and honor and glory and power be unto him.

August 17

Major Malady

Sometimes we arrive in worship with a personal, compelling need. We find our familiar pew. We turn at the appointed hour to the radio frequency. We enter a spirit of prayer. Sometimes we bring, or are brought by, a compellingly particular concern.

In fact, on many occasions of return to worship, after a hiatus, or an absence, or a distance, we come trying to sort something out. We are, after all, "persons becoming persons" as Carlyle Marney used to say, and we'll say. We are in the process of becoming who we are, bit by bit, trouble by trouble, hurt by hurt, scrape by scrape. The more irregular rhythms of the summer, with its heat spots and rain storms and family visitors and office coverages, can sometimes become a kind of summer grace, allowing us to recollect, to reckon with our souls, to seek a summer grace in Word and Table, preaching and sacrament.

Sometimes the malady is major. Our dearest friendship can come in danger, if we do not keep our friendships in good repair. You may come to work to discover that an office mate, a trusted friend, whose friendship you may have taken for granted, has felt unappreciated, and so has gone on to greener pastures, now that there are a few more jobs around from which to choose—not enough, just a few more. Or a regular summer picnic may reveal an absence, someone whose presence you expected, and missed. You may come some Sunday, having realized on Saturday night that your marriage, seemingly so solid, has revealed a human but painful fracture. A most painful weight to bear, for sure. Our reading from Hosea, the loveliest passage in the Hebrew Scripture, comes from a book in the Bible written straight of the pain of infidelity. It can be a ready reassurance to hear that for a long time, and in the heart of sacred writing, there is a shared experience, for yours, the deep recognition of deep hurt. Hosea even makes of his own pain a way to understand the gracious, lasting, love of God—"my compassion grows warm and tender." In the cup and bread today, for you, there is a summer grace, a personal honesty about pain but also a personal witness to endurance. You can get through this. "I am the Holy One in your midst, and I will not come to destroy."

August 18

Martin Luther King

This month, later this month, we shall remember Martin Luther King's great sermon from 50 years ago. August 28, 1963, a sweltering day in the nation's capital. It was indeed a soul, a soulful moment. Some of you listening, some perhaps present, were there. Most have heard King's words, more than once. His was a life "rich toward God." How? How so? What shall we recall fifty years hence? In its remembrance, this month, will our souls come alive that we might be rich toward God? Remember . . .

First, that King was a preacher. He was a preacher first and last. His words, rhetoric, angle of vision were formed in the life of the Christian church, the black church, the pulpit. Taylor Branch tells of an intense Sunday afternoon meeting, King and colleagues, when a knock came at the door. There, an older woman, in Sunday clothes, carrying a basket. She came with something to eat—chicken and biscuits I believe. And they stopped, the planning stopped, the work stopped. She had brought something for the preacher. It was a summer grace to receive it, as is our communion. Today. King was not first an academic, an organizer, a teacher, a prophet, a social leader. He was a preacher. May that be for those of you considering such a calling—then higher in status and lower in stress, now lower in status and higher in stress—a hard vocation, that is, one worth doing—leave the easier things for others, may that be an encouragement to you of what such a calling can mean. Marsh Chapel has every reason to commend and recommend King as a preacher. Further, the series this summer, the primary preachers from the primary northern Methodist pulpits, is meant as a sign for the future when the collapse of general agencies, general conferences, general superintendencies, and generalized discipline will give way, as it is already doing, to real, vocal, preached, pulpit leadership, like that represented in Foundry Church, Washington DC, Christ Church, NYC, Asbury First, Rochester, and Marsh Chapel, Boston.

Second, King was a personalist. That is, he was formed in the philosophical theology of Boston University, Boston personalism. Borden Parker Bowne, Edgar Brightman—the quintessential, even revelatory uniqueness of the human personality as a clue to the divine. Now in our more naturalist age, personalism is less known, less favored. But you can hear it in King when, in Letter from Birmingham Jail, he talks about the clouds and dimness he sees in his little daughters' eyes as they are told that they are not welcome in Funtown, an amusement park. We are all persons becoming persons. The freshmen who come here in a few weeks were all of eleven years old seven years ago when we began our Marsh Chapel work. They are persons, in whose personalities there is a reflection, a revelation of the divine. But they are far from formed, as are we all. Mature in body, perhaps, but not yet in soul. Sent with such high hopes—theirs, their parents,' their schools,' their siblings.' King battled a vast cultural carelessness because of the effect on personality such carelessness has.

Third, King worked at a profound depth. Notice in his sermon that he speaks of dream, not of "a really good idea." That is the sermonic difference between the right word and the almost word, between truth and falsehood, death and life, inspiration and desperation. But there is something for us today, this summer, much harder and truer to his profundity.

King was able to speak in a way that gathered a true solidarity to his cause, the cause of civil rights, racial justice, not later, but now. You hear it and recall it in phrases, "not by the color of skin but by the content of character." His voice brought inspiration and solidarity to a movement. But that was not all. He also somehow had the magic and mysterious spirited rhetoric to evoke more than solidarity, to evoke community. That is, he was able to gather under the wings of his words those, even those, who may not at the moment have agreed with him. Not just solidarity to a cause. But hope, a dream of a beloved community, too. Now that is genius. You hear it in phrases. 'That on the red hills of Georgia the sons of former slaves and the sons of former slave holders will sit down at the table of brotherhood.' Not just solidarity for those who now agree, but the hope of community we those who are not yet with us. I wish I could find the tongue in our time, facing our own issue of humanity and justice, that of the full humanity of gay people, to do the same. Maybe one day that will come . . .

August 19

Class

When you next go to class, make a rough count of the number of fellow students who are sitting behind the screens of lap top computers. We will not even speculate about what they see there. Ask yourself a real, sturdy question: can you really double task or multi task? Studies say otherwise, but you may be the exception, you multi talented multi tasker, you. But ask yourself what is going on when you do so. And, that done, start to probe down a little bit deeper. Ask yourself why. You have 529, 600 minutes a year. Does this give you a million, or does it break down to half the original? Is there such a thing as the integrity of a moment? In class, even? In such a class, Socrates taught Plato the art of the dialogue. In such a class, Jesus taught in the temple, and on the mountain, and on the plain, and in a borrowed upper room. In such a class, the author of the Didache gave an outline of faith. In such a class, Bernard of Clairvaux interpreted the Song of Songs. In such a class, Maimonides guided the perplexed. In such a class, John Calvin, who saw the church as the school of Christ, taught the Scriptures. In such a class, endless numbers of poor Methodists fleeing from the wrath to come found friendship, intimacy, understanding, and faith, just by conferring with one another, without benefit of clergy. In such a class, John Adams learned the classics. In such a class, Emerson taught Thoreau. In such a class, Robert L Calhoun lectured with excellence but without notes on the history of theology. In such a class, Howard Zinn enthused a generation of historians. In such a class, today, Boston University poets Roseanna Warren, Robert Pinsky, Peter Hawkins, and Christopher Riggs handle the magic and mystery of language. In one such class this week, at Boston University, you may, just may, have a revelation, that moment, that click, that insight, that new vision.

August 20

Patriots' Day

Dear Friends,

Grace to you and peace. I bring you greetings from the leadership and community of Marsh Chapel, and three brief words in the wake of yesterday's tragic events.

First, our thanks to you for your concern about us here, and members of the community. Our annual brunch was joyfully and fully attended, with words from Lincoln, bagels and quiche, some Longfellow poetry, and the singing of "My Country 'Tis of Thee." Then, the afternoon. Several of our friends and families were close to the finish line near 3pm, but all have emerged (physically) unharmed. Chapel staff provided hospitality (rest, refreshment, prayer, and counsel) to 120 or so who came in later Monday afternoon. At this writing, we know of one BU student hurt, who is in now in stable condition. We appreciate your contacts, your prayers, and your thoughts. Our brunch and marathon watch will be held, with energy, again on Patriots' Day next year.

Second, we encourage you to continue in ways many have already begun, to find effective modes of help for those well beyond our community who have been hurt, one way or another. A card, a note, a check, a gift, a prayer—we all have things we can do to lean forward and help those harmed. One of our students is active in bringing a blood bank to campus in the next few days. It is healthy and it is helpful, in many directions, to find one thing or two things creatively to do, to bring some good to bear in the face of tragic violence.

Third, and most significantly, we will want to live with faith and courage in the days ahead. The radiance of Easter is still with us, shadowed as it is by Monday's unspeakable violence. Thankfully, from Monday itself, we have examples of people modeling dimensions of healthy spirituality. I will only write here of the runners and the race (a metaphor not unknown to the biblical mind by the way—Psalm 19, 1 Cor 9, Hebrews 12). I picture all the runners practicing months and weeks. I see the lacing of the running shoes. I hear the starting whistle and the throng surging forward. We saw at Kenmore, the brightly attired elderly man, the young guy with blue hair, the student running in a tuxedo, the troop from a nearby college ROTC program, the woman running—as so many—in memory, the folks in wheel chairs, the straining forward, by mile 25, of striving, disciplined energy. They all are models for us of running the race and finishing the course. We can lace up and run, too, in our own ways. God's goodness, love and presence beckon us onward.

At 5:30pm tonight (Tuesday, 4/16/13), the university community will gather on Marsh Plaza for a vigil to remember and honor those hurt and killed on Patriots' Day. At 5:30pm tomorrow (Wednesday, 4/17/13) our community will gather for a formal service of ordered worship, in honor and memory, in the Marsh Chapel nave. And of course we will be together for worship on Sunday (4/21/13) at 11am. Please join us for one or more of these services.

August 21

Prone Float

We grew up along the shores of fresh water lakes, and along the shoreline of the faith once delivered to the saints.

By 1960, in the algae covered, safely shallow, sand bottomed Oneida Lake, playing with no certain direction, and on a sun-dappled August afternoon, I felt my back feet float up, and I paddled along without touching the sand. I told my parents, both then young parents, that I could float. "See," I showed them. We were singing in the car ride home, *amazing grace how sweet the sound that saved a wretch like me.*

By 1968 we were sent off to the woods, with a small scouting troop to a small, now sold, camp ground, along Eaton Brook reservoir. Having learned the strokes, we were sent to swim a mile under the shade of maples and still living elms on the nearby shore. At night we learned the constellations. Our leader sang at night, to himself, and explained later that he was thinking of a winter campout the year before, *O God our help in ages past, our hope for years to come, our shelter from the stormy blast, and our eternal home.* A small time home builder who volunteered with the scouts turned over in his memory and conversation words from a church hymn.

By 1973, unwilling to borrow for an education, debt being a fearful form of sin in our home, I hunted for a job, with little skill to barter, except a love of swimming. I became a lifeguard along the shining big sea water of Owasco Lake. There we kept people from drowning, taught the J stroke and the backstroke, and waterskied for miles at dusk. *It only takes a spark.* We sang that. *Blessed are the poor in spirit, for theirs is the kingdom of heaven.* We read that. *Tireless guardian on our way, thou hast kept us well this day.* We prayed that.

By 1975, with some boating experience, I was invited by a lawyer with a bad leg to help him sail on Cazenovia Lake. Mainsail, Jib, Spinaker, come around, stem, stern, port, starboard, fore, aft, mast, keel. A practical mariner's vocabulary for an ancient mariner's craft. Once back on shore, at the somehow different and somewhat intimidating Yacht Club pool, with people who looked and sounded and acted slightly different from the simpler friends of my parents and my own, I went alone to swim. I had never mastered the butterfly, rhythmic motion not being my strong suit. Until that late afternoon, when the arms went down far enough, and the feet up high enough and the stroke became a natural swaying through the crisp clear water. *Faith comes by hearing. How shall they hear without a preacher. What is your best response to God? The heavens are telling the glory of God.*

By 1988 our three children were paddling around in Bradley Brook, in front of a cottage that needed tender loving care. They learned the strokes, there. They learned to boat, there. They learned to ski, and well, there. They brought their boyfriends, their girlfriends, their friends there. We sang around the fire at night. *Every time I feel the spirit moving in my heart I will pray. Do Lord remember me. This little light of mine, I'm gonna let it shine.*

By 2012 we had a five year old granddaughter. One afternoon, playing with no certain direction, and on sun dappled August afternoon, jumping toward me, she felt her back feet float up, and paddled along without touching the bottom. SheI told her parents, her young parents, that she could float. "See," she showed them. They were singing in the car ride home, *amazing grace how sweet the sound that saved a wretch like me. I once was lost but now am found, was blind but now I see.*

August 22

Reverence

You will finally worship somewhere, somehow. The human being is irretrievably religious—not such good news in the face of pride, sloth, falsehood, superstition, hypocrisy, and idolatry.

Nonchalance about non attendance in public, ordered worship expands the circles of nonchalance about others, about different others, about the hurts of different others, about the willingness to neglect the hurts of different others, about the capacity to harm different others. There is a straight line from absence in church to drone warfare.

If on Easter Sunday you saw and heard only your own kith, kindred and kind, be warned. Brunch with your wife's family, dinner with your parents, a nap in the Easter afternoon. Lack of physical engagement with the physical presence of others, in reverence, narrows the personal imagination about what life is for others.

People all people belong to one another.

We may take five days of prayer. One in a prison. One in a hospital. One in a school. One in a psych unit. One on a farm (R Shankar).

That is John's difference, ironically, universality. Our puny, trumped up differences of size, gender, race, religion, color, orientation, age, creed, tongue, waist and shirt measure—what we see—falls away before what we believe, in love. Love is God. We are loved, so we may love.

We think this week about Martin Luther King and the Letter from Birmingham Jail.

Some of us are habitual. Some of us are spiritual.

Some of us are habitual: morning prayer, daily reading, Sunday worship, tithing, gathering, all. But are we spiritually habitual?

Some of us are spiritual: present, alive, free, gracious, loving, open, all. But are we habitually spiritual?

Let those of us who are habitual, be spiritually so. May we have the power not only the form of faith.

Let those of us who are spiritual, be habitually so. May we have the form not only the power of faith.

Who is your Lord? Who commands your allegiance?

Who is your God? Who inspires your reverence?

Coda

Be happy
Stay happy
Be confident
Have fun
Create fun

Enjoy
Count it all joy
Shine
Live in Love
You so will benefit others

August 23

Robinson on Lent

Come Lent, here at Marsh Chapel, we converse each year with our sibling Christians out of the Calvinist tradition. We grow and learn, from and with, the slight differences, in sibling traditions, wherein we do not always agree, but agree to disagree agreeably. Our interlocutor this year, 2013, is Marilynn Robinson—essayist, novelist, Calvinist. Her love of Scripture, her sense of the eternal, her rendering of John Calvin, her prophetic defense of wonder in our time, her unwillingness to buy the cheap goods of a culture that languishes in the doldrums of a pervasive malaise, her celebration of quiet life, pastoral ministry, providential grace, and the deeps of love: all these human gifts we gratefully receive from her this year. Especially her sense of the extraordinary in the ordinary, health in the clucking of hens, helps us this year.[2]

On Scripture: "One Easter I went with my grandfather to a small Presbyterian church in northern Idaho where I heard a sermon on the discrepancies in the gospel accounts of the resurrection. . . . I was a young child . . . yet I remember that sermon. . .I can imagine myself that primal Easter, restive at my grandfather's elbow, pushing my nickels and dimes of collection money into the tips of my gloves . . . memorably forbidden to remove my hat. . . . It seems to me I felt God as a presence before I had a name for him . . . I was aware to the point of alarm of a vast energy of intention all around me . . . and I thought everyone else must also be aware of it . . . Only in church did I hear experience like mine acknowledged, in all those strange narratives, read and expounded . . . Amen (the preacher) said, having blessed my life with a lovely thing to ponder" (227).

On Speech: "What should we call the presiding intelligence that orchestrates the decision to speak as a moment requires? What governs the inflections that make any utterance unmistakably the words of one speaker in this whole language-saturated world?" (120).

On Sin: "It took, for instance, three decades of the most brilliant and persistent campaign of preachment and information to establish, in the land of liberty, the idea that slavery was intolerable" (249).

On Salvation: "[Calvin's] theology is compelled and enthralled by an overwhelming awareness of the grandeur of God . . . his sense of things is so overwhelmingly visual and cerebral, that the other senses do not interest him . . . heaven's essence for him is that it is inconceivable in the world's terms, another order of experience" (221).

On Service: "We should maintain an appropriate humility in the face of what we think we know . . . encourage an imagination of humankind large enough to acknowledge some small fragment of the mystery we are. . . . The Judeo Christian ethic of charity derives from the assertion that human beings are made in the image of God, that is, that reverence is owed to human beings simply as such. . . . Our civilization believed for a long time in God and the soul and sin and salvation, assuming, whatever else, that meaning had a larger frame and context than this life in this world" (84) . . . I do not think it is nostalgia to suggest that it would be well to reestablish the setting apart of time traditionally devoted to religious

---

2. Marilynne Robinson, *When I Was A Child I Read Books* (New York: Farrar, Straus, Giroux, 2012).

observance" (99) . . . Science cannot serve in the place of religion because it cannot generate an ethics or a mortality" (71).

August 24

Shared Trouble

Sometimes the trouble is a shared trouble, a time of trouble, a time in trouble. The poets often will warn us, even a decade in advance. So TS Eliot wrote The Wasteland in 1922, and envisioned 1932 and 1942. We disregard our poets to our peril. So summer can be a good time to remember them, and to memorize the biblical poetry of the psalms. In Robert Raines' family the children were prized with a soda when they had memorized a psalm. Is that bribery or is that good parenting? Or both? When we realize that at some deep level, the moorings are loosened in our community or culture, then we may come to church a little dazed, a little unbalanced, not quite sure why. Thirsty, in a way, hungry, in another way. I have been preaching and teaching through the summer, and regularly people will ask about Boston. How are you? How are things there? They are not referring—usually—to Whitey Bulger, or even—usually—to the Red Sox. One woman from the Midwest was wearing a shirt that said "Boston Strong." As a guest preacher I usually say something general in response, using a collected vocabulary—'pretty well . . . good people . . . very resilient . . . courageous women and men . . . yes, Boston Strong.' But as a pastor I also have other thoughts, not so easily expressed in a less familiar setting. Yes, strong. But we also have our forms of wandering, as the psalmist puts it. We also know about the soul fainting, as the psalmist puts it. A photo of an innocent middle aged woman, now legless, is all it takes, at least for me, to recognize the truth of the Scripture and its repeated emphasis on cries in trouble. Not only sorrow, but anger, not only grief, but very human rage will bring us to the desert. It takes time, real time, and a long time, to process trauma, and when you least expect it, the desert can envelope you. That may bring you to listen to a sermon, or attend a church, to hunt out again the lasting love of God. If nothing, no one else: "Give thanks to the Lord, for he is good, for his steadfast love endures for ever." Boston Strong? Maybe Boston Getting Stronger?

August 25

Situation

Come with me for a moment, if you will, and by the mind's eye, by the imagination, as we walk a little bit across our beloved city.

We can leave Marsh Chapel and head to the left, due east. The trees and flowers are fragrant and in bloom. We will saunter and wander down the Commonwealth Mall, past the statues and benches and people enjoying a free Sunday. At Dartmouth we will turn right, due south. Now you will want to pause at Copley Square. Take a moment with me to stop by the office of our sister congregation at Trinity Church. We will leave a calling card and say a prayerful word of greeting. Take a moment with me to stop by the office of our brother congregation at Old South church. We will leave a calling card and say a prayerful word of greeting. Take a moment with me to read the cards and notes, see the flowers and gifts, in the people's memorial, there, across from the library. Remembrance, thanksgiving, presence—you feel them all, these emotions of living grace, these sacramental emotions of living grace. I want to give us a moment to pause here. By the living grace of God we can face grief with grace, hatred with honesty, and death with dignity. There is a spirit of truth loose in the universe, to guide us on our walk this morning. Many of us have already, personally or individually, made this same hike, but we have done so together, until now, and now we do so, together, by the mind's eye, by the imagination. There are some things we need to face, again. Here.

Now we will head back to Marsh Plaza, walking west on Boylston. These blocks have become brick to brick familiar to the whole globe, not just to those of us in the 'hub.' It is important for us to take this walk, and it is important for us to take this walk together. You may want to look at some running shoes in Marathon Sports. Or if you like the gracious narthex of the Lennox Hotel, we could rest there a moment. We will stand for a moment in front of the Forum Restaurant, and there, look for a moment, at another makeshift memorial. By the living grace of God we can together make our way into the past, in memory, and into the future, in imagination. We see ourselves being filmed from the camera atop Lord and Taylor. We greet a friend who is seated in a nearby restaurant. The eyes film over, somehow. But we are walking together, and we can walk on. You can walk fast, or, like me, walk slowly. It is after all your own imagination. Take things at your own pace. Coming back, up Boylston, across Hereford, left on Commonwealth, and on to the Chapel, there are some things we need to face, again. Here.

Two young men of limited abilities, armed with the Internet, $100, and some kitchen utensils, brought the fifth largest metropolitan region in the country to a many day standstill. Coffin: God gives us minimum protection and maximum support. In our neighborhood. Loss of life and limb, of property and security. Here. Present together to receive the living grace of God in Eucharist, present together across the airwaves to receive the living grace of God in the spoken word, we face together all the potentials of an open future and the extent of human freedom. This is our shared situation. We need to level with each other about this.

August 26

The Prairie

Robinson is a contemporary novelist and essayist, and a Calvinist, perhaps the strongest living American exponent of Calvinism. Her depiction of the Rev. John Ames, in the novels *Gilead* and *Home*, has been deeply meaningful to many of us. Her writing celebrates the privilege, terror and joy of pastoral ministry. Her writing celebrates the goodness of village life. Her writing celebrates providential grace. Her writing celebrates the power of story, of parable. Her writing celebrates the beauty of the world around us. Listen to her voice in that of the Rev. John Ames, depicting dawn in Iowa:

> I love the prairie! So often I have seen the dawn come and the light flood over the land and everything turn radiant at once, that word 'good' so profoundly affirmed in my soul that I am amazed I should be allowed to witness such a thing. There may have been a more wonderful first moment 'when the morning stars sang together and all the sons of God shouted for joy,' but for all I know to the contrary, they still do sing and shout, and they certainly might well. Here on the prairie there is nothing to distract attention from the evening and the morning, nothing on the horizon to abbreviate or to delay. Mountains would seem an impertinence from that point of view.[1]

August 27

---

1. Marilynne Robinson, *Gilead* (New York: Farrar, Straus, and Giroux, 2004), 246.

The Women

We might ponder especially this Easter the women in Luke 24, the prototypes of faithful people in the church, your own progenitors: sent on a thankless mission. . .heading for the stench of death . . . facing a corrupted corpse and a corrupted hope. . .dreading the visual and spiritual encounter . . . worried too about the practicalities (spices, cloths, stone) . . . together, at least, in their dread and sorrow, together . . . leave the messy things to the women . . . carrying with them, at daybreak, the memory of Passover loss . . . perhaps hoping for one last earthly moment of connection with One who brought meaning, belonging, and empowerment. . . .Jewish women of the first century, not exactly the Lords of creation . . . three for whom the ministry of Jesus was in ruins, consigned to failure . . . it is a tomb after all to which they march, conscripted into the army of the least, last, and lost.

"I dread the sight of him, torn and bloody. I dread the lifting of him, and the stench. I dread the cold of the stone, the darkness of the crypt—it makes me shiver shake. I dread to touch him. I dread facing him and the future, and facing the future without him. I dread how awful the world is, and now that light love glimmer doused. I dread the walk home, full of emptiness."

Come Easter we recall: something happened, with power, to restore the life of a desolated community, and to restore the lives of particular women and men, who have given us the record of the Easter restoration. Easter is about restoration, resurrection, rebuilding, re-creation.

They expected a corpse and found an angel. They expected a stone and found an opening. They expected and ending and found a beginning. They expected death, real pungent death, and found life. No wonder they were perplexed.

The women breathed apocalyptic air. The church breathed messianic air. The evangelist breathed dualistic air. We are recovering naturalists. Some assembly required here, that is, some translation, from worldview to worldview. These are symbols to be interpreted more than doctrines to be propounded.

Easter: *Wherein our worst fears are not realized in dread, in bread, and in spread. Wherein, for once, our experience if far better than our expectation.* For the Easter news of Jesus Christ is not about creation, but about redemption, about restoration. The good news of Jesus Christ is not about building, but about rebuilding. The good news of Jesus Christ not about the beginning, but the next beginning. The good news of Jesus Christ is not about creation but about a new creation.

It raises a personal question for those in their later sixties: with time remaining, what do you hope to restore? Endow? Rebuild?

As said EE Cummings "I thank you Lord for this most amazing day."

As Tug McGraw so well said, "You gotta believe."

As Butch Cassidy told the Sundance Kid, "Kid, I've got vision and the rest of the world wears bifocals."

"I am an old man and have known a great many troubles, most of which never happened." M Twain.

As Judy Collins sang, "I've looked at life from both sides now, from win and lose and still, somehow, it's life's illusions I recall. I really don't know life at all!"

August 28

Wonderfully Created

Wonderfully created, more wonderfully restored . . .

Often our experience falls short of our expectation, even very short. We hope for love and find companionship. We desire friendship and find alliance. We expect vocation and land a job. We have high expectations, but low experience. So, over time, our expectations can diminish, and we find ways both to accept that outcome and to militate against it. Experience ever trumps, and often disappoints, expectation. We want an A and get B. We want a Porsche and get a Ford. We want a full church, and get half of that.

How different Easter! The Easter gospel is so strangely, hauntingly different. It is not just a matter of a church being full (though that is very nice). It is the experience of the women, who come to the tomb, in the face of their expectation. Luke begins and ends this gospel of restoration power with the women. A gathering of women engaged in a traditional task of preparing a body with spices and ointment. Luke revises, not to say restores, Mark's earlier account. Christ has triumphed over the cross and that triumph is based on appearances—experiences—of the risen Lord, experiences of restorative power.

For St. Luke, the resurrection of Jesus brings the restoration of life, the redemption of the world, the re-creation of the church. Hence his location of all these stories in Jerusalem, where the spirit will come upon the church come Pentecost.

August 29

Marsh Spirit: Walk

In 8:18, Matthew strongly affirms the lasting power of such church considerations, even saying, similar to our reading two weeks ago, in the phrase, "the keys to the kingdom of heaven," that what is bound on earth is bound in heaven, what is forgiven on earth is forgiven in heaven. Get things moving in the community—get people walking together!

In verse 19, two or three, when truly together, suffice to form a judgement. Our English words 'symphony' and 'pragmatic' are rooted in the Greek here for agreement and matter. Get things moving in the community—get people walking together!

In verse 20, to conclude, the gospel further celebrates the precious joy of common life in the present, in the here and now, and it only takes a few, "wherever two or three *are* gathered in my name, there I AM as well." Get things moving in the community—get people walking together!

This is the announcement of *presence*, in word and table, in audition and celebration, in pulpit and altar.

In the spirit I call you to the Marsh Spirit of inquiry. *In conversation, memory, and exercise.* If you have not had a real conversation once a day, you have missed something. If you have not memorized something once a week, you have missed a chance to be mindful. If you have not walked along the sea shore, near Boston, once a month, you have missed the cleansing of the spirit. If you have walked down to the harbor and back to BU once a year, you have missed something.

I can not speak to you if I have not spoken for you and I cannot speak for you if I have not spoken with you. To needs for and for needs with.

So the Apostle had made us an urgent appeal, an appeal to love one another.

8 Owe no one anything, except to love one another; for the one who loves another has fulfilled the law. 9 The commandments, "You shall not commit adultery; You shall not murder; You shall not steal; You shall not covet"; and any other commandment, are summed up in this word, "Love your neighbor as yourself." 10 Love does no wrong to a neighbor; therefore, love is the fulfilling of the law.

11 Besides this, you know what time it is, how it is now the moment for you to wake from sleep. For salvation is nearer to us now than when we became believers; 12 the night is far gone, the day is near. Let us then lay aside the works of darkness and put on the armor of light; 13 let us live honorably as in the day, not in reveling and drunkenness, not in debauchery and licentiousness, not in quarreling and jealousy. 14 Instead, put on the Lord Jesus Christ, and make no provision for the flesh, to gratify its desires.

Wind is a gift of the sea. Salt sea breeze is a gift of the great oceans deep. Spirit, a spirit of inquiry, is a gift of God, our gift to share.

August 30

Matthew Changes Mark

Matthew's curt summary of the Markan teaching, gives us a way forward, a way to live out such a common hope. Unlike some philosophy and some religion today, the gospel does not separate head from heart, does not separate, mind from faith, does not separate the spiritual and the cerebral. In fact, here, to love with heart and soul means, emphatically to love with the your mind. Do you? Do you have love in mind?

Matthew has shortened the passage from Mark. He has taken out the positive reference to the Jewish interlocutor. He has winnowed the narrative structure of the text. He has emphasized mind. Especially he has removed the kind response Jesus makes in Mark to his questioner: "you are not far from the kingdom of God." What he has added is an introduction that describes a conniving collusion of the Pharisees and Sadducees to 'test' Jesus. In Mark Jesus is invited to help, and he does. In Matthew he is put to the test. Love of God. Love of Neighbor. On these two depend all the others. That is, even in the darker condition of the church, perhaps in the fear of the terror of Domitian, reflected in Matthew, the gospel stands. Love means love in mind.

And "mind"? Almost every NT use of the mind, is in Paul, as this morning in Romans, a measure of his Greek outlook. There, in Paul, and here, in Matthew, the word refers to the breadth of human intellect, ingenuity, and creativity. But in Matthew there is a prefix, and the word gives a breathing, process, dimension to the root of the noun, which you will recognize, *nous*. Here: Not so much thought, as thinking. Not so much mind, as minding. Understanding as gerund: "if I am understanding you . . ." A disposition. A manner of thinking, like "after a manner of speaking" (BGD, loc cit).

Let us live with love in mind.

August 31

September

September

Confession of Anxiety

We know fear and anxiety. I wonder if my nephew's military service has changed him in a forever way? Does my current lack of a job, given my age and background, forecast something longer and harder? How will I now cope with being alone, having been married, and happily so, for so long? I feel my body changing, aging, and hurting: will one day come when I cannot make it up the stairs? Has the cyber divide which I know individually also managed to bring a break in generational relations? Why am I so regularly down, and sleepy, and lethargic and, should I say, depressed? Can I make my way in this church, with all these PhD's around me? What will I do when I graduate? I feel our marriage changing, as things do over time: should I be worried? Our country seems different than it was ten years ago, and I worry that people are hardened to each other. I am afraid I could have done more with my life than I did in my life.

September 1

Advent confession

Distracted sometimes, or sometimes forgetful, or just tired, we neglect to do something we mean to do, or should do, or want to do. Sometimes sin is as simple as neglecting to do something with or for somebody, when we know we should, could, and would like to.

Lament and compunction help us. They are utterly human feelings. They remind us of who we most want to be, and what we mean to do. The preparation, prayer, penitence of Advent make us ready for God's action, in Christ, and for ours, through Him.

As our choir guides us, let us pray.

September 2

Assisi Confession

As we have again this weekend been reminded
We live in a violent age
We have gathered in the name of the Son, the Beloved
So we bow in confession, and take with us the words of Assisi:
Lord, make me an instrument of Thy peace;
where there is hatred, let me sow love;
where there is injury, pardon;
where there is doubt, faith;
where there is despair, hope;
where there is darkness, light;
and where there is sadness, joy.
Let us pray:
O Divine Master,
grant that I may not so much seek to be consoled as to console;
to be understood, as to understand;
to be loved, as to love;
for it is in giving that we receive,
it is in pardoning that we are pardoned,
and it is in dying that we are born to eternal life.

September 3

Bonhoeffer Confession

We enter the season of Lent in diaspora. Many of our staff, administrators, faculty and students are on winter break these two Sundays. We hold them in prayer in their travels, and enter our time of confession, with two sentences from Dietrich Bonhoeffer:

> Complete truthfulness is only possible where sin has been uncovered and forgiven by Jesus. Only those who are in a state of truthfulness through the confession of their sin to Jesus are not ashamed to tell the truth wherever it must be told.
>
> "Forgive us our debts as we forgive our debtors." Every day Christ's followers must acknowledge and bewail their guilt. Living in fellowship as they do with him they ought to be sinless, but in practice their life is marred daily with all manner of unbelief, sloth in prayer, lack of bodily discipline, self indulgence of every kind, envy, hatred, and ambition. No wonder that they must pray daily for God's forgiveness.[1]]

September 4

---

1. Dietrich Bonhoeffer, *The Cost of Discipleship* (New York: Touchstone, 1995), 167.

Christopher Lasch Confession

Christopher Lasch, now deceased, once summarized well a part of Reinhold Niebuhr's thought about confession and absolution:

The only way to break the "endless cycle" of injustice is through nonviolent coercion, with its spiritual discipline against resentment. In order to undermine an oppressor's claims to moral superiority, (one) has to avoid such claims on their own behalf.

We are about to celebrate a Thanksgiving Feast. Before we do, let us bow our spiritual heads and fold our spiritual hands and purse our spiritual lips and quiet our spiritual centers, and acknowledge our own waywardness, in order that we may acquire a "spiritual discipline against resentment."

September 5

Confession and Contrition

Call to Confession.

Our age, as much as and perhaps more than any other, hungers for the language of contrition, longs for the spirit of compunction, yearns for the courage of confession. We face the contrast of abundance and scarcity. We know for sure that not every investment has been fruitful, faithful or talented. So we sing the one thing needful in a time of various forms of ruin: a desire for pardon. Let us pray.

We worship the God of pardon and peace. You know God to be a pardoning God. This is the gospel.

September 6

Confession and Prayer

From the lands of Zebulun and Naphtali, from the darkness into which light breaks, we pause in prayer.

In the singing of the Kyrie, we confess our slowness to rejoice for what we have been given.

Along the banks of the Sea of Galilee, we confess our forgetfulness to give ourselves in fishing for others.

May our prayer make us kind to one another, tenderhearted, forgiving one another as God in Christ has forgiven us.

September 7

Confession and Pardon

Holy and Just

With happy hearts we receive your lavish grace, loving mercy, and lasting pardon. Confident of pardon, we pray with honesty.

Grant us thy pardon and peace.

Forgive what we have been, what we have become.

Forgive our sloth in giving and visiting.

Forgive our bland preaching.

Forgive our easy acceptance of decline.

Forgive our mistaken choices, elections, selections, decisions, expenditures.

Forgive our willing forgetfulness of our own best past.

Forgive what we have become. Help us to amend what we are. By thy Spirit direct what we shall be.

September 8

Confession : Innocents Harmed

When we witness harm done to innocent people, we are angry, we are shocked, we are deeply saddened, and, at another level, sorely frightened. How could we be anything but? What is wrong with people? We ask. We confess that we do not understand, that we have not yet spread preventive healing to all madness, that to our peril we forget just how fragile, how precious is each life. We confess that our hopes : "have been aborted by a combination of impatience, elitism, the lack of any real consequential sense of history, and the failure to offer even a meaningful outline for a different (future)."[1] Worship invites compunction, inspires confession, invokes contrition, induces lament, reminds us that regret is the beginning of consciousness.

September 9

1. William Appleman Williams as cited by Andrew J. Bacevich, 'Afterward,' in *The Tragedy of American Diplomacy* (New York: W. W. Norton & Company, 2009).

Confession Spill

Friends:

In the confidence of divine love we pause in prayer to consider ourselves under the aspect of divine love.

The good that we would, we do not, and the harm that we would not, we often do.

We recognize the consequences of greed and arrogance.

Spilling out, leaking out, teeming out all around us both in nature and history we face the unintended consequences of measures of greed combined with measures of arrogance.

And we feel sorrow. We truly feel sorry, know contrition, expression compunction, cry out in lament, admit regret, and bow in confession.

We have been called to be stewards, but our stewardship has been far from perfect.

So, come Sunday, we pause and pray, seeking renewal.

For renewal of resolve, renewal of courage, renewal a right minded care, we offer our thanks.

Beloved:

As we welcome you today, we invite you to help us to come to know you by name, through the use of our ritual of friendship, as we pass the red pad from the center to the side aisles.

We invite you into forms of ministry and fellowship. Coffee hour follows worship, please join us. The Marsh Chapel Summer Softball team starts playing soon, please join up. Opportunities for giving for those afar may be found on our website, please join in.

September 10

Confession with Postcard Secrets

Call to Confession
Friends
Confession is good for the soul.

One great treasure which the world's religious traditions may offer our troubled time, is the language of confession. Words for confession, psalms of lament, hymns of contrition, poems of compunction, all offered in the happy confidence of God's lavish pardoning love.

You may want to get something off your chest. You may want to let a secret go. Imagine in your right hand a postcard, and in your left hand a pen. As the choir sings our Kyrie, write out your secret on your card, and as the choir finishes, drop in the mail, and *let it go*. You will be glad you did.

Pens poised?

September 11

Confessions of Sin

Forgive us our trespasses as we forgive those who trespass against us
Forgive us our sins as we forgive those who sin against us
Forgive us our debts as we forgive our debtors
Forgiveness is at the heart of being and being alive
On the trail of mercy we find the trail of life
Stalking the experience of pardon and being pardoned
We find our way to a great meadow, and open meadow, a great open meadow
Where to err is human, to forgive divine
May we gather up our collective and individual prayers of confession during the singing of the Kyrie

September 12

Daughter's Confession

One daughter remembered her father this way: "certainly it was his response to us whenever we complained that some decision or punishment was not fair—Whoever told you life would be fair—that I take out and use on a weekly and sometimes daily basis."

That phrase has served as a steady reminder that we need to take life as it comes and not waste time wishing things we different. His sister and Aunt had saved a few of his Chaplain's corner columns from his experience in the Air Force in the nineteen fifties and this one paragraph is an early embodiment of that philosophy.

"We make our own opportunity and are personally responsible for the development and employment of our talents. If we are to know the true meaning of life and experience, vital happiness, we need to know that every situation in life is both good and bad, and will be for us what we make it."

There is a spirit of wholeness abroad, one expression of which is found in the Judeo Christian tradition. There is a self-correcting spirit of mercy, goodness, truth, and forgiveness loose in the universe, one expression of which is found in the Judeo Christian tradition.

Will you center down now? Will you arrange yourself to center down in the deep river of this spirit? Let us confess our need, dependence, frailty, and mortality, as the choir sings our traditional Kyrie.

September 13

Epiphany Confession

Perhaps this morning we can begin with a personal, even a pastoral word.

Many of us were raised under the aegis of a good proverb, "anything worth doing is worth doing well." A worthy word.

Yet when we come to our giving, this proverb needs the balance of another, "anything worth giving is worth giving imperfectly."

For when it comes to offering what matters most, gifts of love and hope and faith, even simple ones like "come to church with me on Sunday," we may not achieve perfection of form or precision of tone. Real things are often messier than that. In giving, the main thing is the gift, even given imperfectly.

So the poet wrote, for me and you and other recovering perfectionists, "ring the bells that still can ring, forget your perfect offering, there is a crack in everything, that's how the light gets in."

That is how The Light gets in.

In the Kyrie we listen for divine peace and pardon.

September 14

Grace for Dinner 2008

Dear God:

We pause in this hour of memory and celebration

To give thanks to thee, thou God of every time and season

In the quiet of winter we give thanks for moments of reflection, hours of recollection, hints of happiness remembered and expected.

In the vesper stillness of the evening, we offer grateful thanks for careful friends, caring companions, care continued, pardon and rest.

In this minute of grace before dinner, we pray your blessing for Boston University with its storied past and its exciting future, for our President and Provost and all university leaders, for our alumni and alumni leaders, for our students, faculty and staff, for our community, city, nation and world. We are truly thankful for those whose wise, steady, and inventive leadership has and does guide us into the open future.

On this occasion of honor, we give thanks for heart and voice, for those who heal the body and for those who share the arts of communication.

The gentle arts of healing and the artful gentleness of speech do us honor tonight.

We are thankful for such human gifts and graces.

We pray both for the wisdom to avoid the dangers of a graceless perfection and the insight to appreciate the powers of a graceful imperfection.

May the poet's words be our own:

Ring the bells that still can ring
Forget your perfect offering
There is a crack in everything
That's how the light gets in

Now as we receive the nourishment of food and fellowship, we do so with happy hearts, remembering those who have labored to prepare it, as we are nourished by spirit, grace and presence.

Amen.

September 15

H.R. Niebuhr Confession

H. R. Niebuhr: "[R]epentance for the sins of social life is not enough; there needs to be repentance for the sin, for the false faith, for the idolatry which issues in all these sins. Men will be ready for no radically new life until they have really become aware of the falsity of faith upon which their old life is based." (Evans 81)

September 16

Robinson Confession

"There is a saying that to understand is to forgive, but that is an error, so Papa used to say. You must forgive in order to understand. Until you forgive you defend yourself against the possibility of understanding."[1]

September 17

---

1. Marilynne Robinson, *Home* (New York: Farrar, Strass, and Giroux, 2008), 45.

Remembering

"Your father taught us all so much about ministry. I remember him in my early years as DS and often reaching out to me as a new 'woman' in what was then very much still a man's world. I remember too his sense of humor even when dealing with much of the nitty-gritty work of the conference. And I remember his passion and love for the church which he obviously implanted in you. And so I have been thinking of you and I pray that much of who he was, and certainly the best of who he was, will find a home in you and your children—as I have no doubt it has and will continue to do. I hope that in this time of loss you will feel his spirit with you as love and gift."

"I lost my Dad at 27 . . . He would never know a grandchild, retire, take a real vacation. You know, for 30+ years I mourned my father's death at 61, until I saw mother spend the last 5 years of her life with raving dementia. Then I was at peace, knowing that there really is a victory anda glorious next life with the Risen Lord. . .and Bob, you dad must be so proud of you."

"Since I am only a bit more than a year younger than your father, his death is a vivid reminder of how short our life span is, even if we live into our very senior years"

September 18

Bruce Chapman's Prayer

"O God, our Father, from whom we come and unto whom our spirits return; as we draw to completion this service of remembrance, thanksgiving and commendation for your servant, we again give you hearty thanks for all Irving has been, is now, and will be in the ongoingness of eternity; we we pray that you will grant your grace upon all who mourn in this city, these churches, this conference and, especially, this family of Marcia, Bob, Cathy, Cynthia, John, their sisters, spouses, children, grandchildren, and engage them to have your comfort and support until that day breaks and the shadows flee away and we are reunited again in the ongoingness of eternity. This, and so much more, we pray through Jesus the Christ, our Saviour and Lord."

September 19

Persistence Confession

Sometimes we are tempted to pull up the carrots to see whether or not they are growing. We lack patience.

Sometimes we are tempted to try to think 24 thoughts at once, and become befuddled. We lack presence.

Sometimes we are tempted to give up too early, to throw in the towel when we are almost home. We lack persistence.

How good to come to church, where we may confess and so leave bundled behind our lack of patience and presence and persistence.

Let us confess our condition, as the choir sings a traditional Kyrie Eleison.

Grant us thy peace.

Grant us thy peace.

Grant us thy peace.

September 20

Ten-Year Luncheon

Gracious God:

We lift our hearts in thanks, for being, for being here, for being here together.

We honor all being present whose work supports the work of learning. Help us to be mindful, daily, of the shaping of young minds.

We hold up the challenge and privilege of being here, over a decade, engaged in the swirl of a University community, ever growing we hope in virtue. Help us to mindful, daily, of the beating of young hearts all about us.

We celebrate this moment, being here together, in the common piety of a shared meal, to mark ten years of labor, in these hours of fellowship. Help us to be mindful, daily, of the growth of young souls.

We lift our hearts in thanks, for being, for being here, for being here together, in the nourishment of this table and meal.

Amen.

September 21

Weekly Confession

Friends,

The Kyrie sung for us is meant to evoke peace and pardon, to refresh and renew our minds. The Kyrie lifted among us is meant to evoke peace and pardon, to restore us and re-clothe our souls.

Friday evening our Chapel was full of 20 year olds, reciting their poetry, renewing the language of the heart. We seek that renewal today.

Saturday noon our Chapel lawn, the BU beach, was full of 20 year olds, enjoying a moment of sunlight, re-clothing the self in health. We too seek new raiment today.

Let us offer our individual and collective confessions.

September 22

Ministry 101

1. *They need to know how much you care before they will care how much you know.*

2. *You can't shoot 'em if they're in the bushes.*

3. *There are no souls saved after 22 minutes.*

4. *You have to start where the people are*

5. *Preach the Gospel and love the people.*

6. *If you always do what you've always done, you will always get what you've always gotten*

7. *Sometimes you just have to whistle past the graveyard.*

8. *Leadership is example. Period.*

9. *Church renewal requires careful attention to what is said.*

10. *Proper planning prevents poor performance.*

11. *Leaders can get others to attack or defend the Alamo.*

12. *K.I.S.S. Keep it simple silly.*

13. *It takes two wings to fly.*

14. *Visit the people.*

September 23

Sociology: One

First, in the very present, with increasing attention, our nation has recognized a pervasive malady within student life and culture, certainly not limited to any one college or city, a callous disregard for the safety of women. This is not a women's problem, this is a men's problem and a community problem. In this past year, appalling renditions of campus life have gradually brought about a 'raised consciousness' (a phrase whose currency we owe to the women's movement of a generation ago). Read again the March (Caitlin Flanagan) Atlantic article on fraternity life. Look once more, if you can endure it, at the New York Times early August account of assault and rape in Geneva, NY, at Hobart William Smith. Peruse the various columns on acquisition and education, excellence and sheep, like that of William Deresiewicz. Assess the attention last week to Harvard's administrative change, and the objections of their law school faculty. Sift through carefully the daily details of what young adults recount of their own experience. A young friend this week related the chilling experience of being chased for blocks in the early evening on a well-lit street, through no fault of her own. One student at Columbia now carries, cross-like, day-by-day, from class to class, the mattress on which an assault occurred some months ago. Groups of students readily volunteer to help. No campus across this land is free from the responsibility and the opportunity of facing and addressing, in real time, the issue of safety on campus.

Unlike many other problems—tornados, cancer, mortality—these are problems that need not occur and have both consequences and cures. One reads that 20% of college women are harassed, attacked or assaulted during their student years. That is going to change. That has to change. That will change, if only because those funding college tuition payments over time will make sure it does.

September 24

Sociology: Two

The voice of religious life (history, community and leadership) has everything to offer to this dilemma. Where there are still religious voices to be heard, on campus, where that is there are still pulpits, on campus, (a mere fraction of the number a generation ago, a tiny fraction of that two generations ago) religion has been consistently, faithfully and aggressively engaged with issues of safety on campus, in concert with many good people and leaders across campuses like this one.

At Marsh Chapel, while we have breath, we will continue to provide sacred space that is a safe place. Come Sunday, in worship wherein we remember that life is lived before God, and that our experience rests in the presence of ultimate reality. And on weekdays, by employing and deploying sexual and other minorities in ministry and for ministry—the Inner Strength Choir, the LGBTQ work, and all manner of life affirming and spiritual enriching groups, events and programs. Spend a Friday evening with the Seventh Day Adventist student group and you will feel and see this in action. Learning, yes, but also virtue and also piety. Knowing, yes, but also doing and also being. Mind, yes, but also heart and also soul.

A few years ago I met with a group of theologians at Yale. At dinner, a highly accomplished professor approached. 'I picked up that you work with religious groups. What can you tell me about Intervarsity?' His question carried a nervous apprehension. I replied that they were a campus group, more conservative than I, and my tradition, but reliable and experienced. "Why do you ask?" I responded. "Well, my daughter goes to that group here at Yale. She was raised a Presbyterian." I asked why she chose Intervarsity: "did she like the bible study, or the leader?" "Oh, no," he answered. "I think she just was looking for a group her age who were not drinking every night."

September 25

Sociology: Three

At Marsh Chapel, while we have breath, we will also continue to uphold a vision of a beloved community among women and men on campus. A beloved community, and nothing short of it!

A while ago someone asked why religious leaders on campus weren't saying more about campus safety. It took most of what little self-control I have not to blurt out: 'where have you been? Are you interested in these things? Really? Then why aren't you in church with us on Sunday? If you were, you would see, hear and know just steadily we have done so. So if you are really interested in a beloved community of women and men on campus, then I expect to see you in church on Sunday. Put your body where your mouth is! Come to Marsh Chapel'.

Here is a community of faith living weekly in the shadow of a monument to Martin Luther King. His dream is greatly deferred, we confess. But the dream lives, we affirm. The dream of a beloved community, including such a community among women and men on campus.

Here you might be greeted by an African American woman from Atlanta, like one of our former ushers, Jennifer Williams, now researching her PhD dissertation in urban planning at the University of Michigan, with a winter in South Africa. Here you might be greeted by an Asian man like Maadiah Wang, one of our former ushers, now in business in Toronto, who was baptized by immersion on Easter Eve, on the side lawn here, last spring. Here you might be greeted by Dominique Cheung, one of our former ushers, a BU graduate who taught for a year in Taiwan, and who has now returned this fall for a Masters degree in Education, and is an usher again, an usher both former and current. Go ushers!

Here you might find a friend like mine who guided me to a column by Emma Green, Atlantic, 11/14: *Americans born after 1980 are less likely to identify with a religion. But. Religious people report more satisfaction with their love lives and sex lives. Church\service attendance protects healthy people against death. College grads born in the 1970's are more likely than non-grads of the same age to identify with a particular faith. Maybe there's something about contemporary campus life that maes people more, not less, likely to gravitate toward traditional institutions—or maybe college grads have simply learned that religion is pretty good for you.*

September 26

Shakespeare at BU

Here you might catch a glimpse of what love can be, neighbor to neighbor, what loving kindness, chivalry, honor, care can be. We still teach Shakespeare at Boston University:

Let me not to the marriage of true minds
Admit impediments. Love is not love
Which alters when it alteration finds,
Or bends with the remover to remove:
O, no! it is an ever-fixed mark,
That looks on tempests and is never shaken;
It is the star to every wandering bark,
Whose worth's unknown, although his height be taken.
Love's not Time's fool, though rosy lips and cheeks
Within his bending sickle's compass come;
Love alters not with his brief hours and weeks,
But bears it out even to the edge of doom.
If this be error, and upon me prov'd,
I never writ, nor no man ever lov'd

September 27

Stairs

Once after failing in an attempt to build a set of stairs, I put in my journal some thoughts for beginners . . .

1. If you have the right tools you can do almost anything.

2. The first time you do something it is never quite right.

3. Watch the danger spots.

4. Practice.

5. Practice some more.

6. A mistake is a chance to get it right the next time.

7. Don't be afraid to try something big.

8. Things take time.

9. Copy others who know better.

10. Why be discouraged—after all, you're a beginner!

September 28

The Moral Law Within

Conscience. Without conscience your God is too small.

Without wonder your God is too large. Without conscience your God is too small.

Conscience is the beating heart of truth and justice. Conscience is the soul of soul. Let your conscience be your guide, for conscience is soul, conscience is one of the things of God. Conscience reminds that the kingdom of heaven is not a present state of mind but a coming state of affairs.

Conscience recoils at the horror of injustice.

Peterboro, NY is one of the poor, small towns with rich histories that dot the upstate landscape. Like Seneca Falls, known for the birth of the women's movement. Like Palmyra, known for the birth of Mormonism. Like Oneida, known for the birth of a communitarian utopianism which itself gave birth to the children of stirpiculture there. Like New Lebanon, known for the birth of the Shaker community. Like Fort Stanwix and Fort Ticonderoga and Fort Poughkeepsie, where the American Revolution was saved in thwarting British advance. Like Fulton, which with Robert Fulton gave birth to the steamboat. Like the long winding stretch of water forming the remains of the Erie Canal, Albany to Buffalo, the opening the west to commerce. Like Lake Placid of Olympic fame, the retreat, home and burial place of the cloud-splitter himself, John Brown, who in Kansas and at Harper's Ferry, and from his gallows pulpit did ignite the civil war, to free the slaves. Like Orwell and Redfield, tiny northern towns, now home to Unity Acres, a ministry with the poor, and the places of origin for the Berrigan brothers, radical catholic peace activists over the last 50 years. Like Onondaga Lake, the center of the Iroquois confederacy—Mohawk, Oneida, Onondaga, Cayuga, Seneca, and later Tuscarora, and the legend of Hiawatha. Like the gloriously beautiful Finger Lakes, known as the 'burned over district' of religious fervor following the second great awakening. Like Corning, Rome, Oneida, Rochester, Syracuse, Buffalo and Schenectady known for the birth of industrial development in glass, firearms, silver, film, salt, steel, and electricity. Like Rochester, known for Frederick Douglass and his abolitionist paper, the North Star. Like Syracuse, known for world wide leadership in the creation and development of air conditioning. The Southern churches, I chide my preacher friends there, owe a great debt to Rochester and Syracuse, for the two things that make current southern growth possible at all, civil right and air conditioning. Peterboro is one of these now poor, small towns with rich histories.

September 29

The Starry Heavens

Wonder. Without wonder your God is too large. Wonder at the small things, for they are the things of God, as in the details from Exodus 33, the shekinah, the presence.

Wonder marvels that small things make a big difference

A lesson re-learned in the summer . . .

The *boat motor* idled well and even carried the pontoon boat forward, but at a snail's pace. All boats disappoint just like all dogs bite. The summer on our lake is a series of boat breakdowns. I wondered. Old age finally taking the motor? Carburator? Choke? Throttle wires? I am no mechanic. This usually means taking the boat out of the water and towing it 30 miles for repairs. I took a chance, and gave it a try. The motor casing came off easily. In a few minutes, it was apparent even to a non-mechanic that a single connection, throttle to gas line, had slipped undone. Just as easily, without tools, it was reconnected. The motor purred. Small things, little things, can make a big difference.

Our out cottage, a broken down old fishing camp, built probably on weekends by one guy with tools, a six pack and a rod and reel, has a *pump*. On that well and pump depend cooking, eating, cleaning washing, showers and other forms of relief. It is outside, so subject to weather and other beings. The pump stopped one afternoon. I am no plumber, but I know a good one. We called him. You worry when your guest needs water and you have no way to provide it. A new pump? Line problems? Dry well? What is wrong? But it was something very little. Ants had found their way into the electric box and broken the connection. Two minutes of expert attention, ants erased, problem solved. Small little things can make a big difference.

The *dock* itself is new, partly brand new. The dock is our island into the lake, our portal into boating, our entrance into swimming, our bridge into fishing, our outpost of land in water. It is just a wonderful territory in itself. But in order to get from the hillside down onto the dock, a makeshift staircase is required. It is fraction of the size of the dock, a farthing compared to a pound. It is a humble set of six stairs in wood reaching out onto the majesterial dock. Without the stairs, though, the dock is useless. All the weight, all the space, all the expanse, all the expense of the four piece dock lies permanently adrift from the mainland without the simple steps. Small things, little things, make a difference, and open up the possibility of much, much greater things.

Wonder remembers the little things with lasting consequences. Children begin to get hearts of wisdom in learning this.

Back from the fishing camp, and a warm water pumped shower there, now out on the dock beneath the stairs, ready to board the boat for a motor powered ride our 7 year old granddaughter caught something in her younger brother's rhetoric. Brother said, "Eric said to me yesterday that he would take me tubing behind his boat today." Sister said, "I know that is what he said, but that is not what he meant." There is short, short way from birdie to bogie, from right to almost right, from what is said to what is meant. To be able to hear that difference is a spiritual gift, a small, little, powerful, spiritual gift. "I know that is what he said, but that is not what he meant!" Children their age love small things, from riddles to jokes. Small things, little things, make a difference, and open up the possibility of real understanding.

It is a Sabbath reminder for us. Little things can change the world. Remember when someone said something to you that intervened, helped, saved. Sometimes the best medicine is whatever gives you the courage to take one more step forward. Small, little things, make a difference.

Wonder keeps us from making God too large.

September 30

October

Greeting and Welcome

We pause with joy and pride to welcome our Baccalaureate speaker for 2008. As we do so, we recognize the congruence in his life and in this place, Marsh Chapel, of the importance of personal commitment and faithful devotion. Here, we prize person over place.

Take a look around you for a moment. Those who gracefully and wisely constructed Marsh Chapel, most notably President Marsh himself, did adorn our nave with beautiful stained glass windows, Connick windows. Pause for a moment to notice the first level, the lower tier. All of these windows depict places, places of significance, meaning, and devotion. Jerusalem, Rome, Oxford, London. Place is indeed important. Every city and every urban University is acutely aware of the importance of space. Our chapel honors the importance of space, place and common ground. As they say in real estate, it is all about location, location, location.

Yet, take a moment to look higher. The top bank of windows displays people, not places, souls, not spaces. Here, at the higher level, it is all about vocation, vocation, vocation. One's calling in life, one's passion in life. So you find those you might expect. Augustine, Athanasius, Aquinas. St Francis—see him with the birds. You also find some you might not expect. Emma Willard, Abraham Lincoln, James Bashford. The charming gothic nave of Marsh Chapel is meant to lift us to what lasts, what matters, what counts, what works.

It is a place, where persons and personality are lifted in devotion.

So it is fitting that we bring such a fine person, Dr William H. Hayling, to this particular place and pulpit. Take a moment to reflect on his life, his vocation. (Read Biography).

With real appreciation, we welcome Dr. Hayling to Marsh Chapel and Boston University.

October 1

Words of Welcome

Friends Near and Far,

We welcome you to this Sunday service of ordered worship in the nave of Marsh Chapel, Boston University. With this Sunday our liturgical year begins again, as we enter Advent, a season of preparation, prayer and penitence. Especially today we are grateful for our musicians, both vocalists and instrumentalists, as they present the second of four Bach cantatas prepared for this school year.

The liturgy, homily, and music are offered in the praise of God, for our gathered congregation here at 735 Commonwealth Ave, for our New England radio audience through WBUR 90.9 FM, and for our internet listenership around the globe, live at wbur.org.

We encourage your written or emailed responses, your prayerful and material support, and, as the Spirit moves, your presence with us for worship.

Today we hear of the Precursor, John the Baptist, splashing in the murky depths of the waters of trouble. Facing the unforeseen future we are called, challenged to live with graceful vigilance. In that spirit we light our first Advent candle this morning.

This is the day the Lord has made. We shall rejoice and be glad in it.

As we are able, let us stand in the praise of God.

October 2

A Seasonal Greeting

Friends Near and Far,

We welcome you to this Sunday service of ordered worship in the nave of Marsh Chapel, Boston University. This Sunday, 'Sing We Now of Christmas'! Especially today we are grateful for our musicians, both vocalists and instrumentalists, our ushers and readers, our gathered and listening congregation, on this Snow.

The liturgy, homily, and music are offered in the praise of God, for our gathered congregation here at 735 Commonwealth Ave, for our New England radio audience through WBUR 90.9 FM, and for our internet listenership around the globe, live at wbur.org.

Especially this morning we welcome the meteorologically displaced, those who may be listening for the first time, because your own church for one day is snowed in, our out. Pull up a chair, and hum the hymns by the radio. We are glad you are with us.

We encourage your written or emailed responses, your prayerful and material support, and, as the Spirit moves, your presence with us for worship.

Today we hear of the Coming Birth of Jesus, the Son of Man. In his birth, God enters and blesses all and varied human life. In that spirit we light our fourth Advent candle this morning.

This is the day the Lord has made. We shall rejoice and be glad in it.

As we are able, let us stand in the praise of God.

October 3

Opening for First Sunday

Welcome to this service of ordered worship. The liturgy music and homily are offered in the praise of God, for our gathered congregation here at Marsh Chapel, for our radio congregation across New England at WBUR 90.9 FM, and for our internet listenership around the globe.

On this first Sunday of December we happily lift particular forms of welcome: to one and all to receive the Lord's Supper, to all who may wish formally and publicly to join the chapel coming forward during our last hymn, to all to come for lunch following service, to all who desire with us to develop disciplined generosity to engage in creative giving, to you, and you, and you, this day.

This is the Day the Lord has made, let us rejoice and be glad in it.

October 4

Musical Greeting

Beloved:

The Marsh Chapel community warmly welcomes you to this year's service of lessons and carols , a long, lovely, charmed and charming tradition at Boston University. In greeting you, you will want me to offer our thanks to choristers and instrumentalists and readers and others who have created and crafted our worship hour. We remember in particular those whose hands and arms have cleared our path here, and so have protected us from the ravages of this year's semi-annual lessons and carols blizzard. Also, with pride and affection we personally thank Dr. Scott Allen Jarrett and Mr. Chad Kidd, even as greet in verbal embrace Dean Ray Lee Hart and Father Paul Helfrich. Friends, listen, sing and pray, in memory and hope.

October 5

Atonement Greeting

Friends Near and Far,

We welcome you to this Sunday service of ordered worship in the nave of Marsh Chapel, Boston University.

The liturgy, homily, and music are offered in the praise of God, for our gathered congregation here at 735 Commonwealth Ave, for our New England radio audience through WBUR 90.9 FM, and for our internet listenership around the globe, live at wbur.org.

My name is Robert Allan Hill. As the Dean of Marsh Chapel I encourage your written or emailed responses, your prayerful and material support, and, as the Spirit moves, your presence with us for worship.

On this Lenten Sunday we affirm a great watershed of peace, grace and freedom, and commend this living water to slake the thirst of a parched world.

During Lent 2010 we are happily hosting a series of sermons on the theme of the Atonement, offered by our Boston University Chaplains. Their messages will be recapitulated during the Good Friday Service, a 50 year tradition here, on April 2. During this academic year Marsh Chapel has sought to optimize our administration and oversight of Religious Life at BU, by improving communication and coordination through the office of the Chapel Director, by regularizing and our monthly Religious Life Council meetings, by expanding the membership of that Council, by updating our Standards and Expectations document for Religious Life, and by filling openings in our roster of University Chaplains, a team of 8 now finally and finely full. Thus the 2010 University Chaplains Lenten series is an outcome, reflection and celebration of this more latent year long project. Today, on our fourth Sunday in the series, we are proud and pleased to welcome our Chapel Associate for United Methodist students, the Rev. Ms. Victoria Gaskell.

As we are able, let us stand in the praise of God.

October 6

Atonement Greeting 2

Friends Near and Far,

We welcome you to this Sunday service of ordered worship in the nave of Marsh Chapel, Boston University.

The liturgy, homily, and music, including this morning's lovely Lenten offertory anthem, Lo The Full Final Sacrifice, are offered in the praise of God, for our gathered congregation here at 735 Commonwealth Ave, for our New England radio audience through WBUR 90.9 FM, and for our internet listenership around the globe, live at wbur.org.

My name is Robert Allan Hill. As the Dean of Marsh Chapel I encourage your written or emailed responses, your prayerful and material support, and, as the Spirit moves, your presence with us for worship.

During Lent 2010 we are happily hosting a series of sermons on the theme of the Atonement, offered by our Boston University Chaplains. Their messages will be recapitulated during the Good Friday Service, a 50 year tradition here, on April 2. During this academic year Marsh Chapel has sought to optimize our administration and oversight of Religious Life at BU, in several ways, including by improving communication and coordination through the office of the Chapel Director, and by filling openings in our roster of University Chaplains, a team of 8 now finally and finely full. This past Wednesday, we honored and celebrated the 40 years of ministry at Boston University of Rabbi Joseph Polak, director of our Hillel House, with a Religious Life Council gathering and party. Here at Marsh Chapel, the 2010 University Chaplains Lenten series is an outcome, reflection and celebration of our more latent year long work in Religious Life. Today, on our fifth and last Sunday in the series, we are proud and pleased to welcome our University Episcopal Chaplain, Father Joshua Thomas.

As we are able, let us stand in the praise of God.

October 7

Holiday Greeting

Friends Near and Far,

We welcome you to this Sunday service of ordered worship in the nave of Marsh Chapel, Boston University.

The liturgy, homily, and music are offered in the praise of God, for our gathered congregation here at 735 Commonwealth Ave, for our New England radio audience through WBUR 90.9 FM, and for our internet listenership around the globe, live at wbur.org.

We encourage your written or emailed responses, your prayerful and material support, your selection of personal ministries, and, as the Spirit moves, your presence with us for worship.

With joy today we affirm two views of Christmas: the Christmas impulse for lasting good and the Christmas promise that our distinctions need not be our downfall.

Sing We Now of Christmas! This is the day the Lord has made. We shall rejoice and be glad in it.

As we are able, let us stand in the praise of God.

Christmas Absolution

In order to be able to face the mirror, we need the bright confidence of light and love. It is surely and only a sudden awareness of the willingness in another to forgive that empowers us to confess. First we are seized by the Christmas gospel, 'on earth peace, good will.' Then we have the courage to admit, to bow down, to face the music, to the face the mirror, to face ourselves.

Te absolvo

Te absolvo

Free from sorrow, praises voicing, greet the morrow.

October 8

Call to Worship

Here and Now
Where the Dawn of the East
Meets the Twilight of the West
And the Cool of the North
Touches the Calm of the South
Where the Transcendent Grace of God
Touches Ground in the Humility of Christ
On Easter Sunday—In the Spirit—Right Here, Just Now
At Marsh Chapel, Boston University
Where the Head of the Charles meets the Heart of the Country
In this Holy Place, at this Sacred Time
We Assemble to Worship
To Illumine the Imagination by the Beauty of God
To Quicken the Conscience by the Holiness of God
To Warm the Heart by the Love of God
To Devote the Will to the Purposes of God
We Gather to Worship Almighty God

October 9

First Sunday

First Sunday Greeting,

Welcome to this service of ordered worship. The liturgy music and homily are offered in the praise of God, for our gathered congregation here at Marsh Chapel, for our radio congregation across New England at WBUR 90.9 FM, and for our internet listenership around the globe.

On this first Sunday of the month, as is our custom, we welcome all of whatever age, station or background to participate in the Sacrament of Holy Communion. Those listening on the radio may request communion in the home by calling the Chapel office.

On this Sunday we commend to you the ministry of the chapel, and its programmatic offerings, and its sermon offerings, found on our website.

On this Sunday we invite those so moved to identify as members of the Chapel 'chapter' simply by speaking with our director of hospitality, Elizabeth Fomby Hall, or one of the clergy, or by leaving a note in the collection plate.

On this Sunday we encourage all to continue or to commence the practice of tithing, of disciplined generosity, and to indicate interests in giving to our chapel director, Ray Bouchard, by email, phone or voice.

On this first Sunday we ask you to ask yourself what form your ministry here will take in he coming weeks. A community luncheon follows worship downstairs, and all are warmly invited.

This is the Day the Lord has made, let us rejoice and be glad in it.

October 10

First Sunday Brief

Welcome to this service of ordered worship. The liturgy music and homily are offered in the praise of God, for our gathered congregation here at Marsh Chapel, for our radio congregation across New England at WBUR 90.9 FM, and for our internet listenership around the globe.

On this first Sunday of the month, as is our custom, we welcome all of whatever age, station or background to participate in the Sacrament of Holy Communion. Those listening on the radio may request communion in the home by calling the Chapel office.

On this Sunday we commend to you the ministry of the chapel, we invite those so moved to identify as members of the Chapel 'chapter,' we encourage all to continue or to commence the practice, of disciplined generosity, and we ask you to ask yourself what form your ministry, your engagement of gratuitous kindness here will take in the coming weeks.

This is Trinity Sunday, the Day the Lord has made, let us rejoice and be glad in it.

October 11

First Sunday January

Welcome to this service of ordered worship. The liturgy music and homily are offered in the praise of God, for our gathered congregation here at Marsh Chapel, for our radio congregation across New England at WBUR 90.9 FM, and for our internet listenership around the globe.

On this first Sunday of the month, as is our custom, we welcome all of whatever age, station or background to participate in the Sacrament of Holy Communion. Those listening on the radio may request communion in the home by calling the Chapel office.

On this Sunday we commend to you the ministry of the chael, we invite those so moved to identify as members of the Chapel 'chapter,' we encourage all to continue or to commence the practice, of disciplined generosity, and we ask you to ask yourself what form your ministry, your engagement of gratuitous kindness here will take in the coming weeks.

This Epiphany Sunday, this New Year's Day, is the Day the Lord has made, let us rejoice and be glad in it.

October 12

Greeting: Darwin and Faith

The Lord be with you.
And also with you.
Lift up your hearts.
We lift them up to the Lord.

Dean Robert Allan Hill and the Marsh Chapel Community welcome you to this Sunday service of ordered worship, one part of our 2009 National Preacher Series on the theme "Darwin and Faith."

Our guest this Sunday is the Rev Blogs McGee, Senior Minister at St John's by the Gas Station, Gnome Alaska. We also welcome guests musicians . . .

We encourage your written or emailed responses, your prayerful and material support, your selection of personal forms of ministry, and, as the Spirit moves, your presence with us for worship.

Let us offer our praise to God in liturgy, homily, and music, as a gathered congregation here at 735 Commonwealth Ave, as a New England radio audience through WBUR 90.9 FM, and as an internet listenership around the globe, live at wbur.org.

As we are able, let us stand in the praise of God.

October 13

Greeting February A

Friends Near and Far,

We welcome you to this Sunday service of ordered worship in the nave of Marsh Chapel, Boston University.

The liturgy, homily, and music are offered in the praise of God, for our gathered congregation here at 735 Commonwealth Ave, for our New England radio audience through WBUR 90.9 FM, and for our internet listenership around the globe, live at wbur.org.

My name is Robert Allan Hill. As the Dean of Marsh Chapel I encourage your written or emailed responses, your prayerful and material support, and, as the Spirit moves, your presence with us for worship.

As we begin Lent today we consider insight, saving insight, which saves us from being less than truly human, as we walk the mountain path of life.

We are thankful this Lent and this morning
For eyesight and sunlight and insight
For hearing words which make us endearing
For the taste of grace through time and space
For the scent and sense of our need for lament
For touch and such and much and so much
That lies beyond us, the mystery in which we are held
As we are able, let us stand in the praise of God.

October 14

Greeting February B

Friends Near and Far,

We welcome you to this Sunday service of ordered worship in the nave of Marsh Chapel, Boston University.

The liturgy, homily, and music are offered in the praise of God, for our gathered congregation here at 735 Commonwealth Ave, for our New England radio audience through WBUR 90.9 FM, and for our internet listenership around the globe, live at wbur.org.

We encourage your written or emailed responses, your prayerful and material support, your self-identification with your own form of ministry, and, as the Spirit moves, your presence with us for worship.

With joy today continue to embrace our shared epiphany. In our shared epiphany this early winter, we have prepared to start. This morning we affirm the strength to start.

This is the day the Lord has made. We shall rejoice and be glad in it, grateful as we are for the gifts of sustaining relationships.

As we are able, let us stand in the praise of God.

October 15

A Little History

Peterboro was founded by Gerrit Smith. Smith was an ardent abolitionist with a trust fund. He spent his father's money to buy land southeast of Syracuse, along the high ridge at the northern end of the Allegheny plateau. He used the land to provide safe dwellings for free slaves, who came up from the south in dark, crossing various rivers, Susquehanna, Genesee, Delaware, with dogs barking and slavers chasing, and the occasional Harriet Tubman as guide, armed with prayer and a pistol. The tracts he gave to these people of misfortune and found fortune are still farmed today, and in some few cases by the familial descendants of Gerritt Smith's abolitionist largesse. He also built an almshouse, a kind of hospital for the poor, in Eaton NY, nearby Peterboro, which as an 8 year old I remember entering as my father made a pastoral call on a dying man there. It has long since closed. The Methodist church in Peterboro, the remains thereof, includes people of color who are of the lineage of Gerritt Smith's abolitionist generosity. There is a rare more colorful hue in the pew than one finds in other upstate churches.

That is, there is much good, of good conscience, in the length and breadth, the history and legacy of Upstate New York. That is, there is much good in the very village, the little town of Peterboro, a poor hamlet with a rich history.

Yet this summer on July 8 at 7pm a tornado took the lives of four people in and near Peterboro, NY. A four-month old little girl and her 35 year old mother died when their mobile home was crushed in the wind. The local paper carried photographs of them both, two beautiful pictures on the front page. Two others died, an elderly woman, and also the male partner of a female oncologist in the region.

Tornados are rare in New York, some ten or so per year, almost all minor and inconsequential. Tornados are unknown, or had been, in this part of the upstate region, as Governor Cuomo said in his remarks about the tragedy, and the new normal in radical weather events.

Why do such things happen? Why?

October 16

Greeting November A

Friends Near and Far,

We welcome you to this Sunday service of ordered worship in the nave of Marsh Chapel, Boston University.

The liturgy, homily, and music are offered in the praise of God, for our gathered congregation here at 735 Commonwealth Ave, for our New England radio audience through WBUR 90.9 FM, and for our internet listenership around the globe, live at wbur.org.

We encourage your written or emailed responses, your prayerful and material support, your self-identification with your own form of ministry, and, as the Spirit moves, your presence with us for worship.

With joy today continue to explore the intersection of Christ and culture, Commonwealth Avenue and our commonwealth of heaven, as we travel in the company of the blessed.

This is the day the Lord has made. We shall rejoice and be glad in it, grateful as we are for the gifts of sustaining relationships.

As we are able, let us stand in the praise of God.

October 17

Greeting November B

The Lord be with you . . .

Friends Near and Far,

We welcome you to this Christ the King Sunday service of ordered worship in the nave of Marsh Chapel, Boston University.

The liturgy, homily, and music are offered in the praise of God, for our gathered congregation here at 735 Commonwealth Ave, for our New England radio audience through WBUR 90.9 FM, and for our internet listenership around the globe, live at wbur.org.

My name is Robert Allan Hill. As the Dean of Marsh Chapel I encourage your written or emailed responses, your prayerful and material support, and, as the Spirit moves, your presence with us for worship.

Today we receive the good news of the possibility of peace and the things that take us across the New Frontier of peace.

This is the day the Lord has made. We shall rejoice and be glad in it.

As we are able, let us stand in the praise of God.

October 18

Greeting October

The Lord be with you . . .

Friends Near and Far,

We welcome you to this Sunday service of ordered worship in the nave of Marsh Chapel, Boston University.

The liturgy, homily, and music are offered in the praise of God, for our gathered congregation here at 735 Commonwealth Ave, for our New England radio audience through WBUR 90.9 FM, and for our internet listenership around the globe, live at wbur.org.

My name is Robert Allan Hill. As the Dean of Marsh Chapel I encourage your written or emailed responses, your prayerful and material support, and, as the Spirit moves, your presence with us for worship.

Today we are summoned by a courage to be. In word and table, you are invited, grasped by Grace. You are invited to join us for a community meal following worship, to provide your name and address for further communication on the bulletin card and ritual of friendship, to speak to one of the clergy when you are moved to profess faith through Marsh Chapel, to attend with us the Boston University lecture, at 6:30pm on Tuesday October 9 in the Tsai Center, given by Professor Andrew Bacevich, on the enduring significance of Reinhold Niebuhr. Due to the holiday there are no meetings nor community dinner tomorrow night.

This is the day the Lord has made. We shall rejoice and be glad in it, grateful as we are for the gifts of sustaining relationships.

As we are able, let us stand in the praise of God.

October 19

Greeting September

The Lord be with you . . .

Friends Near and Far,

We welcome you to this Sunday service of ordered worship in the nave of Marsh Chapel, Boston University.

The liturgy, homily, and music are offered in the praise of God, for our gathered congregation here at 735 Commonwealth Ave, for our New England radio audience through WBUR 90.9 FM, and for our internet listenership around the globe, live at wbur.org.

My name is Robert Allan Hill. As the Dean of Marsh Chapel I encourage your written or emailed responses, your prayerful and material support, and, as the Spirit moves, your presence with us for worship.

Today we are summoned by a courage to be. In word and table, you are invited, grasped by Grace. You are invited to join us for a community meal following worship, to provide your name and address for further communication on the bulletin card and ritual of friendship, to speak to one of the clergy when you are moved to profess faith through Marsh Chapel, to attend with us the Boston University lecture, at 6:30pm on Tuesday October 9 in the Tsai Center, given by Professor Andrew Bacevich, on the enduring significance of Reinhold Niebuhr. Due to the holiday there are no meetings nor community dinner tomorrow night.

This is the day the Lord has made. We shall rejoice and be glad in it, grateful as we are for the gifts of sustaining relationships.

As we are able, let us stand in the praise of God.

October 20

Greeting September B

Friends Near and Far,

We welcome you to this Sunday service of ordered worship in the nave of Marsh Chapel, Boston University.

The liturgy, homily, and music are offered in the praise of God, for our gathered congregation here at 735 Commonwealth Ave, for our New England radio audience through WBUR 90.9 FM, and for our internet listenership around the globe, live at wbur.org.

My name is Robert Allan Hill. As the Dean of Marsh Chapel I encourage your written or emailed responses, your prayerful and material support, and, as the Spirit moves, your presence with us for worship.

With joy today we begin a new semester and a new season. In a way we all 'matriculate.' In our worship today we give thanks for the various persons involved in our emerging ministry at Marsh Chapel. As you discover your sense of place and purpose in our shared ministry we encourage you to name it and claim it!

This is the day the Lord has made. We shall rejoice and be glad in it, grateful as we are for the gifts of sustaining relationships.

As we are able, let us stand in the praise of God.

October 21

Greeting and Confession

Welcome to Marsh Chapel.

The Chapel's gothic nave, built to lift the spirit, welcomes you.

The Chapel's sixty-year history, at the heart of Boston University, welcomes you.

The Chapel's regard for persons and personality, both in its Connick stained glass windows and in its current ministry, welcomes you.

The Chapel's familiar love of music, weekday and Sunday, welcomes you.

The Chapel's congregation of caring, loving souls, in this sanctuary "built to last a thousand years," welcomes you in spirit.

But nave, history, regard, love and spirit lack voice, so, there is also a Chapel Dean, to give voice to such otherwise sincere but necessarily silent welcome.

The Dean welcomes you.

We pause to compose ourselves, in an attitude of prayer.

Our pause we trust will return us to our rightful mind, in purer lives good service to find, in deeper reverence, praise.

We trust the Spirit at work in the world to make and keep human live human.

Erazim Kohak once wrote, "A life wholly absorbed in need and its satisfaction, be it on the level of conspicuous consumption or of marginal survival, falls short of realizing the innermost human possibility of cherishing beauty, knowing the truth, doing the good, worshiping the holy."

We bow in confession as the choir offers our Kyrie Eleison.

October 22

Greeting at Christmas

We gather to worship Almighty God
In whose light we see light
Sing we now of Christmas
For we celebrate together
The birth of the Prince of Peace
The presence of Peace
The limitless circumference of Peace
Our voices and prayers are lifted
In harmony with those present and those virtually present
Our congregation in the nave of Marsh Chapel
Reaches in spirit across New England by the gift of Radio, WBUR, 90..9fm
And out internationally across the internet, wbur.org
For all, the hand of hospitality is extended,
And for those listening, especially, we encourage sometime
Your visit and presence here at 735 Commonwealth
We gather together to worship Almighty God

October 23

Lessons and Carols

Beloved:

The Marsh Chapel community warmly welcomes you to this year's service of lessons and carols, a long, lovely, charmed and charming tradition at Boston University. In greeting you, you will want me to offer our thanks to choristers and instrumentalists and readers and others who have created and crafted our worship hour. We remember in particular those whose hands and arms have cleared our path here, and so have protected us from the ravages of this year's semi-annual lessons and carols blizzard. Also, with pride and affection we personally thank Dr. Scott Allen Jarrett and Mr. Justin Blackewell.

On this particularly beautiful, snowy Sunday, we offer a special word of welcome to those of you who may be with us, by radio, for the first time. The peace of God to you. Our national offering of historic worship, in liturgy, music and homily, is offered to you, in your home, with a Christmas prayer for peace and joy. Marsh's service is your service, and we are at your service.

Friends, listen, sing and pray, in memory and hope.

October 24

Thanksgiving

The word of grace is spoken and heard from faith to faith.

It is a Spirit of Grace which embraces us this morning.

We give thanks for this grace.

Welcomed in this nave, and across the radio at WBUR 90.9 FM, and around the globe at WBUR.org, we listen for grace.

As Isaiah did prophesy: "For Behold I create new heavens and a new earth; and the former things shall not be remembered or come into mind. But be glad and rejoice for ever in that which I create."

Lord of All to thee we raise this our prayer of thankful praise.

As we are able may we stand.

October 25

Invitations

How shall we respond to the gospel?

Can we summon the discipline to continue to worship every Sunday and to be faithful in partnership evening and morning, and to tithe at the end of the month?

Shall we invite our neighbor or colleague to accompany us to service?

Will we find a way to do good this week?

Will some join our students in the CROP walk at 12:30 today, beginning on Marsh Chapel Plaza?

Will others plan to worship on Wednesday evenings, starting again 11/28, 5pm for eucharist, and 9pm for *one prayer*?

Is one ready to adhere to faith in this community in this season?

How shall we respond to such bounty as we are given in Christ?

The ushers will wait upon us.

October 26

Transfiguration

Greeting Friends Near and Far,

We welcome you to this Sunday service of ordered worship in the nave of Marsh Chapel, Boston University. This Sunday, 'Sing We Now of Christmas'! Especially today we are grateful for our musicians, both vocalists and instrumentalists, our ushers and readers, our gathered and listening congregation, on this Snow.

The liturgy, homily, and music are offered in the praise of God, for our gathered congregation here at 735 Commonwealth Ave, for our New England radio audience through WBUR 90.9 FM, and for our internet listenership around the globe, live at wbur.org.

We encourage your written or emailed responses, your prayerful and material support, and, as the Spirit moves, your presence with us for worship.

On this day of Transfiguration we hear a call to bear witness.

Our life flows on in endless song

Above earth's lamentations

We hear the clear though far off hymn

That hails a new creation

This is the day the Lord has made. We shall rejoice and be glad in it.

As we are able, let us stand in the praise of God.

October 27

Mary Elizabeth Moore Welcome

Welcome to Marsh Chapel.

President Brown, Provost Campbell, Bishops May, Weaver and Hassinger, Reverend Clergy, Honored Guests, Esteemed Colleagues and Faculty, Dedicated Students, Gathered Congregation.

The Chapel's gothic nave, built to lift the spirit, welcomes you.

The Chapel's sixty year history, at the heart of Boston University, welcomes you.

The Chapel's regard for persons and personality, both in its Connick stained glass windows and in its current ministry, welcomes you.

The Chapel's familiar love of music, weekday and Sunday, welcomes you.

The Chapel's congregation of caring, loving souls, in this sanctuary, welcomes you in spirit.

Welcome today as we enhance our endowment.

Endowment. Yes, a word brings a lift to the decanal eyebrow, a stirring to the Episcopal soul, a tingle to the Provostial spirit, a warming to the Presidential heart.

A welcome word, today. Now, endowments are crucial for chapel, for school, for university. We shall other days on which to build such.

But today we celebrate the endowment we already have. It is a rich and treasure. It is an endowment vocal not visible, audible not audited, psychic not physical, moral not material. Listen for its echoes . . . listen.

October 28

Summer Greeting

From the banks of the Charles River the Marsh Chapel Congregation and Dean Robert Allan Hill greet you this morning.

From the streets of Boston, the cradle of liberty, we greet you this morning.

Streets adorned by preaching statues: Phillips Brooks, William Ellery Channing, Abigail Adams, William Lloyd Garrison, Harriet Tubman.

And, from above the front door of Marsh Chapel, John Wesley.

Our summer Marsh Chapel Summer National Preacher Series, beginning July 10, addresses the theme, 'Evangelism in the Liberal Tradition: South, North, Youth,' with guests the Revs. D Wade, C. Garner, G. Thomas, and R. Olson.

The liturgy, music and homily of this hour, which is meant to begin in delight and end in wisdom, is offered for our summer congregation here in Marsh Chapel, for our regular radio community across New England on wbur 90.9fm, and for our internet listenership around the globe.

We invite your responses, gifts and participation. We especially invite you to come and worship here with us.

October 29

The Joy of Faith

You are invited into the 60 minute poem of this hour of worship
To remember some word that is true
In the joy of faith, when grace is present
To see someone who is good
In the joy of faith, when grace is present
To hear something beautiful
In the joy of faith, when grace is present
You are invited into the 60 minute poem of this hour of worship

October 30

The Things That Are God's:
Matthew 22:15–22

We are left to wonder in conscience about "the things that are God's." What are they? We are not told. There is no live interview from the heavenly conference room. There is no point-by-point bulletin, with details promised at 11pm. There is no footnote, or explanatory second conversation. We are left on our own by our Lord to wonder in conscience about "the things that are God's." We are given a fair and good amount of freedom in doing so.

In conscience, do you wonder about 'the things that are God's'?

Give to Caesar the things that are Caesar's. Give to God the things that are God's. (In the Gospel of Thomas, (110ad?) a bit yet later than Matthew (85ad?) who is a bit yet later than Mark (70ad?) who is a good bit later than whatever Jesus might actually have said (30ad?), the Lord adds, "and give to me the things that are mine."

Give to Caesar what belongs to Caesar, give to God what belongs to God, and give to me what is mine (GT, logion 100).

Matthew, true to form, intensifies the bitterness of Jesus toward Pharisees, of church toward synagogue, of Christian to Jew. He hikes up "entrap" (Mark) to entangle. He is "aware of their malice." To the question, "why put me to the test" he adds, for good measure, "you hypocrites." His Jesus demands not just a coin, but "(all) the money for the tax."

Through the year, from this Marsh pulpit, we have tried continuously to trace the moves Matthew makes in 85ad away from what Mark, his source, had written in 70ad. Mostly, we want to be crystal clear about the way the expression of the gospel changes, with the setting, changes with the occasion, changes, with the time and season and year. *New occasions teach new duties. Time makes ancient good uncouth. One must upward still and onward, who would keep abreast of truth.*

A standard reading of the passage is that the Herodians (supporters of Herod who is the Simon Legree of Rome in the cotton fields of Palestine) would want the tax paid to Caesar whereas the Pharisees (the French Resistance of Palestine against the Third Reich of Rome) would want resistance to payment of the tax. Jesus is caught. If he agrees with the Herodians, the people will kill him. If he agrees with the Pharisees, the Romans will kill him.

And yet, he finds a way, a way toward the things of God.

"Two things fill the mind with ever-increasing wonder and awe the starry heavens above and the moral law within," wrote the German philosopher Immanuel Kant at the end of his Critique of Practical Reason (1788), and these words were inscribed on his tombstone.

We are left to wonder in conscience about "the things that are God's." What are they? Are they wonder and conscience—the starry heavens above and the moral law within? Wonder and conscience? Wonder and conscience, spirit and soul?

October 31

November

Pastoral Prayer

Great art thou, O Lord our God, and fully to be praised, morning by morning.

We pray for thy blessing in this our, thy gifts of confidence, certainty and sureness for the days to come.

Help us to receive, with confidence, the many surprising gifts embedded in our personal lives. Help us to notice the unexpected possibility, the new friend, the unusual word, the strange connection. Help us to see more than we plan to see, to receive more than we expect to receive, with the confidence born of obedience.

Teach us to claim some certainty in the midst of uncertainty, as a church and as a congregation. Teach us we pray the path we best should trod into the unforeseeable future. Teach us rightly to connect yesterday with tomorrow, in the light of thy certain love.

Shower with cool saving rain and moist power the leaders of this world, with sureness to seek justice and peace. Help those in the torn out conflicts of our day to continue daily, surely, to seek the promise of the Prince of peace. Kindle daily in the hearts of great leaders an even greater desire for peace, with a sense that surely goodness and mercy shall follow.

Through Jesus Christ our Lord

November 1

Morning Prayer

Dear God:

We pause in prayer to place before you all the past year has taught.

Our learning from this year we present to you. We bundle together what we have known and the ways we have grown in tasks partly completed, in challenges met, in losses unexpected and foreseen, in spurts of creative energy, in disappointments, in surprises, in changed relationships. All this past experience we give over to your care and keeping.

Together we seek your blessing for what is yet to be. We seek your blessings of imagination and insight for the learning in the year to come. For keen eyes to sense unexpected opportunity. For faithful ears to hear a call to speak truth. For steady obedience to Christ Jesus, his teaching, his healing, his church, his spirit. For curiosity to discern the odd joys embedded in trials. O Lord, we pray, make of all that will come toward us a pattern of meaningful learning and growth.

For all that has been, we offer Thanks

For all that will be, we say Yes.

Through the same Jesus Christ our Lord.

Amen

November 2

Memorial

Opening:

We offer a word of greeting to the family, friends, classmates and colleagues of Alan Stern, whose life we remember, honor and celebrate today.

The community of Boston University, and particularly of the School of Law, is now gathered here for a time of grieving, remembering, accepting, and affirming. The space and time afforded us, here, give us a chance to pause, in peace, together.

Through our loss and tears we wait for a sense of peace.

Through our words of remembrance we wait for a sense of peace.

Through our recognition and acceptance we wait for a sense of peace.

Through our shared experience, today, and through our shared experience of Alan Stern, we hope for a sense of peace.

The generous thoughtfulness and creative hospitality of all those who have prepared this hour, especially members of the Stern family, we gratefully acknowledge, as we begin.

Our service will follow the printed order of speakers. We invited them, now, to come and speak with us, and for us. Dean O'Rourke?

Closing:

May the sun who warm and bright on you. . .

Your darkest night a star shine through. . .

Your dullest morn a radiance brew. . .

And when dusk comes, Love's hand to you.

Please join the Stern family in a reception immediately following the service.

November 3

Conscience

During that tornado week, other kinds of cyclones hit. A fine young woman gave birth to a baby daughter with a whole in her heart. A salt of the earth carpenter, a laboring gentleman, had to clean off the car door against which his older brother had shot himself after years of financial difficulty and depression. A 60 year old saintly woman who has given her life to pre school children and the Methodist church, in equal measure, was told she would need chemotherapy for the rest of her life. A father of four, a recovering alcoholic, grandfather of nine, community leader and faithful soul discovered he has esophageal cancer. We do not mention global rates of infant mortality, especially in the first month of life, statistics that have not improved at all in our time. We do not mention 180,000 civilian dead in Syria, surpassing the number slain in Iraq. We do not mention the hundreds of deaths in Gaza, in the mini war of the same fortnight. Just to say, that during that tornado week, scores of other cyclones, microbursts, wind blasts of various types and size did touch ground, in the heart of human lives.

Why? Why do such things happen?

We do not know why these things happen. We know in our experience of random hurt the biblical truth in Jesus' teaching that rain falls on just and the unjust alike. We know in our experience of horrible, unspeakable tragedy the biblical reference to the tower of Siloam that fell killing dozens who were no better nor worse than those spared. We know in our experience the falsehood of Job's friends and counselors who in mistake and error tried to explain to Job his misery, which they had not themselves suffered. We know in our experience of sin, death, meaninglessness the gut cry of Jesus in debate, "none is good but God, and in the garden, 'let this cup pass from me,'" and on the cross, "why have you forsaken me?"

And in our experience, we confess, we find it far easier to discount in size, scope, measure and meaning the pain of others than we do to discount our own. For instance. How often have I thought, and heard, in some arguments, "things in this world would be different if men bore children and knew the pain of childbirth." 6 to 3 votes in the Supreme Court can on this score be quite revealing. We do not know why these things happen, and we are prone to discount others' lacerations by comparison with our own. How many of us wish we had Syrian passports, Iraqi citizenship, or Ukrainian bank accounts this morning?

Conscience keeps us from making God too small.

November 4

People

Gay people are people, at least 5/5 human, endowed by their creator, and ours with Life, liberty, happiness—they deserve to enjoy these too, including ordination and marriage. *Jesus* can teach us this if we will let him. Remember he said to consider the lilies of the field, and how much God loves even these slight floral creatures in God's garden. Gay identity is creation, not fall, God's gift, not human sin, as is straight identity. Love the Lord your God, and your neighbor as yourself. Try to imagine what it must be like to be a 9 year old, who knows he is in the sexual minority. *Paul* can teach us this if we will listen to him. Paul? Yes, Paul. He places the pinnacle of the good news at Galatians 3:28: 'in Christ there is neither Jew nor Greek, slave nor free, no male and female.' And no gay and straight. The gospel is about redemption, not about tradition. Gospel finally and ever trumps tradition. Gay people have integrity, are beloved, by God's grace, just as you are and just as you do. *John* can help us, if we will read what he says. He says there will be another advocate, even a spirit of truth, which will lead us, lead us out into further truth, which is not in that gospel, or, even, in the Bible. There is a self-correcting spirit of truth loose in the universe. Truth involves continuity with past teaching and also discontinuity through new insight, by the gift of the spirit of truth. Our failure regarding gay people is theological. Our doctrine of creation could use a recollection of Jesus. Our doctrine of redemption could use a re-reading of Galatians. Our doctrine of the Spirit could use the voice of John. Gay people are people: the Bible tells me so. This is not only an issue of justice, nor only an issue of clerical integrity, nor only an issue of theological truth. *It is most profoundly an issue of pastoral care.* The physician has responsibilities to many institutions—her practice, her board examinations, her hospital, and her community. But in the end, all these and others are eclipsed by the care for the patient, the health of the patient. The pastor also has many responsibilities to institutions, or conferences—charge, annual, jurisdictional, and general. But in the end, all these are eclipsed by the requisite care for the parishioner, for the 8 and 9 year old children who are among the sexual minorities. Gay people are people.

November 5

Luncheon, Tim Kunzier

Tim Kunzier, in his rolling wheel chair, and regular greeting, reminds us of kindness. He often gave me a poem, or a prayer, or both. In the shadow of his kindness, and to honor yours, today, a poem, from George Herbert, and a luncheon grace from John Wesley, the founder of Methodism, whose statue adorns the portal of Marsh Chapel, and out of whose zeal did spring, over time, Boston University, in 1839.

Our poetic friend George Herbert wrote:

> Love bade me welcome: yet my sould drew back, Guiltie of dust and sinne.
> But quick-ey'd Love, observing me grow slack From my first entrance in,
> Drew nearer to me, sweetly questioning, If I lack'd any thing.
> A guest, I answer'd, worthy to be here : Love said, You shall be he.
> I the unkinde, ungratefull? Ah my deare, I cannot look on thee.
> Love took my hand, and smiling did reply, Who made the eyes but I?
> Truth Lord, but I have marr'd them : let my shame Go where it doth deserve.
> And know you not, sayes Love, who bore the blame? My deare, then I will serve.
> You must sit down, sayes Love, and taste my meat. So I did sit and eat.
> Our forebear John Wesley wrote:
> Father for this noonday meal
> We would speak the praise we feel
> Health and Strength we have from thee
> Help us Lord to faithful be.

November 6

March Employees Prayer

Dear God:

Holy and loving.

We pause in this evening hour to offer our thanks and praise.

For the very gifts of life and faith, of community and work, of safe space and gracious time, we are deeply thankful.

Bless our time together in this place, we pray.

For the daily chances to encourage one another, to give another generation a place to grow in learning and virtue and piety, we are truly thankful.

Bless our work together on this campus, we pray.

For the example of those honored tonight, whose steady service, valued loyalty, and hard work we celebrate here, we are happy and thankful.

Bless our life together across this great University, we pray.

Spirit of Life: Thou our source of meaning and hope,

Before we break bread together, we pause to be thankful for bread to break together, remembering those, far and near, who are in need.

Now on land and sea descending brings the night its peace profound.

Let our vesper prayer be blending with the holy calm around.

We invoke thy blessing this hour.

Amen.

November 7

Sketch of a Hard Pastoral Week: Meditation on Suffering

Week Past: Ray Hart, Simone Weil.

Weekend: Hal Garman, 60\65, friend of Neil Fisher, attends Foundry, Dean Snyder "ministers to their pain."

Sunday: Ben Dewinter, wife Susan, sick Thanksgiving, dead Epiphany, Del Sentimiento Tragico de la Vida, centenary.

Monday, Regina Walton, Hawkins\Klemperer\KWT\ Little Gidding, Farrars, worship wars, Proustian tableau—windows, wood, river, voices—end with this.

Wednesday, reminder of ten years ago. 100,000; 30,000; 4400; 2T$; almost total silence of protestant pulpits (UMC etc) David Buttrick\David Shnasa Jacobsen\R Neville. . .distance killing 3/2/03 . . . this is why curriculum decisions (languages, scripture, history, philosophy, and all—so important.

Thursday: Pakistani woman, forties, international students discussion, BU..Marcia—name, mother from Pakistan, given methodist scholarship to a Methodist school, SU—befriended by a neighborhood minister and wife and young children—the minister died driving from annual conference 1969, Ithaca, small VW—when her daughter was born, named her after oldest daughter . . . sacrifice and suffering of ministry, limited discretionary income—one reason, in addition to freedom of pulpit that guaranteed income so important.

Friday (coming): worship—I know you want to worship Wed and Sun—I know you mean to—Dean Moore, Ass Dean Lightsey, others—a cry a prayer and a word . . . a bit of Palm Sunday coming. . . . Deliver us from evil.

That is, let us sing with our hearts the beauty of holiness of George Herbert.

November 8

G B Caird on the New Testament

Caird addresses Jewish nationalism, pessimism and legalism, before turning to the problem of evil, to which academic question the NT gives no answer, but rather responds to what can be done about it: "God has done something. His kingdom of righteousness has broken in upon the kingdom of Satan." The NT supplants the above three with universalism, optimism, and spiritual freedom.

The Destiny of Man. "The NT always regards the life of man in the light of eternity . . . NT thought is always eschatological." NT combines vertical Greek with horizontal Hebrew eschatology. "The essence of sin is self-love and the essence of salvation is that the old self dies in order that out of it may rise a new self with its love set on the proper objects of love—God and neighbors.

"The Christian who knows and practices the New Testament faith regards the world not as a vale of tears or as a house of correction, but as a fit setting for a life of heavenly citizenship. . .Perfection is a social achievement and only in the corporate perfection of the new society of God's kingdom can a man find his own subordinate perfection."

The Argument from Experience. "Life in the New Testament is viewed in the light not of theory but of experience. . .It is impossible to describe an experience to one who is incapable of sharing it. . . . It is no criticism of St Paul as a theologian if we say that he touches the deepest springs of our spiritual life when the theologian yields to the poet. . .The New Testament does not leave us in any doubt as to the nature of the equipment required for the appreciation of its testimony. To the humbling of all University professors, let it be admitted that it is not intellectual; there are things hidden from the wise and learned which are revealed to babes. The equipment is moral. Blessed are those who hunger and thirst for righteousness, for they shall be filled. . .Whatever be the relation in other faculties between pure and applied science, we in the Faculty of Divinity are ever conscious that the science of theology must be subservient to the practice of Christian living.

"To the fatalism of those who see the world hustled by a blind impulse to an unknown destiny the New Testament proclaims that behind the manifold workings of the mysterious universe there is a personal and purposing power; to the loneliness of those whom the friendship of this world has failed to satisfy it offers the fellowship of a new society; to the optimism which still hopes to build utopia by social reform it declares that that society is already in being; to the materialism which has submitted to the facile attractions of worldly security and comfort it asserts that the kingdom is not of this world; to the rationalism which demands logical proof it responds with the testimony of personal experience; and to the pessimism which is overwhelmed by the burden of the world's shame and sorrow it gives the assurance that the Lord God omnipotent reigns."

November 9

Meditation on the Passion

L: To the question of evil let us live our answer by choosing the cruciform path of faith.

P: Let us meet evil with honesty, grief with grace, failure with faith, and death with dignity.

L: Let us carry ourselves in belief.

P: Let us affirm the faith of Christ which empowers to withstand what we cannot understand.

L: Let us remember that it is not the passion of Christ that defines the Person of Christ, but the Person that defines the passion.

P: Let us remember that it is not suffering that bears meaning, but a sense of meaning that bears up under suffering.

L: Let us remember that it is not the cross that carries the love but the love that carries the cross.

P: Let us remember that it is not crucifixion that encompasses salvation, but salvation that encompasses even the tragedy of crucifixion.

L: Let us remember and that it is not the long sentence of Holy week, with all its phrases, dependent clauses and semi-colons that completes the gospel, but it is the punctuation to come in seven days, the last mark of the week to come in 168 hours, whether it be the exclamation point of Peter, the full stop period of Paul or the question mark of Mary—Easter defines Holy Week, and not the other way around. The resurrection follows but not replace the cross. The cross precedes but does not overshadow the resurrection. It is Life that has the last word and there is a God to whom we may pray, in the assurance of being heard: "Deliver us from evil."

November 10

Pastoral Prayer

In a season of change, may we embrace what lasts.
In a time of loss, may we hug the new.
In an era of decrease, may we find the unexpected.
In an epoch of debt, may we (sacrificially) endow the future.
In a day of disappointment, may we savor simple gifts.
In a month of worry, may we undress our anxiety.
In a year of decline, may we again see winter's gifts.
In an hour of depression, may we, with effort, accept kindness.
In a moment of fear, may we grasp the gift of faith.
In a morning of acedia, may we enter our prayer closet.
In an afternoon of besetting sin, may we recognize, humbly, our humanity.
In an evening of loneliness, may we experience graceful solitude.
As dusk comes, gracious God, help us walk in newness of life.

November 11

Generosity

We offer our prayers to thee, O Lord, thou source of life and refreshment, of spiritual irrigation.

In the quiet of this hour, and the beauty of this space, with the meditation of music to guide us, we remember and are refreshed.

We remember a moment of generosity in our youth.

We recall an act of generosity which impressed us.

We uncover a reminder of generosity in our hearts.

Thou whom we have loved, even when loving thee late.

November 12

Gracious God

Gracious God:

God of Moses and David and Matthew and Peter:

Thou by whose power Moses did split the rock, and by whose grace David did fell the giant with five smooth stones and by whose spirit Matthew did teach us about a house well founded, and by whose wisdom was the church built upon Peter, Cephas.

Thou Rock of Ages: Come Sunday we lift our hearts to thee: Help us we pray.

When a man in middle age breaks the commandments of Moses, or better said, is broken by them, bring a stream of remembrance of mercy, thou whose property it is always to have mercy.

When a student hunting for a manifest destiny wonders whether one person can make any difference, conjure for us again the story of David, an unknown shepherd, one boy with five stones, and remind us of what we have to offer—our five fingers on each hand, our five senses head to toe, very blessed pentagonal promise of potential to strike a blow for freedom, somehow.

When a child learns the faith, its hymns and psalms and words, may they become, today as they long have been, for that seven year old, a sure foundation, against which the rain may fall, the flood may come, and the wind may blow, but will not prevail.

When a community of faith, this morning, gathers to worship, help us to remember those who came before, on whom the church was built, and help us resolve in their shadow, to offer something to those who have not yet had a first serving of faith—a prayer, an encouragement, an invitation, a ride to church.

God of Moses, David, Matthew, Peter

We long for thy mercy, thy power, thy wisdom, they love

God of our weary years

God of our silent tears

Thou who has brought us far on the way

Thou who has by thy might

Led us into the light

Keep us forever in the path we pray

In the name of Christ, who taught us to pray.

November 13

Prayer

O Thou:

Loving us into love and freeing us into freedom

We offer thanks for tokens of love, the welcome of this home, the graciousness of this welcome, the earnestness of this evening, all reflections of the light of your love.

We offer our thanks for signs of freedom, for the freedom of faith, for the liberty of expansion, for this moment in the cradle of the cradle of liberty.

Help us to be the salt of the earth. Help us to be the light of the world, offering liberty, freedom and emancipation.

November 14

An Affirmation

In less mythological terms, and more general biblical phrases, we express something of this same, first, belief, in future hope, in grace at the dislocation of death. As we said last week, during the memorial for one of our greatest saints:

If we believe that life has meaning and purpose

If we believe that the Giver of Life loves us

If we believe that divine love lasts

If we believe that justice, mercy, and humility endure

If we believe that God so loved the world to give God's only Son

If we believe that Jesus is the transcript in time of God in eternity

If we believe that all God's children are precious in God's sight

If we believe grace and forgiveness are the heart of the universe

If we believe that God has loved us personally

If we believe in God

. . . And we do

Then we shall trust God over the valley of the shadow of death

Then we shall trust that love is stronger than death

Then we shall trust the mysterious promise of resurrection

Then we shall trust the faith of Christ, relying on faith alone

Then we shall trust the enduring worth of personality

Then we shall trust that just deeds, merciful words are never vain

Then we shall trust the Giver of Life to give eternal life

Then we shall trust the source of love to love eternally

Then we shall trust that at death we rest protected in God's embrace

Then we shall trust in God

. . . And we do.

November 15

Sam Needham Welcome Words

Sixty-three years ago, the Rev. Dr. Samuel DeWitt Proctor donned his brand-new scarlet robe with three red bars on the arm and gave a talk at Crozer Divinity School. In the audience was another STH doctor-to-be, Martin King, who was sufficiently impressed by Dr. Proctor that he started to think about graduate school in Boston.

Twenty-four years ago, the same Samuel DeWitt Proctor reflected on his life in ministry and civil rights with the following words: "[Eternal life is] the refinement of the inner life with moral coherence, selfless love, a symphony of thought and deed, and the peace and wisdom that come from communion with the living God. We live in time, but eternity impinges upon our days now, and time becomes incidental." (Samuel Proctor: My Moral Odyssey, 119.)

Mindful of the legacy of Rev. Dr. Proctor, we too come to the recognition that God's love is so deep, and so real, that time becomes incidental. Our fifty minutes together in this space today, and our two or three or five or fifty years spent at the School of Theology, are little opportunities to appreciate how big God's love is for us. How eternity impinges upon our days, connecting us intimately to one another and to the Holy One, creator and sustainer of us all.

And so, my fellow symphonies of thought and deed, welcome. I invite you to take a look at your bulletins to see just a small sampling of the amazing things that are happening at STH, including announcements and information about our preacher, Dr. Robert Neville. And be welcome here. Welcome to you who know peace, and to you who seek peace. Welcome to you who have much, and to you who have little. Welcome to you who love song, to you who love story, to you who love men, to you who love women, to you who love God, and to you who seek that which you love. Welcome to you.

November 16

Sesh Memorial

1. A Psalm of David. 2. A Poem of Gandhi. 3. A Prayer of Invocation
I offer you peace.
I offer you love.
I offer you friendship.
I see your beauty.
I hear your need.
I feel your feelings.
My wisdom flows from the highest source.
I salute that source in you.
Let us work together.
For unity and peace.
Our prayer today
Gracious God:
We invoke your blessing and presence.
For the gift of the life of 'Sesh,' we offer our thanks.
For the goodness and grace of his life, we are grateful.
For the grief we feel and know in the hour of his untimely loss, we await your healing.

For his family and friends, near and far, who mourn his loss, we offer our heartfelt condolence.

For his school and University and community, and their leaders, who have helped us to gather and remember, we lift our thanks.

Help us we ask to find the faith to withstand what we cannot understand.

Helps us to find the courage, in and memory and hope, to honor his life by living honorable lives.

Help us in this memorial hour to grasp and hold what matters most, means most, lasts longest and is most deeply true in each of our lives and in every life.

O Lord support us.

November 17

Silber Memorial: John Silber, 7th President of Boston University

Ladies and Gentlemen, good friends all.

We greet you and welcome you to this memorial service in honor of the life, service and leadership of Dr. John R. Silber, the seventh President of Boston University. In this hour we hold several dear things in common, as a community of One Boston University, gathered this afternoon in memory and celebration.

We have in common the experience of loss, the loss of a uniquely gifted person and leader. One chapter closes, others open.

We have in common our heartfelt, shared condolences for the Silber family. As we did privately in Marsh Chapel on September 29, so today in public we offer our support, our thoughts, our prayers, and a willingness to offer any form of help that might be in our capacity to offer.

We have in common a recognition, surely personal to each one, inevitably partial, probably still evolving, of the legacy, gift and history we together receive, and do inherit from the decades of Dr. Silber's leadership.

We have in common a quickened sense of our own mortality, our fragility, our shared humanity—the daily gift of life itself, so precious, and also the honest reminder of the limits of life, brought together today.

We enjoy a special recognition of the good gifts offered to Boston University by all our Presidents: Warren, Huntington, Merlin, Marsh, Case, Christ Janer, Silber, Westling, Chobanian, and Brown.

We have in common a deep gratitude to President Brown and our University leadership for their voice and witness today, and to our honored guests and speakers, for their presence and remembrance.

We have in common a desire to remember John, to meet this moment of his passing, to match the moment, to master it, and to be mastered by it.

Last January a couple of us had dinner with John. As we sat down, I saw a copy of a book of my sermons on the coffee table—a gift to him from a previous Christmas, I believe. Ooh, I thought, here we go. I wonder what he will say? Then, adding anxiety to anxiety, I noticed post it notes, placed through the volume, about thirty in total I think. His response could not have been more generous. We talked in earshot of the great Kantian themes of God, and freedom and immorality. We talked about religious experience, and how one enters another's personal, deep experience. In short, we talked about faith, hope and love—the things that last and count and matter. This is what we are doing today, talking about faith and hope and love—the things that last and count and matter. (He did also say that evening, "There are some typos in here," but then quickly added, "you can readily correct them for the second edition." Curiosity, a rough and rugged humility, and the optimism, the hope for a second edition—a graceful word, and so, a graceful memory).

We shall offer our own remembrances today. The service will proceed without further introduction or interruption, speaker to speaker, beginning with our tenth President, Dr. Robert A. Brown. As we listen and speak, reckon and recollect, perhaps we may hold in mind the verse of the psalmist, who acclaims the lasting, divine presence: Whither shall I go from thy spirit? Whither shall I flee from thy presence? If I ascend to heaven, thou art there. If I make my bed in Sheol, though art there. If I take the wings of the morning and dwell in the uttermost parts of the sea, even there the hand shall lead me, and thy right hand shall hold me. If I say 'let only the darkness cover me, and the light about me be as night'—even the darkness is not dark to thee, the night is as bright as the day, for darkness is as light with thee.

We all hope our books will have second editions. We all hope in a promise of second editions for our lives, a house not made with hands, eternal in the heavens, wherein the various inevitable typos are resolved and remade. To the divine presence, to the freedom of grace, to the eternity of love, we now commend President Silber.

And we shall rise and depart this place, knowing that we too have work to do. Things to do before the sunsets. May we have a measure of that rare combination of idealistic vision and pragmatic skill, that Lincoln-like blend of commitment to excellence and attention to detail. For we have our work to do. And we shall do it. In words on our minds, of late, we shall do it, with malice toward none, we shall do it, with charity for all, we shall do it, with firmness in the right as God gives us to see the right. And in that spirit, of John Silber we shall say, "now he belongs to the ages," or, "now he belongs to the angels," or, "now he belongs to the ages and the angels." He surely belongs to both.

Please join us, following our musical benediction, for a time of fellowship, in the hall just behind us here.

November 18

Phelps

The presence near our campus of an ostensibly "Christian" organization devoted to the hatred of gay people, to the hatred of people of other religions, and to the hatred of Christians of non-protestant denominations, is a sorry, tragic, affront to our University, to its history, to its stated mission, to its motto, to its ethos and practice, to its various communities, and to its religious life leadership, chaplains, and groups. It is difficult to find words strong and true enough to convey the shared disdain of our community for this most unwelcome intrusion. Particularly for those of Christian orientation, the reminder of the lasting vitality in our time of bigotry and anti-Semitism, cloaked in the garb of religion, brings measures of pain and shame. We recognize the right of free speech on city streets, but we unequivocally deplore what is said by this group.

November 19

Thurman Litany

L1: As we close our worship service, let us do so in memory and hope, for those who have come before us, and still guide us from afar.

L2: As we enter another week, let us do so in memory and hope, for Howard Thurman, who came before us, and guides us still.

L1: For Howard Thurman, who was a hundred years ahead of his time, fifty years ago.

L2: For Howard Thurman, the champion of the disinherited, the officiant at the marriage of heart and head, the angelic herald of common ground.

L1: For Howard Thurman, who said:

S: "People, all people, belong to one another"!

L2: For Howard Thurman, who wrote:

S: "The ocean and the night surrounded my little life . . . death would be a small thing in the sweep of that natural embrace!"

L1: For Howard Thurman, who sang:

S: "Today I make my sacrifice of thanksgiving!"

L2: For Howard Thurman, who preached in silence, admired penguins, taught a King, and celebrated what is shared in love.

L1: "The religion of Jesus makes the love ethic central"

L1 and 2: Amen.

Nave left: Amen.

Nave right: Amen.

Leaders and congregation: Amen.

November 20

Old Prayers

Gracious God, loving and holy and just,
We lift our hearts in thanks and praise this morning.
We come to this sanctuary ready again to live as glad hearted women and men.
With glad hearts, curious minds, and eager spirits we offer ourselves in worship. Bless us, we pray, by thy presence, which we invoke in the name of Jesus Christ our Lord. Amen.

November 21

Almighty God

We gather to worship Almighty God
In whose light we see light
Our voices and prayers are lifted
In harmony with those present and those absent
Our congregation in the nave of Marsh Chapel
Reaches in spirit across New England by the gift of Radio, WBUR, 90..9fm
And out internationally across the internet, bu.edu\chapel
For all, the hand of hospitality is extended,
And for those listening, especially, we encourage sometime
Your visit and presence here at 735 Commonwealth
We gather together to worship Almighty God

November 22

Haydn Mass

It is my happy honor and personal privilege to welcome you tonight.

I do so in partnership with Ms. Vita Paladino, Director of the Gottlieb Archival Research Center, and Dr. Robert Dodson and Dean Walt Meissner, of the School of Music and the College of Fine Arts. These University leaders and their staffs have well brought us both the possibility and the hospitality of this evening.

Welcome.

Our most heart felt welcome, tonight, is reserved for our musicians, Cambridge Concentus, and University Professor Joshua Rifkin, conductor.

Tonight's performance draws together many Boston University luminaries. We are keenly aware of the significance of our Haydn festival and its honoree—H C Robbins Landon. Robbins Landon's legacy in Haydn scholarship is one of the most regarded and cherished in all music research.

Marsh Chapel is also involved in celebrating Haydn's anniversary and will soon present a performance of his great oratorio, "The Creation," here with the combined forces of our Chapel Choir and Collegium, in collaboration with the School of Music's Chamber Chorus, under the baton of our own Dr. Scott Allen Jarrett. Dr. Jarrett sends his regrets tonight, as he is busy rehearsing 'Papa' Haydn's fugues down the street at this very moment.

As a Professor of Music at the Boston University College of Fine Arts, School of Music, Joshua Rifkin teaches in the Department of Musicology and Ethnomusicology. He is one of the world's most known and sought after Bach scholars, and, in this field, has published the most recent score and performance materials on Bach's masterpiece, the B Minor Mass.

In addition to his scholarly endeavors, Prof. Rifkin is an extremely gifted conductor having worked with many of the world's professional performing ensembles. His most recent collaboration with the Cambridge Concentus was an extensive tour to Japan with Bach's St Matthew Passion this past summer.

Prof Rifkin is certainly one of Boston University's most distinguished scholars, teachers, and performers. Bach's music lives and breathes here at Marsh through the Bach Cantata Series so I am personally delighted to welcome him here tonight.

Will you please join me in welcoming Prof Joshua Rifkin and the members of the Cambridge Concentus.

November 23

The End of Words[1] A

Two of the finest church organists in America during the late twentieth century both lived in Rochester, New York. They lived on the same suburban street, nestled in the leaves and furrows of the upstate lake region. In fact, they lived in the same house. As husband and wife, it seemed the right thing to do. David Craighead brought his wife Marian, in the last month of her life, to sit one last time on her organ bench. It was a mortal struggle for her to make it from home to church, this last time, a trip that she had made with relative ease, hundreds of times, since 1960. The Austin organ had been refurbished, at her direction and with her supervision and on her approval. Before she died she wanted to sit at the bench and assess the work. They came in the afternoon of Ash Wednesday, 1996. Few words were spoken in the hour visit. She sat and looked and touched. She did not play. At last, with a lifted eyebrow, she summoned her husband to take her home. Home. As we left, in the deepest of pain that one loving human can have at the imminent departure of another, and in some tears, David said, "Watching her there . . . So hard . . . It is like Moses on Nebo . . . She can see the land ahead, but it will not be hers to enjoy . . . Like Moses, on Mount Nebo." One heard that afternoon a distinctively faithful, distinctively loving, Christian way of speaking, the Biblical narrative summoned without preparation or pretense, to give voice and response to the day's own trouble.

A similar distinctively Christian way of speaking provides the subject of Richard Lischer's Lyman Beecher lectures, now in book form as *The End of Words: The Language of Reconciliation in a Culture of Violence*. The lectures are intended to expand the range of Christ-like thought, speech, and experience. This book brings the preacher many wonderful gifts, and is well worth purchase and perusal. We note two primary gifts below. Dr. Lischer's formal apprehension of preaching here will be a welcome addition to the minister's library, especially for the preacher who has already have enjoyed his memoir of an early pastorate, *Open Secrets*. "The preacher models for the community a distinctively Christlike way of speaking in an uncomprehending and often hostile world"(8). Perhaps the two most intriguing sets of insights offered in *End of Words* (again, there are many others as well) are its use of Luther and its meditation on sermon design.

November 24

---

1. Richard Lischer, *The End of Words: The Language of Reconciliation in a Culture of Violence* (Grand Rapids: Eerdmans, 2005).

The End of Words B

Our time benefits from a reminder, like this one, of Martin Luther. The Lutheran spirit and legacy provide this book its theological core (*crux sola nostra theologia*), its decision about the 'theme sentence' of the New Testament (2 Cor. 5:19—"God was in Christ reconciling the world to Godself"), its worldview (Christ and Culture in paradox), its cast of characters (Luther himself, Bonhoeffer, the Niebuhrs, Tillich, Lindbeck, Augustine, Buechner), its primary nemesis (pride—rather than sloth, with Wesley, or falsehood, with Calvin), its early and high view of Scripture, its mood and mode, its realism. "In all American literature you would be hard pressed to find one happy, well adjusted preacher" (20). Well, one thinks of the colorful and happy clerical characters in *Moby Dick, the Grapes of Wrath, Gilead, Rabbit is Rich, Blood Done Sign My Name,* and so on, and disagrees, but the mode is clear, and, in the main, helpful. It is a hard time to be a preacher, as most times are. High stress, low status. Hence, a little dose of Luther feels sobering and healthy. On the days when we feel that we have spent enough time among the Canannites in 'happy clappy' worship, singing 'Jesus is my girlfriend' music, and the promoting the gospel of 'Every Morning is Easter Morning from Now On,'" this refreshing book will nourish us. On the days when we wish the bongo drums were out on the curbs and the horizontal worship spaces had reverted to Walmarts, *The End of Words* will feed the imagination. A realistic word of the cross, in hymnody that mentions that cross and churches that still house one, will have a broader hearing. In time. Of course, every morning is not Good Friday morning either. But as one teacher had us memorize and repeat, "the resurrection follows but does not replace the cross." Fair enough. "The Christian story pivots on the execution of a teacher who claimed to be the Messiah. . . . According to Luther, the theology of the cross protects us from total knowledge of God. When we preach from that jagged perspective, the empowerment we receive comes at the expense of a triumphal mastery of life" (102). One thinks of Edmund Steimle, and his chaste, cruciform sermons, and is glad for this sibling tome of Lischer's.

But is there not something also of practical help here? Yes, in fact, there is much. One finds and enjoys here a careful and balanced kind of a hermeneutic of affirmation, like that L. Keck acclaimed at Yale some years ago ("a reading strategy of trust in the faithfulness of God who is revealed in the text" (87)). One also finds a detailed response to narrative preaching—itself worth the price of admission (real narration needs a preacher, the cross, an open future). Yet, what (from one perspective at least) is most significant here lies in Lischer's threefold treatment of matters of design. Lischer recommends the use of *focal instances*, rather than sermon illustrations; *perspectival retelling* of the narrative (crux sola); and the regular use of the *master metaphor* (think 'Knock at Midnight'). Most experienced preachers will quickly appreciate his appeals here. To benefit from his insight, his practical advice, you will of course need to read the book! But you will readily pick up what he is putting down. You may not agree with everything here. For instance, I do not agree that the mediocrity of much current preaching is due to overemphasis on personality, but rather to a combination of disease of personality, overuse of the lectionary, and too much watery, narrative preaching, which together have taken their toll on the Methodist pulpit.

Lischer ends with Tutu and King, to exemplify reconciling preaching. A last word about, and from, the End of Words: "Ultimately it is the promise of the gospel and the power of the Holy Spirit and not the nagging of the preacher that makes for change in people's lives. . . . Reconciling speech is not our native language. . . . In Christ, however, we are released from treating our fellow believers as an audience to placated, persuaded, or impressed" (162–164). Well, while not placated, this reader at least was persuaded and impressed, and grateful for the chance to learn from Lischer.

November 25

What is in a Name?

As Methodism continues to shrink and diversify, we may need to look at the courageous examples of those who gave up their denominational names for the sake of a healthier future. As a cradle Methodist, and one who loves to tell these stories, this is a difficult admission for me. Yet, particularly in the Northeast, we may need to remember, sometime, the willingness others found to leave older names behind. Two nearby examples come to mind.

The United Church of Canada was born out of the willingness among Methodists to leave their name behind for the sake of a greater good. Some of the best people I have known have come out of this tradition, like Douglass John Hall.

The Evangelical and United Brethren church gave up its own name to become a part of a larger whole, the United Methodist Church. Pastors and lay leaders lost traditions, hymns, campgrounds, influence, and the various other intangible but significant relations that go into extended family life. They did so happily, to a great degree. Some of the most caring pastors I have known have come out of this tradition, like Joe Yeakel and David Lubba.

November 26

SUPE Reflection 1

The Sustaining Urban Pastoral Excellence Concluding Conference, 10/9–10/10 was an inspiring and inspired moment. I was delighted to participate in parts of the event, and to connect with a couple of long time friends who were a part of the project. From 1984–2006 we were engaged in urban ministry in upstate New York, and in 1978 we worked with George Todd at the WCC in the Office of Urban and Industrial Mission. Urban ministry is a subject of some interest for me.

The presentations, hospitality, organization, small group sessions and fellowship of the conference were inspiring. They were conducted with excellence. The diversity of the participants in the conference was heartening. The clearly expressed gratitude and satisfaction of the members of the teams was also encouraging. I believe this was the largest gathering of clergy at BUSTH during my limited tenure here.

I was able to hear most of Dr. Wolfteich's presentation on Tuesday morning. As a newcomer to the project I found it very helpful, since it summarized by citation and example much of what had transpired in the sabbaticals. Many of the quotations were poignant and powerful. The delivery included moments of lightness and humor that kept the gathered attention of the audience focused and alert. It seemed to me, from the range of reflection given, that most of the participants had been able to formulate a considered understanding of Sabbath, Sabbath-keeping, renewal, and health in ministry. The use of Heschel's venerable and still reliable book was an additional gift.

In the interstitial time I was able to talk with my two aforementioned friends. Both expressed sheer delight at what they had found in the project. One named the developed bonds of the friendships within the four member group as the most significant. The other spoke more generally of the impact on pastoral life of the chance to be away, to get away, to get distance. One reflected at length on his own field education experience here at BU, a generation ago, as "the two happiest years of my ministry." I found that unprovoked reflection a ringing endorsement, from the long past, of some things still accentuated here (praxis, self-understanding, collegial connections).

As I said at lunch, I have two suggestions for further conversation. First, I believe that the actual condition of the churches, now, in 2007, in which our urban pastors find themselves, is important to assess. Across the north, and extended north, at any rate, the condition of the churches is different from what it was fifteen years ago. Churches in the urban settings, with some exceptions, are high in need, and low in resource, as are their neighborhoods. As the churches' conditions weaken, the demand on the leadership expands, the stress rises, and the need for Sabbath, both as rest and as reflection of the creativity of the divine, dramatically increases. In particular, the conditions of the buildings and of the lay leadership ranks (and hence of the churches' finances) have a claim on attention. Second, if the desire is to sustain pastoral excellence, then what constitutes excellence becomes something of an issue, as one thinks about what sustains it. I found the conference strong on sustaining pastors. I wondered, though, what pastoral excellence was in view. My understanding I guess is that what sustains excellence is excellence itself. In other words, what nourishes the minister, most strongly, is not the absence of work, but work, not disengagement, but fruitful engagement in the practice of ministry—the work itself, enjoyed for its own sake, and practiced happily with excellence. Something to think and talk about, perhaps.

I appreciate the chance to participate in this process, and wish you all the best. Let me know if and how I can be of any other help.

November 27

SUPE Reflection 2

I was not able to be present at the November 8 dinner, due to another commitment (an evening with John Ashton, whose text we are using this term in my Gospel of John class). That said, the notes from the table conversation which Holly kindly composed and graciously shared provide something of an entrance into further thought. In response and in ongoing reflection about a topic we all find central and significant, I offer the following few thoughts.

First, settings and gatherings like these which pose the question of personal health on the part of clergy and future clergy are commendable, and should not be taken for granted. The endless potential for endless engagement in the practice of ministry and in the preparation for the practice of ministry requires forcible interruption and intervention. The project underway has provided one healthy intervention on behalf of ministerial health, simply by virtue of the time and energy devoted to the topic. I am grateful for this, and glad to spend some time as a supporter and partner in the work. It is worth doing. Much of ministry is listening. Some of ministry is speaking. All of ministry depends on the capacity of minister to protect a modicum of personal space and personal health.

Second, I wonder about the book the faculty read or were to have read for the autumn 2006 faculty retreat, C Foster's *Educating Clergy*. Did this manuscript ever see any daylight in faculty conversation? I have known Chuck for twenty years, and our family has known him for forty years. He has some good things to say in that book (at one point he quotes Dale Andrews, to good effect, by the way.) In particular, the exploration of pastoral imagination in Foster's book I find compelling. There are many applications of his thought in the life and work of ministry in general, which I bypass for the moment. There also is a singular significance, in the play of the imagination, for the prospect of ministerial health. Where the imagination quickens and is quickened one finds passion, happiness, and effectiveness. I wonder if we have fully exhausted the reading of his book and conversation about it.

Third, and a matter closely related to the previous two meandering paragraphs, encouragement of reading itself, clergy reading itself, perhaps deserves more attention. I note in the notes that the matter arose. Wesley divided the day into morning for reading, afternoon for visiting, and evening for meetings. Allan Knight Chalmers taught his 1950's students to read a book a day. We certainly continue to emphasize the spiritual significance of reading the curriculum here, don't we? Or don't we? I mean wide, fun, imaginative, idiosyncratic reading, as well as professional reading. Do our students graduate loving reading or not?

Three errant thoughts for your disposal.

November 28

SUPE Reflection 3

Let me begin with a word of gratitude. Your invitation to participate in this autumn conversation has been a healthy interruption, in the best sense of interruption, for me. I appreciate your including many and different people in this circle of interest and mutual enrichment. Thank you!

Furthermore, the matter of pastoral excellence and personal health is crucial to present and future study and service. It matters for the church and for the school in equal measure. Particularly it matters for the laity of the church, who engage and are engaged by the ministry of the clergy. Unhealthy ministerial leadership hurts most the laity. The gospel of grace and freedom (granted the native Methodist weight of this way of speaking) requires preachers who can exhibit grace and freedom, who can model dimensions of 'spirituality' (like excellence, undefined in our talking) that are freely gracious and gracefully liberating. How can we preach a gospel of grace and freedom without ministers who embody grace and freedom?

You have found and funded a fecund form of conversation.

Let me next set out some complementary assumptions or perspectives with which I think I participate in this kind of conversation. These are angles of vision or points of view that are perhaps different from, though not contradictory to, the largely unspoken assumptions and perspectives we have used together. It is hard to change the carburetor while the vehicle is cruising down the turnpike, so we often leave systemic or perspectival discussions to rest stops like this one. That is as it should be.

First, the mission of the school of theology is to educate clergy. Two words is a good number for a mission statement, and 'educate clergy' are the two words I would choose. By educate I mean twenty things, among them the intention to form life-long learners who are self taught on the basis of a robust exposure to classical materials. By clergy I mean twenty one professionals, among them teachers, preachers, leaders, executives, and those who teach all these, who will bring dimensions of meaning, belonging and empowerment to the new creation, during their day in the Day of God. In saying this I do not deny or contradict the lengthy mission paragraph we have affirmed as a faculty. It is good, but not easily remembered. In saying this I do not deny the important ongoing discussion of theology as the core of theological study, largely because pastoral excellence absolutely requires, utterly depends on every shred of decent theological study available. (In the long run.) In any case, of the 5 funding streams I can dimly perceive which currently pay our rent and grocery bills, 5 assume that our mission is to educate clergy. For this reason I think Foster's book, *Educating Clergy*, has something to offer us.

Second, the faculty is the curriculum. 90% of curriculum choices and teaching enhancements are made at the point of permanent hire. Who teaches largely answers the questions about what is taught and how it is taught and when it is taught and so on. In the church, we talk in terms of 'conference program' or 'denominational ministry,' but the dynamic is the same. The ministers of the conference are the conference program. Period. The faculty is the curriculum. Forgive a New Testament digression, but this is what the irascible Apostle to the Gentiles meant, I think, in 2 Corinthians 3: 1ff, a most difficult chapter to translate well. He contrasts print documents with the human being. "Do we need, as some do, letters of recommendation to you, or from you? You yourselves are our letter of recommendation, written on your (our?) hearts to be known and read by all (men). . .written not with ink but with the Spirit of the living God, not on tablets of stone but on tablets of human hearts." You yourselves are the curriculum. Again, I do not here deny the importance of collegial conversation, learning with and perhaps teaching with each other, sharing best practices, and growing steadily ourselves. We, though, come, each one, with decades of commitments made, investments undertaken. We are the curriculum. But I seldom hear us acknowledge this.

Third, as just one person around the table, and speaking from 30 years of preaching twice each week, many visits each week, etc., I cannot think of one paragraph, sentence, phrase, word or syllable that I heard, read or learned in seminary that was not helpful in ministry. The issue is not that some of it is good and the rest is hooey. The issue is that we have 3 years (actually more like 18 months) in which to provide a sound basis for sound ministry. It is all essential, and all helpful, particularly what may seem most unhelpful at the time. The challenge is to provide enough excitement about the documentary hypothesis and the synoptic problem, enough intrigue about Chalcedon and the reformations, enough tensive enjoyment of Aquinas and Guttierez, enough admiration for Steimle and Chalmers, that a whole of life of learning in ministry ensues. Not one shred of Bible, History, Theology, and Rhetoric is superfluous to real ministry, let alone to 'pastoral excellence.' In other words, I assume that the dichotomy, learning vs. piety, is a false one.

November 29

Winter Dawn

The dawn is breaking, slowly, over the snow-blanketed city. You have assembled your-self for the morning, with your coat and hat and mittens. You stand like a medieval knight with his standard, you with your great-mouthed shovel in hand, and dawn is breaking, slowly, over the fourth day of Nevada, the great snowfall. You are ready to start.

In our shared epiphany, this early winter, we have prepared to start. We encouraged you to begin by breathing. We pondered the possibility of a New Birth of Freedom. We noticed the early, first light of love in music, love and music. We announced and received a winter grace. We meditated on starting over. You have had already a homiletically busy year.

Yet there is a relationship between knowing and doing that dies without the strength of choosing. It is one thing to know the true and good and beautiful. It is another thing to do the true and good and beautiful. How do we move from knowing to doing? By choosing. Learning becomes virtue through piety. Learning becomes virtue through piety. Learning becomes virtue through piety. . . .

In some way best only known to you, by faith, you are ready to start. You have practiced the breathing of prayer. You have seen the horizon of freedom. You have heard the loving angels sing. You have admired a winter grace. You have seen the need to start over. Somehow. I do not know, fully, all of your new starts, though some are pretty clear, and shared. All share this: it takes strength to start. To change to a new path requires strength to start.

Shakespeare knew the beauty and terror of the dawn:
The grey eyed morn smiles on the frowning night
Chequering the eastern clouds with streaks of light
And flecked darkness like a drunkard reels
Form forth days path and Titan's fiery wheels
Now ere the sun advance his burning eye
The day to cheer and night's dank dew to dry

November 30

December

Lay People

Lay people are people. Beloved, it will do us no good only to open up the church. We also have responsibility to build up the church. The needs, longings, reports and voices of lay people count, matter, last, and have meaning. The church exists for mission, as fire for burning. Fishing and planting, evangelism and stewardship—these are the joy of faith. And the fun, too. Lay people deserve and desire enchanting worship. We have every reason to provide vibrant, warm, ordered, traditional worship. Sixty minutes of fire and love, every Sunday. We will want to draw on the deep well of tradition—not traditionalism but tradition. Listen to the lay people. They have no need for bongo drums, shallow hymns, neglected liturgy, or bad music. They respond to excellence. They deserve it. Traditional worship is what we owe them. Likewise, lay people deserve loving, intelligent, devoted, competent pastoral ministry and preaching. We once knew that so deeply we needed no reminder. Traveling preachers, taking grace and freedom and love from post to post—this is what we once did best. Please: no more lay pastors, local pastors, deacons than absolutely necessary. Give us excellent ministers, educated and ordained, the brightest and the best! And are some of these local pastors excellent? Excellent! Then educate them and ordain them. Put up or shut up. And lay people deserve the best that money can provide, and the best exemplary teaching about money we can provide. If nothing else, our tradition provides stellar disciplines about giving. Our people need to be taught, by the example of the clergy, to tithe. Well led, they will and do well follow. Tradition in worship, Traveling elders in the pulpit, Tithing all day long—I cannot begin to tell you how much difference these three currently neglected features of spiritual life make when they are practiced, and especially when they are practiced together!

December 1

Kings of the Earth[2]

In May each year I watch our M.Div. and other graduates at Commencement. We send them out with a degree, with too much debt, and with minimum exposure to what they will soon encounter, especially if they are called to preach. All, and more than all, we give them, in Bible and History and Theology and Practice, they will need. Every scrap. They are digging a well from which they will want to drink for many years. It should be well dug. Yet I wonder sometimes how to begin to provide some exposure, early on, to life in ministry, or to ministry, or to life. Then, now and then, a book will appear, and I will read it, and I will think: "While this will never appear in a seminary curriculum, and shouldn't, I wish all graduates would read it, between graduation and their first Sunday in the pulpit and their first autumn stewardship drive."

And when the book (in this case a novel) opens the particular world they will enter in a magnificent way (in this case I am most concerned about those students going to rural churches in the Northeast, where many begin), I get excited enough to write up a review. Those entering the ministry will see here a part of the world they are entering. Those already in ministry will recognize what a couple of decades of pastoral experience can also reveal: people, poor and hard working people, forgotten laboring people, who have the *imago dei* splashed all over them, in the midst of the mire and struggle of the farm and the barn and the field.

Jon Clinch's novel is one of the best of our generation. Its lyrical beauty and narrative verve recall M Robinson's *Gilead* and A McIntyre's *No Great Mischief*. It has been a long time since rural upstate New York inspired such a work (do people still read *The Damnation of Theron Ware?* or *Drums Along the Mohawk?*). The novel is loosely based on the thirty year-old story of the Ward brothers, in which one brother is charged with murdering another, and which inspired the documentary *My Brother's Keeper*. Clinch tells his hard, glad, generous story in several voices, each of which, chapter by chapter, has a kind of genius. He describes three post-war brothers, of limited everything, milking a few dozen cows, and living a kind of life that pastors will recognize or soon recognize, a life imbued with a kind of 'antique strangeness.' That one phrase captures much of the mood of the book. The novel compels its reader also to consider the merits and virtues of what is an increasingly antique kindness, yet one still visible at milking time, in the winter, out beyond the bright lights of the big city.

If you decide to read the novel, you will hear the voices of these three struggling brothers. You will hear the heroic voice of their neighbor, a man named Preston, who attends church as a way of honoring his wife (his comment about one pastor is choice: 'on Sunday he was everywhere and during the week he was nowhere'). The competing and conflicting voices of lawyers, police and a district attorney themselves are ample preparation for what one will find once the committee or Bishop assigns a pulpit. The haunting memories of what it took for young men to leave home for war and return home from war are justly evoked

2. : *Kings of the Earth*. Jon Clinch (author of *Finn*). NY: Random House, 2010. 393pps. $26.00

here. One of the truest voices is that of the sister of the brothers, who has made her escape, somehow, from the family's dysfunction, and yet continues to care and heal and pray. It is this quality embedded in the novel that perhaps most fits, and proudly heralds, what one finds moving from classroom to kitchen table, from library to pulpit. The writer has found a way to show just how powerfully, personally, ably, and fully these characters—and their real life counterparts—"watch over one another in love," without much aid or interference from organized religion.

As a people we don't always remember the past and we don't well plan for the future and we don't regularly notice the heroism of people like those depicted in *Kings of the Earth*. We somehow forget them. Then we get appointed to a rural parish, or pick up a recent novel, and we are powerfully reminded.

In 1981 we moved from Ithaca and Cornell to two rural, tiny villages an hour southwest of Montreal. Imagine my surprise to discover that while the communal levels of formal learning were lower up north, the communal levels of real wisdom were higher. It is that kind of surprise, discovery, and delight that await the reader of *Kings of the Earth*.

December 2

Canada: One

A popular refrain in Montreal runs like this: "Canada could have had the best of three worlds: British government, American industry, and French culture; instead, Canada collected the worst of all three: French bureaucracy, British economics, and American culture!"

But don't you believe it. As that proverb's tangled contents and tone of wry self-criticism tell, Canada has a great deal to offer you and me. We can learn from our northern neighbors. This is part testimony and part admonition: Take a look at the Dominion of Canada. In particular, let me suggest three things that United Methodists can bring across the border.

First, there is the Anglican Church of Canada. Its influence far exceeds that of its sister Protestant Episcopal church in the Unite States. Though still statistically small, Canadian Anglicanism in one sense is the ecclesiastical leader of its land. We United Methodists-especially those out of the Methodist Episcopal tradition-need to hear the voice of the Church of England. After all, we are called to honor our father and mother; where would Methodism be without its Anglican mother? In this age when theological judgment is so frightfully difficult, the history and tradition and liturgy of this parent church have such to offer us. To take just one example: We Americans sometimes make much of religious experience. But there are some things that should not have to be learned from experience. The richness of our Anglican heritage can remind us of this.

December 3

Canada: Two

Second, there is Doug Hall, teacher at McGill University in Montreal, former student of Paul Tillich, and author, His book *Lighten Our Darkness* sounds like a voice of realistic truth crying in pious wilderness. For example:

> The test of theological authenticity is whether we can present *Jesus as the crucified.* To be concrete: Can one perceive in the Jesus of this theology a man who knows the meaning of meaninglessness, the experience of negation, the anguish of hopelessness? Does he encounter the absurd, and with trembling? Would a man dare to confess to this Jesus his deepest anxieties, his most ultimate questions? Would such a Jesus comprehend the gnawing care of a generation of parents who live every day with the questions: Will my children be able to survive as human beings? Will there be enough to eat? Will they be permitted to have children? Would he, the God-Man of this theology, be able to weep over the dead bodies of little children in Southeast Asia and Brazil, as he wept over his friend Lazarus? Would he be able to agonize over the millions of other beings-not quite little-children, fetuses-for whom there was no place; and over the mothers. . .Could he share our doubt: doubt about God, about man, about life, about every absolute? Could he understand why we cling to expectations that are no longer affirmed or confirmed by experience, why we repress the most essential questions? Would such a Christ understand failure? Could he participate in *our* failure? Or is he eternally above all that?[1]

December 4

---

1. Douglas J. Hall, *Lighten Our Darkness: Toward an Indigenous Theology of the Cross* (Philadelphia: The Westminster Press, 1976), 211–212.

Canada: Three

Third, there is the United Church. It was formed in 1925 as a union among Methodists, some Presbyterians, Congregationalists, and other Protestant groups. Today it is a church of some 2 million members (in a country of only 25 million), built out of a combination of Methodist and Presbyterian policy. It is not a church without problems. But for those of us who are still interested in walking a little further down the road toward ecumenism, the experience of the United Church in both its victories and defeats offers a glimpse of what our future might be like.

Canadian tourism commercials entice us to the natural, scenic, and cultural wonders of Canada, our neighbor to the north, "the world next door." United Methodist, I believe, have at least three other reasons for interest: Anglicanism, Doug Hall, the United Church. Take a look

December 5

Equality

You love the tradition of the church as well. Though with a scornful wonder we see her sore oppressed. John Wesley loved the church's tradition too, enough to study it and to know it, and to seek its truth. The central ecclesiastical tradition of his time, the tradition of apostolic succession, he termed a 'fable.' It would be like political debaters today using charged language like "fairy tale." Likewise, we lovers of the church tradition will not be able to grasp for certainty in it, if that grasping dehumanizes others. The Sabbath was made for the human being, not the other way around, in our tradition.

Baptism is as traditional and central a variously understand practice as Christianity possesses. It is in some ways the very doorway to our traditions. Yet listen to Paul today. In his context, he rejects baptism. For him gospel trumps tradition.

Our linkage of the gifts of heterosexuality and ministry, however traditional, fall before grace and freedom. Further, on a purely practical level, another generation will not be impressed by church growth strategies rooted in the exclusion of 10% of the population. There is a serious upside limit to the use of gay bashing to grow churches. My three children in their twenties are not going to stay around for it.

It is theologically tempting to shore up by keeping out. But it has no future. Equality will triumph over exclusion. It is coming like the glory of the morning on the wave.

If I were convening a Lenten study in suburban Washington DC I would have the group read G. Wills' *Head and Heart: American Christianities*, for some perspective on the way traditions change.

December 6

Evolution

You love the mind, the reason. You love the prospect of learning. You love the life of the mind. You love the Lord with heart and soul and mind. A mind is a terrible thing to waste. You love the reason in the same that Charles Darwin, a good Anglican, loved the reason. You love its capacity to see things differently. (Marsh Chapel will host a series of ten sermons on the theme "Darwin and Faith," offered by preachers from around the country, during the summer of 2009).

Of course reason unfettered can produce hatred and holocaust. Learning for its own sake needs virtue and piety. More than anything else, learning to last must finally be rooted in loving. Did you hear the one thing requested in our vibrant Psalm? To inquire in the temple. Inquiry.

The universe is 14 billion years old. The earth is 4.5 billion years old. 500 million years ago multi-celled organisms appeared in the Cambrian explosion. 400 million years ago plants sprouted. 370 million years ago land animals emerged. 230 million years ago dinosaurs appeared (and disappeared 65 million years ago). 200,000 years ago hominids arose. Every human being carries 60 new mutations out of 6 billion cells. Yes, evolution through natural selection by random mutation is a reasonable hypothesis, says F Collins, father of the human genome project, and, strikingly, a person of faith.

If I were the chaplain of a small private school in New England I might have my fellowship group read this winter F Collins, *the Language of God*. He can teach us to reason together.

It is tempting to disjoin learning and vital piety, but it is not loving to disjoin learning and vital piety. They go together. The God of Creation is the very God of Redemption. Their disjunction may help us cling for a while to a kind of faux certainty. But their conjunction is the confidence born of obedience. Falsehood has no defense and truth needs none.

December 7

Existence

You love experience. The gift of experience in faith is the heart of your love of Christ. You love Christ. Like Howard Thurman loved the mystical ranges of experience, you do too. Isaiah, in looking forward, can sing of the joy of harvest. We know joy. Joy seizes us. Joy grasps us when we are busy grasping at other things. You love what we are given morning and evening.

You love experience more than enough to examine your experience, to think about and think through what you have seen and done.

But beloved, a simple or general appeal to the love of experience, in our time, in 2008, is not appealing or loving. It is not experience, but our very existence which lies under the shadow of global violence. To have any future worthy of the name we shall need to foreswear preemptive violence. How the stealthy entry of such a manner of behavior could enter our civil discourse without voluminous debate and vehement challenge is a measure of our longing for false certainties. Our existence itself is on the line in discussions or lack of discussions about violent action that is preemptive, unilateral, imperial, and reckless. One thinks of Lincoln saying of slavery, 'those who support it might want to try it for themselves.' Not one of us wants to be the victim of preemptive violence. We may argue about the need for response, and even for the need of some kinds of anticipatory defense. But preemption? It will occlude existence itself.

If I were gathering a book club in downtown Boston to read this winter I would select the articles and books of Andrew Bacevich. Our future lies on the narrower path of responsive, communal, sacrificial, prudent behavior and requires of us, in Bacevich's hero Neibuhr's phrase, "a spiritual discipline against resentment."

There are indeed theological temptations in the unbalanced love of Scripture, tradition, reason or experience. As we come soon to Lent let us face them down. Let us face them down together. Let us do so by lifting our voices to admit errancy, affirm equality, explore evolution, and admire existence. The measure of preaching today in the tradition of a responsible Christian liberalism is found in our willingness to address errancy, equality, evolution and existence.

December 8

To Repeat:

Perhaps we could set to music a hymn with these verses, in some combination:

God is love.

Love is both mercy and justice, both compassion and holiness.

Compassion is more important than holiness.

God loves the world (not just the church).

The church lives in the culture. The church lives *in* the culture to transform it. (Not above it to disdain it, not below it to obey it, not behind it to mimic it, not before it hector it).

The church is the Body of Christ.

Christ is alive. Wherever there is way, truth, life . . .

Life is sacred.

Life is a sacred journey to freedom.

The Bible is freedom's book.

The Bible is *a* source, not *the* source, of truth

The Sabbath was made for man, not man for the Sabbath.

War is hell.

Peace is heaven. Jesus is the prince of Peace.

Gay people are people.

Women's bodies are *women's* bodies.

Women and men need each other.

There is a self correcting spirit of truth loose in the universe.

The founder of Methodism is John Wesley (not John Calvin).

The ministers of the conference are the conference. Period.

Ministry is preaching.

The fun of faith is in tithing and inviting. 'Remember the poor.'

Tithing is required. It is core, not elective.

Death is the last enemy. As Forest Gump said, atop his beloved's grave, "My momma told me that 'death is a part of life.' But wish it weren't."

God's love outlasts death.

December 9

Christmas: School of Theology

After graduation from Boston University School of Theology, and following close on the heels of the mid-May joyful commencement ceremony in Marsh Chapel, some students suddenly find themselves, July 1, in a pulpit on Sunday, in meetings during the week, living in a parsonage, and wondering how to stoke the fires of a stewardship campaign (by November 1, svp).

When Christmas starts to roll around, a set of specific seasonal questions may arise, one of which is about preaching. How do I preach coming to Christmas? What shall I say, or how shall I say what I say, coming to Christmas? How do I get started as I design a sermon in December?

One thought.

Coming to Christmas, you may confidently rely on the narrative and on narrative in general. I am not generally a fan of narrative preaching, though I respect the work F Craddock and others did to rejuvenate preaching a generation ago. But the narratives at Christmas carry well, as do stories resting upon them. There is something in the journeys at the heart of the season that calls for, or calls out, narrative. Some narrative is right in the Scripture—Samuel, Mary, John, Jesus. Some comes from the tradition (have you read Luke 2 in the KJV lately?) Some is reasonable, a recognition of the way our individual smaller stories fit into the one great story of the one great day of God (when you can pastorally connect someone's personal story with an aspect of the gospel story you have given a powerful gift). Some is in our own experience. Here are two examples, as a merry Christmas gift and wish, Marsh Chapel sermons from 12.4.11 and 12.11.11: (http://blogs.bu.edu/sermons/2011/12/04/grace-upon-grace)

December 10

Winthrop, Lincoln, King, Rickey

Out on the Massachusetts Bay, in the autumn of 1630, Governor Jonathan Winthrop speaks to the frightened pilgrims. The Governor is brief, in his sermon for the day: "We must consider that we shall be a city upon a hill. The eyes of all people are upon us, so that if we shall deal falsely with our God in this work we have undertaken, and so cause Him to withdraw His present help from us, we shall be made a story and a byword through the world." A remarkable, truly remarkable warning, to our country, at the moment of its inception.

It is a cold day in early March 1865. Four score and nine years after Independence, the nation has indeed become, as Winthrop prophesied, "a story and byword through the world." Nearly 600,000 men will have died by the time Lee and Grant meet at Appomatox; approximately one death for every 10 slaves forcibly brought to the New World. This day in March, Mr. Lincoln delivers his own sermon: "The Almighty has His own purposes. . .Fondly do we hope, fervently do we pray, that this mighty scourge of war may speedily pass away. Yet, if God wills that it continue until all the wealth piled by the bondsman's 250 years of unrequited toil shall by sunk, and until every drop of blood drawn with the lash shall be paid by another drawn with the sword, as was said 3000 years ago, so still it must be said, 'The judgments of the Lord are true and righteous altogether.' With malice toward none, with charity for all, with firmness in the right as God gives us to see the right, let us strive on to finish the work that we are in, to bind up the nation's wounds, to care for him who shall have borne the battle and for his widow and his orphan, to do all which may achieve and cherish a just and lasting peace; among ourselves and with all nations."

A hundred more years pass. It is August 28, 1963, a sweltering day in the nation's capital. Thousands of women and men have gathered in the shadow of Lincoln's memorial, and within earshot of his Second Inaugural- maybe some of you were there. A Baptist preacher captures the moment in ringing oratory: "I have a dream that one day on the red hills of Georgia the sons of former slaves and the sons of former slaveowners will be able to sit down at the table of brotherhood."

Winthrop. Lincoln. King. 1630.1865.1963. These are possibly the three greatest sermons ever preached in our country's history. Do you notice that not one of them was delivered in a church? Yet they all interpret the church's Gospel to the land of the free and home of the brave. They warned of tragedy, they endured tragedy, they honestly acknowledged tragedy. What Winthrop prophesied, and what Lincoln witnessed, and what King attacked is our national tragedy still. Too often we still judge-by color of skin and not by the content of character.

The dual achievements of Sammy Sosa and Mark Mc Gwire, this year, though, remind us that some hopeful progress has been made. Baseball, at least, has achieved a measure of racial integration and harmony. We have Branch Rickey to thank for that.

Last year, without much fanfare, we passed the 50th anniversary of Jackie Robinson's entrance into major league baseball. In America in 1947, the armed forces were still legally segregated. So were public schools. But a tee-totalling, Bible-quoting Republican business-man from Ohio-—Branch Rickey—integrated major league baseball.

Rickey was one of those people who just never heard that it can't be done. He was someone who would not take "no" for an answer. For 30 years, slowly, painstakingly, he ma-neuvered and strategized and planned and brought about the greatest change in the history of our national pastime. He brought Jackie Robinson into the game, and so brought some real progress and hope. William McClain, an African American preacher, tells about grow-ing up in Tuskegee, Alabama, and listening to the team Branch Rickey fielded in Brooklyn. "When Jackie Robinson stood at the plate, we stood with him," McClain recalls. "When he struck out, we did too. When he hit the ball, we jumped and cheered. When he slid home, we dusted off our own pants. When he stole a base, he stole for us. When he hit a home run, we were the victors. And when he was spiked we all felt it a long way away, down South. He gave us hope. He gave us hope."

Branch Rickey—one lone person, in one lone lifetime, in one lone sport, in one lone generation—brought to life a sermon, a sermon on the mound. The best preaching hap-pens beyond church. Some is spoken and some is lived. God has not left us, nor does God abandon God's children. God works through human hearts, to bind up the nation's wounds. Finally, it is the love of neighbor which brings peace.

Where is the Branch Rickey of Wall Street? Where is the Branch Rickey of the local church? Where is the Branch Rickey of the public school? Where is the Branch Rickey of your neighborhood? Where is the Branch Rickey of the urban/suburban split in Monroe County?

Where is that secular saint who doesn't realize it can't be done? Where is the preacher of the next sermon on the mound?

Maybe she or he is reading this today.

Don't let people tell you things can't change for the better. They can. This country can work. We just need a few more Branch Rickeys, and a few more sermons on the mound.

December 11

Preaching and Conflict Resolution

Some conflicts in church life have no resolution. No forgiveness, nor reconciliation, nor resolution. When the stakes involve income and employment, on the one hand, or honor and shame, on the other, there often is no early or short-term resolution. Disdainfully, almost thirty years ago, I took a book from a larger church pastor whose secretary he had fired, and whose secretary now sat in my pews. He asked that I give her the book, his greetings, and his affection. I thought: you low life pervert. How could you possibly resort to such an indirect, passive, easy attempt at reconciliation? Now, having terminated two secretaries on unfriendly terms, I understand. People are not happy or reasonable when someone moves their cheese, particularly a Pastor. 'Pastoral administration' is an oxymoron. These things are driven out only by prayer and fasting. Thus, they really have no place in the sermon.

Other typically church conflicts may be avoided or avoided and ameliorated, "finessed," by wise, sensitive, and politically savvy pastoral conniving. People usually back off if they feel they have been heard, truly heard. Hence the need for a 'cast iron fundament' on which pastorally to sit through many useless meetings, useful only to air the grievance of the aggrieved. "Up in the Old Hotel" includes a story of a man who allegedly spends thirty years writing 100 or more books of history about New York City. He leaves them in packages around town—with a bartender, in the library, under a friend's porch. At his death they are collected and found to be thousands of repetitions of a single grief: the author's piteous relationship with his dad.

December 12

Edwards

If you would be in the way to the world of love, see that you live a life of love — of love to God, and love to men. All of us hope to have part in the world of love hereafter, and therefore we should cherish the spirit of love, and live a life of holy love here on earth. This is the way to be like the inhabitants of heaven, who are now confirmed in love forever. Only in this way can you be like them in excellence and loveliness, and like them, too, in happiness, and rest, and joy. By living in love in this world you may be like them, too, in sweet and holy peace, and thus have, on earth, the foretastes of heavenly pleasures and delights. Thus, also, you may have a sense of the glory of heavenly things, as of God, and Christ, and holiness; and your heart be disposed and opened by holy love to God, and by the spirit of peace and love to men, to a sense of the excellence and sweetness of all that is to be found in heaven. Thus shall the windows of heaven be as it were opened, so that its glorious light shall shine in upon your soul. Thus you may have the evidence of your fitness for that blessed world, and that you are actually on the way to its possession. And being thus made meet, through grace, for the inheritance of the saints in light, when a few more days shall have passed away, you shall be with them in their blessedness forever. Happy, thrice happy those, who shall thus be found faithful to the end, and then shall be welcomed to the joy of their Lord! There "they shall hunger no more, neither thirst any more; neither shall the sun light on them, nor any heat. For the Lamb which is in the midst of the throne shall feed them, and lead them to living fountains of waters, and God shall wipe away all tears from their eyes.[1]

December 13

1. Jonathan Edwards, "Heaven, A World of Love." http://www.biblebb.com/files/edwards/charity16. htm

Elections

Elections are about winning.

We have elections and count votes to determine winners. Elections are events you enter if you are interested in winning. If you get into it, 'get in it to win it.' Otherwise, don't get into it.

I am thankful for recent reminders of this.

Elections are not about being right.

They are about winning. It is not enough to be right. Or smart. Or wise. (Though these may matter to some who cast votes on these bases). Do not, do not, do NOT enter an election to prove a point, to win an argument, or to show that you are bright and right. Do not.

Why? Because you will crowd out someone who wants to win, which is the only reason to run. Prove your point in a book. Win your argument on a talk show. Show how smart you are in a documentary film. Only get into a real election if you are interested in winning. Winning is not everything. It is the only thing. When it comes to elections, winning is the only thing that matters in the end.

But didn't he speak so well? Yes, he did. But didn't she run an exciting campaign? Yes, she did. But wouldn't he have made a great leader? Yes, he would have. But aren't the people foolish, even stupid, for not supporting him? Yes, they truly are. But doesn't being right count for something? Yes, it sure does. But didn't he bring change just by representing his people? He did that. But aren't political campaigns a nasty, ugly business? Yes they are.

If you agree with all this, then why did he\she lose?

Because he did not get enough votes.

But he is so eloquent, so energetic, so competent, so smart, so representative, so good! Yes, and he lost.

But why?

Because people did not vote f or him.

But why not?

Because they did not want to vote for him, and it is their choice, their vote, theirs.

December 14

Embodied Theory Chapel Classroom

In the course of preparing students to preach, one addresses the issue of exegesis. Within that major, massive undertaking, the teacher may want to highlight the movement from text to sermon that occurs in preaching on passages from the gospels. One particular approach here involves a choral image. The students are asked to imagine the passages of the Gospels, not as solos, but as hymns sung in four- part harmony. So every passage will potentially include soprano, alto, tenor and bass lines: the soprano melody of the voice of the historical Jesus to the limited extent one may yet hear it; the profoundly significant alto voice of the early church which developed the notes sung well before their appearance in the canonical score; the tenor of the author, Matthew, Mark, Luke or John; and the ongoing basso profundo, the baritone line of interpretation of the passage, starting right in the Bible itself (for Mark, beginning with Matthew and Luke, for example; for John, beginning with 1 John, for example), and continuing on in some ways to yesterday and today and next Sunday when the sermon is finally preached. The gospels are sung in four-part harmony, as many congregations once regularly did sing hymns. The preacher will watch carefully to hear and overhear the various 'parts' within the fully harmonic beauty. To this point, standard instruction in homiletics can proceed without any interaction with the argument of this paper.

Suppose, however, that the teacher is also a preacher, who is responsible every Sunday for a sermon within the context (a highly particularized context) of a University Chapel, located not more than 100 yards east of the offices of practical theologians, the library stalls of graduate students, and the very classroom setting for learning and teaching about exegesis. On one hand, now, the stakes have been radically raised. Sunday arrives, and the text Luke 13. Is there an exegetical chorus heard in the sermon? For those students who are seized by the confession of the church, and who have become a part of the addressable community in the University Chapel, an interpretive moment has arrived. And for the teacher, a moment of truth has come. Do the pods of church and school, ecclesia and academy stick to each other, in R Osmer's image, in ways that allow for transversal reason to engage both student and teacher? The worship service in question is a real, live service, with real living and dying humans. Real ammunition is in use. On any given Sunday the possibility stands that one student or one retiree may hear his or her last earthly benediction, that morning. The setting is not a contrived 'preaching club' quasi-service, nor even a seminary only mid-week devotion. The church has gathered and the hope still lives for something to hear and something to eat, through preaching meant to teach, to delight, and to persuade. Moreover, and quite visible to the eye of the worshipping homiletics student, there stands a person, now robed, who looks quite like the disheveled teacher she remembers from Tuesday's homiletics lecture, which dealt with exegesis and the gospels.

We have here 'a theory-praxis relationship embodied within the vocation of a practical theologian who is working concurrently in the academy and in the pastorate.' Furthermore, for teacher and student and congregation, the experience in worship of the sermon may therefore take on either a greater sense of risk or a greater possibility of benefit. If the sermon bears faithfulness to the teaching earlier in the week about the sermon, the student may benefit. Having offered some preliminary description and empirical observation of a weekly pattern actually found in at least one setting, we pause to provide some reflection upon and interpretation of the experience, the pattern. The preacher may on occasion refer, in passing, to the SATB critique of Luke 13 by saying, "as we teach our students across the plaza, passages like this in the gospels are like our own favorite Methodist hymns. . . ." In fact, the preacher may not be able to avoid saying something like this, given the intertextuality, the interpsychic connection in his own life between pulpit and lectern.

December 15

Embodied Theory Pastoral Imagination

I believe that the actual condition of the churches, now, in 2010, in which our urban pastors find themselves, is important to assess. Across the north, and extended north, at any rate, the condition of the churches is different from what it was fifteen years ago. Churches in the urban settings, with some exceptions, are high in need, and low in resource, as are their neighborhoods. As the churches' conditions weaken, the demand on the leadership expands, the stress rises, and the need for Sabbath, both as rest and as reflection of the creativity of the divine, dramatically increases. In particular, the conditions of the buildings and of the lay leadership ranks (and hence of the churches' finances) have a claim on attention. Second, if the desire is to sustain pastoral excellence, then what constitutes excellence becomes something of an issue, as one thinks about what sustains it. I found the conference strong on sustaining pastors. I wondered, though, what pastoral excellence was in view. My understanding I guess is that what sustains excellence is excellence itself. In other words, what nourishes the minister, most strongly, is not the absence of work, but work, not disengagement, but fruitful engagement in the practice of ministry—the work itself, enjoyed for its own sake, and practiced happily with excellence.

C Foster's Educating Clergy affirms the argument of this paper. I have known Chuck for twenty years, and our family has known him for forty years. In particular, the exploration of pastoral imagination in Foster's book I find compelling. There are many applications of his thought in the life and work of ministry in general, which I bypass for the moment. There also is a singular significance, in the play of the imagination, for the prospect of ministerial health. Where the imagination quickens and is quickened one finds passion, happiness, and effectiveness. I wonder if we have fully exhausted the reading of his book and conversation about it.

A matter closely related to the encouragement of reading itself, clergy reading itself, perhaps deserves more attention. John Wesley divided the day into morning for reading, afternoon for visiting, and evening for meetings. Allan Knight Chalmers taught his 1950's students to read a book a day. We certainly continue to emphasize the spiritual significance of reading the curriculum here, don't we? Or don't we? I mean wide, fun, imaginative, idiosyncratic reading, as well as professional reading. Do our students graduate loving reading or not?

Let me next set out some complementary assumptions or perspectives with which I think I participate in this kind of conversation. These are angles of vision or points of view that are perhaps different from, though not contradictory to, the largely unspoken assumptions and perspectives we have used together. It is hard to change the carburetor while the vehicle is cruising down the turnpike, so we often leave systemic or perspectival discussions to rest stops like this one. That is as it should be.

The mission of a school of theology is to educate clergy. Two words is a good number for a mission statement, and 'educate clergy' are the two words I would choose. By educate I mean twenty things, among them the intention to form life-long learners who are self taught on the basis of a robust exposure to classical materials. By clergy I mean twenty one professionals, among them teachers, preachers, leaders, executives, and those who teach all these, who will bring dimensions of meaning, belonging and empowerment to the new creation, during their day in the Day of God. In saying this I do not deny or contradict the lengthy mission paragraph we have affirmed as a faculty. It is good, but not easily remembered. In saying this I do not deny the important ongoing discussion of theology as the core of theological study, largely because pastoral excellence absolutely requires, utterly depends on every shred of decent theological study available. (In the long run.) In any case, of the 5 funding streams I can dimly perceive which currently pay our rent and grocery bills, 5 assume that our mission is to educate clergy. For this reason I think Foster's book, *Educating Clergy*, has something to offer us.[2]

The faculty is the curriculum. 90% of curriculum choices and teaching enhancements are made at the point of permanent hire. Who teaches largely answers the questions about what is taught and how it is taught and when it is taught and so on. In the church, we talk in terms of 'conference program' or 'denominational ministry,' but the dynamic is the same. The ministers of the conference are the conference program. Period. The faculty is the curriculum. Forgive a New Testament digression, but this is what the irascible Apostle to the Gentiles meant, I think, in 2 Corinthians 3: 1ff, a most difficult chapter to translate well. He contrasts print documents with the human being. "Do we need, as some do, letters of recommendation to you, or from you? You yourselves are our letter of recommendation, written on your (our?) hearts to be known and read by all (men) . . . written not with ink but with the Spirit of the living God, not on tablets of stone but on tablets of human hearts." You yourselves are the curriculum. Again, I do not here deny the importance of collegial conversation, learning with and perhaps teaching with each other, sharing best practices, and growing steadily ourselves. We, though, come, each one, with decades of commitments made, investments undertaken. We are the curriculum. But I seldom hear us acknowledge this.

Further, as just one person around the table, and speaking from 30 years of preaching twice each week, many visits each week, etc., I cannot think of one paragraph, sentence, phrase, word or syllable that I heard, read or learned in seminary that was not helpful in ministry. The issue is not that some of it is good and the rest is hooey. The issue is that we have 3 years (actually more like 18 months) in which to provide a sound basis for sound ministry. It is all essential, and all helpful, particularly what may seem most unhelpful at the time. The challenge is to provide enough excitement about the documentary hypothesis and the synoptic problem, enough intrigue about Chalcedon and the reformations, enough tensive enjoyment of Aquinas and Guttierez, enough admiration for Steimle and Chalmers, that a whole of life of learning in ministry ensues. Not one shred of Bible, History, Theology, and Rhetoric is superfluous to real ministry, let alone to "pastoral excellence." In other words, I assume that the dichotomy, learning vs. piety, is a false one.

I would like to lift up again the possibility of some sustained, communal conversation about Foster's book, perhaps with Foster present. His overview of current theological education, has several distinctive advantages, only one of which I will lift up here. In this largely positive, even happy travel through various theological schools and seminaries, Foster regularly returns to the issue of pastoral imagination, as he terms it: How does a seminary

2. Charles Foster, *Educating Clergy: Teaching Practices and Pastoral Imagination* (San Francisco: Jossey-Bass, 2005.

education cultivate a pastoral, rabbinic or priestly imagination that integrates knowledge and skill with religious commitment and moral integrity for professional practice?"[1] The exploration of his work is directed at those educators who have found ways to answer that question: Clergy educators innovate or adapt by drawing on resources of inherited religious and academic traditions to convey or model for students' pastoral, priestly, or rabbinic imaginations. In our study, students often spoke of moments in their learning as awakening or discovering new meanings in sacred texts, alternative strategies for the conduct of some clergy practice, or new dimensions to their calling and vocation."[2]

I hope that the next several years will allow us to consider the integration of theology and practice with regard to the pastoral imagination, as it is discussed by Foster. In fact, I think that both the long history of BUSTH and the exciting present faculty at BUSTH have everything to offer this discussion.

December 16

1. Foster, 327.
2. Foster, 23.

Forms of Ministerial Imagination

1 John 4:7–12

(Parentheses note hours per week)

1. *Preaching* (25): A faithfully excellent sermon 50 times a year over 40 years becomes an oasis in the desert for listener and speaker and all; the "Fosdick rule" still applies.

2. *Visitation* (20): Two dozen pastoral conversations a week, initiated by the minister (hospital, home, office, third place), model the invitational welcome of the church, and can become communion, heart to heart.

3. *Spiritual Health*: You deserve to have a life, and time off (an hour a day, a day a week, a week a quarter, a quarter a year), to use in prayer, reading, camping, traveling, studying, exercising.

4. *Continuing Education*: CE is best engaged as the pursuit of another, complementary degree (law, health science, teaching, business, music).

5. *Pastoral Counseling* (1): One (at most two) hour long session (s) per person, with the sole agenda being referral, and the door always open.

6. Money: There are two "secrets" to raising money—giving and asking; if you tithe they (some) will tithe and if you ask they (some) will give, but you have to do it and you have to ask for it.

7. Stewardship (4): If you have to have a committee in church, have this one, with three members, one for estates (bequests), one for assets (capital campaigns), and one for income (annual pledges).

8. *Verbal Arsonists*: Psychologically ill people must be helped to leave the center stage, either through your benign neglect or through your private confrontational address ("a dysfunctional system focuses on the identified patient").

9. *Presence* (5): Worship, sacraments, liturgy, little league, concerts, basketball, graduations, parties, weddings, dinners, group teaching, lollygagging on Main Street, praying over the Memorial Day Canon, and otherwise "living in the community" are your pastoral work.

10. *Compensation:* You should be paid at least as much as the principal of the Junior High School in your town.

11. *Negotiation*: "A poor minister is a poor minister" (Brooks): early you will need to develop the difficult arts of conversational negotiation, especially if you are in a denomination that has no significant history of such.

12. *Denomination*: The best defense is a good offense, so pick one thing that is worth supporting and do so, but recognize the difference between the ministry of the churches and the inheritance of the over-church (one is connection, the other is dissolution).

13. *Farewell:* The most important thing you do is to leave well, and the most important thing in leaving well is arranging the process for finding your successor (no one else is going to want or know how to do this).

14. *Meetings* (5–10): Attend only when absolutely necessary; be sure the meeting lasts only 60 minutes (get up and leave thereafter); be sure there is one focal purpose to the meeting; 1/3 devotions, 1/3 discussion, 1/3 deliberation (one focal outcome).

15. *Team Members* (5): From staff, colleagues, lay leadership, or other partners you need two things in equal measure: loyalty and creativity.

16. *Prospects and Students:* The constituent list is where you spend your time (the minister is present for those not present), so to gather recovering and healing people, in part to dislodge those who need to leave the church for another, and sometimes need to be directly invited to do so.

17. *Crises:* Another's lack of planning does not constitute your personal crisis—'"Why don't we talk about this on Friday?"

18. *A Formula:* for Medical and Pastoral Practice: ability plus affability plus availability yields success.

19. *Buildings and Maintenance:* Either you get to maintenance, or maintenance gets to you; the building becomes either sacred shared space, or a millstone around the neck of the future.

20. *Ministry:* Ministry is service, to preach the Gospel and love the people; ministry is service, in a healthy way for a healthy outcome, to put yourself at the disposal of others.

December 17

Four Interviews

Social institutions as well as personal habits have an almost irresistible tendency to perpetuate themselves in disregard of the demands of creative justice in a new situation or under unique conditions both in the communal and in the individual life. (Tillich)

What kind of knowledge can create moral action? It cannot be the detached knowledge of pre-scientific or scientific inquiry, nor can it be the knowledge of the day to day handling of things and people, even if such knowledge is elevated to the level of technical expertise or psychological skill, for any of this can be used for the most anti-moral actions. (Our most flagrant example of this is the Nazi system).

December 18

Facts from Francis Collins

Francis Collins: *The Language of God*

The universe is 14 billion years old.

The earth is 4.5 billion years old.

Amino Acids somehow emerged 150 million years later.

The second law of thermodynamics states that 'in a closed system entropy (disorder) increases'.

Science cannot yet explain the origin of DNA and RNA (our hard and zip drives).

500 million years ago, multi celled organisms appeared. This is the so-called Cambrian explosion.

400 million years ago, plants sprouted.

370 million years ago, land animals emerged.

230 million years ago, dinosaurs emerged.

65 million years ago, dinosaurs disappeared. (perhaps in connection with a collision with an asteroid).

200,000 years ago, hominids appeared.

60 new mutations occur in every new human birth (out of 6 billion cells).

4004 BC, Usher's date of creation, is not a plausible date of creation.

The universe is ancient and all life is interrelated through evolution and selection.

A high pressure cardiovascular system where leaks must quickly be stopped.

The God of the Bible is also the God of the genome.

'Science without religion is lame. Religion without science is blind.' (Einstein).

The death rate will be one per person for the foreseeable future.

16 times more men go to prison than women.

December 19

Huffington Post

Katie Matthews was awake at 3am. Her good friend, she learned hours earlier, had died in New Zealand, one of three Boston University students lost in a car accident. Katie wondered what to do. She could hardly believe Austin was dead.

Katie is about to graduate. She is an education major, a future teacher, a native of Albany NY, a parishioner at BU Marsh Chapel, a leader, a person of faith. She felt something needed doing. Could she do something?

Katie thought maybe 20 or 30 of her closest friends could get together on the plaza of Marsh Chapel, Boston University, a space centered on the monument to Martin Luther King, Jr., to honor her friend. The Chapel website has a page about vigils. She made some notes. She froze for a moment. Could she carry this off? She began to reach out on Facebook in the wee hours of the morning. Could she do something? She decided she would try to do something. One of the chaplains at BU saw her posting and pledged support.

At 10am the next morning, unbeknownst to Katie, 20 BU administrators met to consider the dreadful tragedy of 3 deaths a half a world away, and just a week before Commencement. They began to plan for various responses. Could we do something, they wondered? The chaplain reported that a student group was planning a vigil that night at 8pm. Would they like some help?

By 8pm not 20 but 300 students, faculty, and staff were gathered with candles on Marsh Plaza. The President spoke. The Provost spoke. The Dean of the Chapel spoke. Students spoke. Live streaming carried the moment around the globe, especially arranged for those other students studying in so many places around the world. And for their parents. Katie spoke too. 'I knew I had to do something' she said. Here are some other things said at the vigil:

Tonight we are One BU in mourning.

We lift the names of those who died: Austin, Roch, Daniela.

May we help one another find our way to some solace.

Our hearts go out to their parents and families.

We want to face loss with love, grief with grace, disappointment with honesty, and death with dignity.

May we find the power and faith to withstand what we cannot understand.

Standing beside the monument to the Rev. Martin Luther King Jr., let us remember him not only as a prophetic national leader, but also as a wise and caring pastor, who said in a similar time of tragedy and loss. "when it gets dark enough you can see the stars."

Against a dark backdrop, brightness stands out. The brightness of friendship, relationship, youth, hope, dreams, faith, and love.

It is important to speak. But as the dusk settled in the Cradle of Liberty, Boston MA, and as the stars came out in the dark, and as the candles flickered in the gentle breeze, speech gave way to presence. Speech is important. Presence is more important. The vigil lasted 40 minutes, the gathering around candles lasted 2 more hours. Stories. Hugs. Tears.

Hugs. Stories. *Will somebody light my candle? . . . I wish we had Southern California weather, we could use this plaza like this all year long, this way. . . . Do you remember that time we were in Rhode Island and . . .*

Dusk comes. When dusk comes it is good to gather together, to grieve, to remember, to accept, to affirm. Our limited tenure walking on this green earth—our mortality, our fragility—is not easy to face, especially if we try to do so alone. That may be what Katie Matthews felt at 3am. So she found a way, just before Commencement, at a time of great joy, to help to gather our community in grief, in a time of great sorrow. Maybe she remembered the Apostle, "rejoice with those who rejoice, weep with those who weep" (Rom. 12:15). Maybe she recalled the psalmist, "weeping may tarry for the night, but joy comes with the morning" (Psalm 30:5). Or maybe she was thinking of her fellow Bostonian Robert F. Kennedy, "one person can always make a difference."

At Commencement on Sunday Boston University will try to strike this same spiritual balance of celebration and mourning, in opening words, in invocation, and in benediction. Katie Matthews has led the way.

December 20

Robert Kysar

Robert Kysar, *Voyages with John*:

"What then is the character of Johannine eschatology? This study (Kysar) affirms that Bultmann's theological interpretation (though not his literary-historical judgements) of the gospel is essentially correct. The evangelist seems to have undertaken an interpretation of the primitive Christian eschatology in the direction of what—for lack of better terminology—has been called 'existential eschatology.' That is, the evangelist appears generally to have demythologized the primitive eschatology, which means that the author detemporalized it. The hope which was inherent in the futuristic eschatology of the primitive church became understood as a hope which was realizable in the present, in one's encounter with the kerygmatic Christ. The future was made present, and the present became impregnated with the hope that was previously assigned to the future."[1]

December 21

---

1. Robert Kysar, *Voyages with John: Charting the Fourth Gospel* (Waco: Baylor University Press, 2006), 25.

Methodism in Perspective at Boston University

Today is a beautiful, sun-dappled, bright Friday on Marsh Plaza. Thanks to the College of Arts and Sciences, ice cream is right now served from four formal stations, and hundreds have come to partake. The chapel organ is booming, as musicians prepare for a busy weekend. The Charles River glistens beyond "the beach." Blue sky, cool air, communal gathering—and ice cream. A happy hour or two, on September 6.

I watch as Terriers older and younger sample the ice-cuisine. Some look into the chapel—named for a Methodist minister, our fourth president, Daniel Marsh, as is the plaza itself. Some squint up at John Wesley, above the front chapel door, in a robe, reading his Bible—the founder of Methodism, an English Protestant movement, in the 1700's. A couple, finished with their cones, look in at the Connick stained glass windows, glance at the Methodist hymnals in the pews, and peer at Abraham Lincoln (not a Methodist himself, though his biography—personal faithfulness, and social responsibility—epitomized the best of Methodism in his nineteenth century). Three young men ring the Boston University seal, next to the Martin Luther King, Jr. monument, and, avoiding stepping on the seal, read its motto, crafted long ago by Daniel Marsh, a thoroughly Methodist triad: *learning, virtue, and piety*. I wonder: how could I briefly say to these hundreds just what lasting meaning the Methodist provenance of Boston University continues to have? What difference does it make that in 1839 John Dempster—a Methodist minister from upstate New York—founded the theological seminary that later became our University? After all, BU today is a large, urban, non-sectarian, northern, private, research university, which includes women and men from the whole inhabited earth. What lingers from its birth out of Methodism?

December 22

Methodism in Perspective at Boston University

Learning

The seal tells the story. From its inception in America, Methodism, more energetically than any other tradition, established schools and colleges, from Beacon Hill in Boston all the way to route 66 and Claremont in California. Today 128 universities, seminaries, and other schools adorn America, all fruit of an early love of learning, exemplified by John Wesley himself—an Oxford Don, a classics scholar, a biblical theologian. Speaking of his beloved Bible, said Wesley, 'I desire to be *homo unius libri*,' 'a man of one book.' Methodism never invested all authority in the Bible, because learning about the Bible pointed Wesley and his followers to other truths, in history and in reason and in experience. Learning was the key. My namesake, Professor Allan Knight Chalmers, a mentor to ML King and others, implored his graduate theological students to read 'a book a day.' The old saying that, *nihil humanum,* that 'nothing human is foreign to us,' expresses the love of learning inherited from our Methodist past. Recognizing, with John 8:32, the crucial treasure of learning, of knowledge, we drank education with our mother's milk at the birth of BU.

December 23

Methodism in Perspective at Boston University

Virtue

But Methodism has more than academic rigor to offer us, in reflection on our past. Learning and virtue and piety—knowing and doing and being, if you will—all are part of becoming fully human. Methodism emphasized, and emphasizes, the shared experiences in life: "that which has been believed always and everywhere by everyone"; "in essentials unity, in non-essentials liberty, in things charity"; "a people happy in God"; "the best of all is, God is with us." Our BU history comes out of a movement of 'doers,' in the main—dreamers, yes, and doubters, too, but largely doers. They put a church in virtually every county in the country. They split, north and south, ahead of the civil war, over slavery. Having been poor, they ministered always and fully with the poor. They tithed (as most still do—giving away 10% each year of their earnings). Wesley put it this way: "do all the good you can, at all the times you can, in all the ways you can, by the all means you can, to all the people you can, as long as every you can." Faith without works is dead. Our modern BU work with the Chelsea schools can stand as an example of a dozen other great BU transformative gifts, which well up out of the ancient Methodist bone structure of the school. BU over 170 years has defined itself, not by whom it excluded, but by whom it included—the children of the poor, the working class, former slaves, people of color, different religious traditions, women—and in our time, the otherwise abled, the gay and lesbian community, internationals, and others.

December 24

Virtue

Methodism has more than academic rigor to offer us, in reflection on our past. Learning and virtue and piety—knowing and doing and being, if you will—all are part of becoming fully human. Methodism emphasized, and emphasizes, the shared experiences in life: 'that which has been believed always and everywhere by everyone'; 'in essentials unity, in non-essentials liberty, in things charity'; 'a people happy in God'; 'the best of all is, God is with us.' Our BU history comes out of a movement of 'doers,' in the main—dreamers, yes, and doubters, too, but largely doers. They put a church in virtually every county in the country. They split, north and south, ahead of the civil war, over slavery. Having been poor, they ministered always and fully with the poor. They tithed (as most still do—giving away 10% each year of their earnings). Wesley put it this way: *'do all the good you can, at all the times you can, in all the ways you can, by the all means you can, to all the people you can, as long as every you can.'* Faith without works is dead. Our modern BU work with the Chelsea schools can stand as an example of a dozen other great BU transformative gifts, which well up out of the ancient Methodist bone structure of the school. BU over 170 years has defined itself, not by whom it excluded, but by whom it included—the children of the poor, the working class, former slaves, people of color, different religious traditions, women—and in our time, the otherwise abled, the gay and lesbian community, internationals, and others.

December 25

Piety

I admit this is a superannuated word. It sounds vaguely and curiously cloistered. But what it means is vital and crucial for you, and me. That is, what we learn and how we act finally shape who we are. There is a lasting, soulful dimension to the human being, an own-most self behind the public persona, a multi-dimensional *person* (in the tradition of Boston University's own philosophical tradition of Personalism) down deeper than the one-dimensional surface. At heart, for the Methodists, piety meant love, to love one another, even as God has loved us (1 John 4:7). If we are not both lovers and knowers, both learners and lovers, we have left behind part of our souls. But if we do love one another, these Methodists taught, God abides in us. There are many ways to keep faith. The tolerant, magnanimous openness of Methodism, at its best, reminds us so. 'If thine heart be as mine, give me thine hand,' said John Wesley. Under the seal on Marsh plaza, on a sunlit, gleaming day, there lies the wonder and promise of love. And after all, without love, and an experience of love, what is life for? Charles Wesley, John's 18th century musical brother sang it this way, in a hymn written for the opening of an elementary school in 1762: *Unite the pair so long disjoined, knowledge and vital piety, learning and holiness combine, and truth and love, let all men see.*

December 26

Paideia

John 14:15-17, 25-26

Education, theological education, and ministerial education all have their claim on limited hours and energies, and all feed the preacher, shape the sermon, and protect the pulpit. A sermon centered curriculum needs them all. A sermon needs them all. Yet it is the last, ministerial education, which inspires my own passionate interest. A liberal arts education, a liberal theological education, and a liberal ministerial education were given many of us before we knew how to map their contours, borders, countries and boundaries. (My thanks to Lloyd Easton, J Louis Martyn, and Edmund Steimle.)

Today I am located at the torn intersection of these three dimensions of paideia. As the University Chaplain at Boston University, I have the privilege to pray, to murmur piously, at the high moments in University life: matriculation, commencement, funerals and weddings, Parent's Weekend, Martin Luther King Day, orientation sessions, and the occasional presidential inauguration. After September's matriculation prayer, a teacher in the School of Communication generously sought me out to say thank you for one phrase in the prayer which, he said, 'I have quoted in every class since.' (The phrase was a riff on what I think originally was a F Buechner line. My version: 'where your personal creativity meets the globe's crying hurt.') Strict theology aside, there is worth in those moments of communal quiet and humility in which we make some space for wonder, for vulnerability, for self-criticism—for being human. I loved calculus, once I understood that we were measuring areas underneath curves. I loved chemistry, once I could appreciate its biological implications. I loved earth science and its planets and meandering rivers, once the grandeur of the scope of the study was described. I loved economics, history, literature, poetry, languages, music history, psychology, and cultural anthropology. Once there were no longer chads, I even learned to like computers. The whole educational project I do affirm, I do embrace. My religious role therein, I hold with honor.

Not too long ago, education and theological education were the same thing. Even Boston University at 170 years old has spent a third or a half of its life in such a state of self-understanding. Learning is meant to lead to virtue and virtue is meant to lead to piety. All knowledge is knowledge of God, if God is the creator of all, the healer of all, the protector of all. But that is of course no longer the case. The nineteenth century attempts to keep religion within the range of reason (James, Dewey, Peirce) are a long time gone. The pulling away from the disciplines of theology, and to some degree from philosophy as a whole, has been in process for 100 years. The tearing in many places is complete.

The recent occasion of an invitation to consider the presidency of a liberal arts school, however, caused some self-assessment regarding the range or limits of my affection for education in the large. Parker Palmer's similar story of his decision at this curve in the trail

I do remember. My passion for renovation dining halls, roofing dormitories, expanding fit-rec centers, explaining the raptures of new laboratories, paying the basketball coach and athletic director, and listening with interest to the political intricacies of life in the theater department, that passion is not limitless. In fact, resting on the oars here for a moment in my mid-fifties, with the morning's news of a dear pastor and friend who retired last year and died last night, the sharp keen interest I might have displayed—feigned?—in these things last decade has dulled. Theological education, not education in general, has been my place of investment, even in the undergraduate teaching that has been so meaningful to me. Biblical studies has for a long, good time fed my spirit, soul and body. Yet what has been meaningful within these years of reading and writing about the John, the Coptic Gnostic treatises, and other related matters has been truly and centrally a part of the educational project as a whole. History and exegesis both have needed the full educational curriculum.

The tearing of the two apart does not come only from the engineering school or the physics department. Oddly, theological educators themselves have found their seat at the longer table either inadequate or uncomfortable. I teach now as a full professor in the School of Theology. All the rights and privileges thereof are now mine as well—the meetings, conflicts, rivalries, intrigues, and also the friendships, engagements, enjoyments and improvements. I am earnest about the teaching, and the writing I do. I enjoy it. But I do not view it as necessarily distinct from other forms of learning. I resist those voices who strangely argue that it is the mere location of theological study in the modern university that eviscerates theology. The two so long conjoined, education and theological education, ride uneasily together today. Our BU conflict over 'DRTS' is evidence of this. The as yet unnamed financial weakness of the school itself—both the weakness and the silence about the weakness—is further evidence. In fact, from my vantage point, the only place one would want to teach and study theology is from within the context of the university. But both sides of the equation tear at each other today. The chasm is becoming unbridgeable.

 I find though that, as important as the formal study of theology has become for me, and as crucial as I understand it to be for ministry (contrary by the way to the disregard given it both by fundamentalists and by liberationists), it is not a place where I would lay down my life. Our choice to return the offer of the Presidency of Colgate Rochester Crozer in retrospect was entangled with this, or some of this. I believe in theological education, and am much more sanguine about raising money for Biblical Studies than for the physical sciences. But to be honest the coddling of whining overpaid underworked faculty, the raising of funds from various not so savory persons in church and society, the balancing of persons and personalities and conflicts in schools of theology, our own included, is not my ownmost self. I can do it, have to some degree done it, and may at some point do it again. I certainly have spent enough time interviewing for these positions, with some success and failure both. The passion in this is connected to the connection to the pulpit and to pastoral ministry.

In the same way that education and theological education have torn away from each other, partly intentionally and largely out of blinded habit, so now and increasingly theological education is tearing away from ministerial education. It was once upon a time the case that a liberal arts education paved the way for a liberal theological education which paved the way for a liberal ministerial education (the so-called practical theology in the school of theology and the so-called ministerial preparation in the churches). The whole three dimensional paideia was sermon focused, sermon centered, sermon directed. J L

Martyn concluded his grading of my master's thesis: 'of course, much more could be done, and will be—-in preaching.' Easton, Martyn and Steimle were all of the same cloth. They felt no tearing away, no needed destruction of relationship. Today, though, just as theology has looked askance at education, so too it somehow looks askance at ministry. Baffling as this must seem, it is the case. The idea that schools of theology educate clergy, like schools of medicine and law and philosophy educate doctors and lawyers and philosophers, is not a shared view. Here, it is a minority view, though a vocalized minority view, largely due to Boston's history and the age of key faculty. Just as USC dispensed with its school of theology, so Iliff is dispensing with its education for ministry.

I am teaching John this fall. I am intentionally twisting the lectionary so that I can preach on John too. I am doing this for educational reasons. Last week, praise God, I received an email from one of my best students: "After my own service, I tuned in to your service and heard your sermon on John 1. I will remember it and refer to it in my own preaching." Yes. That is ministerial education. Located in a great university. Prepared in a theological school. Exemplified, practically exemplified, in the Chapel, which is the laboratory of the School, and the heart of the University. It is sermon centered. Not in the sense that anything of the liberal arts can be lost, nor that anything in the history of theology can be forgotten, but in the sense that, finally, the preaching of the gospel is the point of education and theological education and ministerial education. This is where my heart and passion are most fervent. This is why the three part role here—preacher, professor, pastor—is so perfect and so unusual for me.

The tearing, though, tears right at the intersection in which I live. It is a creative tension to be sure, but it is a tough, hurting tension as well. Ray Hart was right, and could see, that as the Dean of Marsh Chapel I would become in fuller measure my "ownmost self." And those who know me best have agreed.

December 27

Alone

This note is for those women and men who are suffering, little or much, on your own. Loneliness compounds all hurt. It has been on my mind and heart to write you a note, all who labor and are heavy laden. As alone as we are, we are not ultimately alone.

December 28

Practical Pedagogical Suggestions

1. Draw international students into conversation by giving out discussion questions in the preceding class session.

2. To cover unknown territory with a student whose interest lies outside the teacher's area of expertise, say, 'that's great, that's a great idea, let's work on this together.'

3. Offer King and Thurman courses. (To undergraduates and others as well?)

4. Follow the inclusive teaching examples of Stone and Ammerman

5. Review course outlines to check for diverse materials (sources, references, bibliography) in the syllabus.

6. Continue to provide a new vocabulary, a diverse lexicon, like Dr. Darr using and explaining the term 'ethnocentrism.'

7. Aim to produce students who are 'evolving learners.'

8. Provide more reference to multiple cultures in worship and liturgical studies.

9. Recruit and *retain* ethnic people in faculty positions.

10. Don't make the few ethnic faculty and staff handle all the 'others.'

11. Hire more and more diverse adjuncts

12. Continue to connect with the life of the church.

13. Provide courses for diverse lay people.

14. It does matter to students that 'people who look like you' teach here as full professors.

15. Create a stronger sense of community.

16. Imitate the Walker Center model for inter religious housing and life.

17. If you have no sense of community in the school you cannot expect to have any in worship on Wednesday.

December 29

Ray Hart: Notes from an off-the-cuff Speech

Speaking "out of the overflow," depending on the Holy Spirit (though he clearly had prepared). Straight, honest, humble, funny, tough.

Our curriculum: 1. Develop self-directed learners, people who have learned how to learn and who love to learn, for whom learning is not misery but thrill and adventure. 2. Prepare our students for change, fast change, five major reorientations within the span of a career, a professional development. 3. Provide a knowledge base in the classics.

Time, a meditation. 'One can only imagine the present' (Aristotle). One cannot read the first several books of Augustine's confessions often enough. The present is a great mystery. It is never available. It is either remembered, or it is anticipated. We can live thousands of years, through learning. Never trust anyone under 2000 years old. Knowledge expands my existence. We are responsible to teach our students WHY they need to know what they need to know. As Wesley said, we must *experiment*. His great grandmother never used the term civil war, just "the late unpleasantness."

December 30

Bryan Stone's Evangelism after Christendom[2]

A dear friend, a superannuated preacher and weathered good man, remembers deciding to join our annual conference, fifty years ago, because he entered the gathering as they sang, beautifully, verses of "Peace, perfect peace." It was not the action but the beautiful, hymnic habits of the church, there, which embraced him. It was the music not the words.

Bryan Stone's rigorous, challenging new argument for a post-liberal evangelism heralds the crucial centrality of ecclesiology. The practice of evangelism, is the practice of faith, particularly understood. "The argument of this book is that the prevailing model of practical reasoning employed to a great extent by contemporary evangelism is inadequate to the Christian faith, ecclesiologically bankrupt, morally vacuous, and tyrannized by a means-end causality that is eschatologically hopeless insofar as it externalizes means from the end"(p52). In the course of defending this claim, Stone will argue, compellingly, that evangelism's first concern ought to be the actual lived habits of the very church which invites the world around to consider its habituated gospel: "Christian witness in the shape of 'ordinary nonconformity' is . . . the central and defining logic of evangelism" (314). Being not doing, music not words, are the focus of this book.

Because the book is clearly structured, and its argument is periodically summarized and re-introduced, one is able to offer a brief overview, a bird's eye view of Stone's own look at evangelism. *Evangelism After Christendom*, as the author repeatedly affirms, is an extended meditation upon the writing of John Howard Yoder. Other partners in reflection include the following familiar surnames: MacIntyre, Willimon, Hauerwas, Abraham, Outler, Lohfink, Ogden, Segundo, Brueggemann, Haight, Lindbeck, Newbigin, Guttierez, Barth, Hutter, Long, Volf, Lischer, Tanner. Other than Yoder, Hauerwas and Lindbeck are the most influential. Countervailing arguments are presented, and critiqued (Bultmann, Hybels et.al., James Adams). In conversation with these partners, Stone steadily mounts his argument. Evangelism should be understood as a 'practice,' particularly understood (in the light of Macintyre). This practice depends upon careful rehearsal of the story of the people of God (Israel, Jesus, the Church). The story needs freeing from two competing, opposing stories (Constantine and the Enlightenment). Such liberation occurs in the life of the *ecclesia* (with special attention to its being, spirit dependence, and context). Liturgical, bodily, eschatological, and 'heterological' formation, in particular, constitute the 'eucharistic economics' of the church. Presence, patience, courage and humility are the habituated virtues required of the ecclesiological evangelism here envisaged. Oscar Romero and a church for street people exemplify these virtues.

Stone's book is a great asset, and an important reading, especially for pastors. You may disagree with his uniformly "Christ against culture' perspective. You may judge that he finally does not get around Bultmann. You may feel that he is too positive about the church and too negative about the world. You may not share his pacifism. You may not fully concur with his agreements with Yoder. You may find that he mistakenly minimizes the role

---

2. Bryan Stone, *Evangelism After Christendom* (Grand Rapids: Brazos Press, 2007).

of preaching. You may think that he romanticizes poverty. Your experience may suggest that Constantinian and Enlightenment shadows still do shade our Christian existence, and not entirely in bad ways. You may wonder whether salvation is, simply, 'a distinct form of social existence" (188). Still, Stone's book is one you should read, especially for its rigorous advancement of these and other points on which you may not agree. Walk with him. He is a trustworthy guide, with a destination to share with you: "A common denominator of any Christian evangelistic strategies has been their basic distrust of the Holy Spirit to work through the simplicity of Christian obedience, lived out in daily practices, habits and gestures" (227).

December 31

CPSIA information can be obtained
at www.ICGtesting.com
Printed in the USA
LVHW101248140920
665959LV00005B/63

9 781625 649812